WITHDRAWAL

Introducing
LISREL

ISM   Introducing Statistical Methods

Series editor: Daniel B. Wright, *University of Bristol*

This series provides accessible but in-depth introductions to statistical methods that are not covered in any detail in standard introductory courses. The books are aimed both at the beginning researcher who needs to know how to use a particular technique and the established researcher who wishes to keep up to date with recent developments in statistical data analysis.

Editorial board

Glynis Breakwell, *University of Surrey*

Jan de Leeuw, *University of California, Los Angeles*

Colm O'Muircheartaigh, *London School of Economics*

Willem Saris, *Universiteit van Amsterdam*

Howard Schuman, *University of Michigan*

Karl van Meter, *Centre National de la Recherche Scientifique, Paris*

Other titles in this series

Introducing Social Networks
Alain Degenne and Michel Forsé

Introducing Multilevel Modeling
Ita Kreft and Jan de Leeuw

Introducing ANOVA and ANCOVA: A GLM Approach
Andrew Rutherford

Introducing
LISREL

A Guide
for the Uninitiated

ADAMANTIOS DIAMANTOPOULOS
JUDY A. SIGUAW

SAGE Publications

London • Thousand Oaks • New Delhi

SAGE Publications Ltd
6 Bonhill Street
London EC2A 4PU

SAGE Publications Inc.
2455 Teller Road
Thousand Oaks, California 91320

SAGE Publications India Pvt Ltd
32, M-Block Market
Greater Kailash – I
New Delhi 110 048

QA
278.3
.D53
2000

British Library Cataloguing in Publication data

A catalogue record for this book is available
from the British Library

ISBN 0 7619 5170 9
ISBN 0 7619 5171 7 (pbk)

Library of Congress catalog card number is available

Typeset by Mayhew Typesetting, Rhayader, Powys
Printed in Great Britain by Athenaeum Press, Gateshead

August 14, 2003

To Heidi, Holly, Winkie and Legend
for making me happy
Adamantios Diamantopoulos

To my husband and my daughters for all
their support and encouragement
Judy Siguaw

CONTENTS

About the authors   iא

Preface   xi

Acknowledgements   xiii

1   WHAT IS LISREL ALL ABOUT?   1

    A brief background   4
    Sequential steps in LISREL modeling   6

    APPENDIX 1A
    Variance and covariance   10
    APPENDIX 1B
    Implied covariance matrix   11

2   MODEL CONCEPTUALIZATION   13

    APPENDIX 2A
    Reflective and formative indicators   21

3   PATH DIAGRAM CONSTRUCTION   22

    APPENDIX 3A
    Path diagram construction for a LISREL model   28

4   MODEL SPECIFICATION   30

    APPENDIX 4A
    Covariance matrix to be analyzed   41
    APPENDIX 4B
    Direct entry of covariance matrix into the SIMPLIS input file   42
    APPENDIX 4C
    Selected output from SIMPLIS input file for illustrative model   43
    APPENDIX 4D
    Parameter matrices of a comprehensive LISREL model   45
    APPENDIX 4E
    Illustrative model in matrix form   46

5   MODEL IDENTIFICATION   48

6   PARAMETER ESTIMATION   55

    Reading the program output: SIMPLIS format   57
    Reading the program output: LISREL format   62

APPENDIX 6A
  Estimation problems   76
APPENDIX 6B
  Path diagram as produced by LISREL 8 program   79
APPENDIX 6C
  Standardized and completely standardized indirect and total
  effects   80

7   ASSESSMENT OF MODEL FIT   82

     Overall fit assessment   82
     Assessment of measurement model   89
     Assessment of structural model   92
     Power assessment   93

     APPENDIX 7A
     Different types of discrepancy in evaluating a LISREL model   101

8   MODEL MODIFICATION   102

     Specification searches   103
     Diagnostics for model modification   105
     Modification of illustrative model: fit improvement   118
     Modification of illustrative model: model simplification   122

9   MODEL CROSS-VALIDATION   129

     Cross-validating the illustrative model (final version)   131
     Cross-validation and model comparison   135
     Equivalent models   138

     APPENDIX 9A
     SIMPLIS input file for validation sample   142

10   AN INTRODUCTION TO PRELIS 2   143

     APPENDIX 10A
     Thresholds for ordinal variables   156

References   157

Index   167

ABOUT THE AUTHORS

Adamantios Diamantopoulos (BA, MSc, PhD, MCIM, MMRS) holds the chair of Marketing and Business Research and is Research Director of Loughborough University Business School. Previously he held the Chair of International Marketing at the European Business Management School, University of Wales Swansea, where he headed the Marketing Group. He has held full-time appointments at the University of Edinburgh and the University of Strathclyde and Visiting Professorships at the University of Miami, Vienna University of Economics and Business, Université Robert Schuman (Strasbourg) and University of Dortmund. During 1997–99 he was also the Nestlé Visiting Research Professor of Consumer Marketing at Lund University, Sweden. His research interests are in pricing, sales forecasting, marketing research and international marketing and he is the author/co-author of some 160 publications in these areas. He has presented his research at more than 60 international conferences and has been the recipient of several Best Paper Awards. His work has appeared, among others, in the *International Journal of Research in Marketing, Journal of Business Research, International Journal of Forecasting, Journal of International Marketing, Journal of the Market Research Society, Journal of Strategic Marketing, European Journal of Marketing* and *Journal of Marketing Management*. He sits on the editorial review boards of eight marketing journals, is the UK Country Coordinator for the European Marketing Academy (EMAC), a founder member of the Consortium for International Marketing Research (CIMaR), Associate Editor of the *International Journal of Research in Marketing*, and a referee for several academic journals, professional associations and funding bodies. He is also a member of the Senate of the Chartered Institute of Marketing (CIM).

Judy A. Siguaw is an Associate Professor of Marketing in the School of Hotel Administration at Cornell University. Prior to entering academia, Dr Siguaw spent ten years in the corporate environment, including a stint as a sales representative with General Foods Corporation, a subsidiary of Philip Morris. She has published numerous journal articles including those appearing in the *Journal of Marketing Research, Journal of Marketing, Journal of the Academy of Marketing Science, Journal of Strategic Marketing, Industrial Management, Journal of Business Ethics* and the *Cornell Hotel and Restaurant Administration Quarterly*. She is co-author of *Marketing: Best Practices* and *American Lodging Excellence: The Key To Best Practices in The U.S. Lodging Industry*. She is also a contributor to four other textbooks and the author/co-author of 25 national and international conference papers. She has been the recipient of prestigious Marketing Science Institute research award, a Jane Fenyo Award from the Academy of Marketing Science, a research fellowship, a CIBER travel award from Duke University, a grant from American Express and the American Hotel Foundation, and eight university research grants. Dr Siguaw has been listed in *Who's Who Among America's Teachers* and has been awarded the Chancellor's Excellence in Teaching Award. She is currently serving as the faculty advisor for the Cornell student chapter of Hotel Sales and Marketing Association International (HSMAI) and is a trustee on the HSMAI Foundation Board. She sits on the editorial board of four journals, including the *Journal of Marketing Management* and *Cornell Hotel and Restaurant Administration Quarterly*. Her research interests include personal selling, sales management, channels of distribution, and market orientation.

PREFACE

There are two ways to learn LISREL. The first is to start by brushing up on your matrix algebra, follow this by a course on regression and factor analysis, learn a good deal about path analysis, multiple indicators, and econometric models, and then – after recovering from at least one nervous breakdown – confidently venture into the world of latent variable models in general and covariance structure models in particular! The second, and arguably, simpler way is to read this book first and then decide whether LISREL is for you. If the answer is yes, then you can build on this *basic introduction* by consulting more advanced sources to which you will be often referred.

There are also two ways *not* to learn LISREL. The first is to buy/borrow the computer program and fit *some* model to your data by following a trial-and-error strategy. While this may work after a few sleepless nights grappling with the LISREL manual, at the end you will probably feel more confused than when you started. The second is to embrace LISREL as *the* solution to your theoretical, methodological and/or analytical problems. At best, what LISREL will do for you is highlight how really bad your data, measurements, or models are. At worst, it may tempt you to sacrifice theoretical substance in your quest for a better statistical model fit. You should never forget that while 'it is relatively easy to find a structural model which fits the data quite closely . . . it is extremely difficult to demonstrate (a) that a model simulates reality, (b) that it provided better simulation than another model, (c) that the constructs defined in the model have greater explanatory power from the observed variables from which they are derived, and (d) that these constructs are in any sense useful in promoting better research'.[1]

Finally, there are two ways of using this book. The first, recommended for 'absolute beginners', is to read it chapter-by-chapter so as to get an overall feel of what LISREL is all about and what it can do for you. Subsequently, you can put your knowledge into practice by setting up a few simple models and, in the process, make new friends with the LISREL manual. The second approach, recommended for 'advanced novices', is to apply the material of each chapter to an actual data set (you can use your own data, an example from the LISREL manual, or an already published study). By the time you have finished all chapters you should have a complete application of LISREL in practice. And what about the 'expert reader' you might ask? Well, if you already are an expert in LISREL, you bought the wrong book – talk to your bookshop nicely and you might get your money back!

Note

1   Werts, C.E., Linn, R.L. and Jöreskog, K.G. (1974) Quantifying Unmeasured Variables. In
    Blalock, H.M. (ed.) *Measurement in the Social Sciences: Theories and Strategies*, Chicago:
    Aldine.

ACKNOWLEDGEMENTS

Irene Moody is the real hero behind this book. She typed most of it (often from disgracefully sloppy hand-written notes), produced all the figures, checked and re-checked for errors, and kept one of the authors constantly supplied with copious quantities of coffee (and the occasional chocolate biscuit!). Irene also acted as liaison officer between the authors by exchanging numerous e-mail attachments of chapters and ensuring that all files were up-to-date. In fact, Irene did everything short of actually writing the book (unfortunately, our efforts to convince her to do this as well, failed miserably). Thank you Irene.

The editorial team at Sage also deserves our warm thanks, not least for its patience when we repeatedly failed to meet deadlines (but since one of the authors is Greek, what do you expect?). The cheerfulness and wicked sense of humor of Beth Crockett is particularly appreciated.

Last but not least, our thanks go to our partners Heidi and Kevin for putting up with our unsociable behavior and blank looks after our (often traumatic) sessions with the LISREL program. Writing books and leading a normal life don't always go together but, then again, who wants a normal life anyway?

Adamantios Diamantopoulos
Judy Siguaw

1 WHAT IS LISREL ALL ABOUT?

'Man's the only species neurotic enough to need a purpose in life'

David Nobbs, *The Fall and Rise of Reginald Perrin*

An acquaintance of yours has been trying for some time to set you up with a blind date. Since you have hit a dry spell in the dating scene lately, you begin giving the set-up more serious consideration. From your discreet enquiries, you have been able to determine that the potential date has a 'great personality'. Having experienced particularly bad blind dates in the past during which you were either terminally bored by the date's incessant chatter or frightened to death by your date's appearance, you feel almost certain that this great personality relegates this person into the 'dog' classification in terms of sex appeal! However, being the great researcher you are, you decide to test the relationship between sex appeal and personality to see if your belief that unappealing physical looks equate to a great personality is actually justified.

So, you have two **constructs** you must measure – personality and sex appeal. You obviously need to collect data on these constructs to test your hypothesized relationship, but neither construct is easily observed; both are **latent variables**. So how can they be measured? You could, for example, subjectively rate (e.g. on a scale from 1 to 10) various aspects of personality and sex appeal that *can* be observed. For example, personality might be measured by 'cheerfulness' or 'friendliness'; similarly, sex appeal might be measured by 'glamour' or 'magnetism'. These measurable indicators of personality and sex appeal are known as **manifest variables**. Figure 1.1 illustrates the relationships between the latent variables and their indicators.[1] Note that, according to the direction of the arrows, each manifest variable is depicted as being determined by its underlying latent variable (as in factor analysis). In other words, manifest variables reflect latent variables; for this reason they are known as **reflective indicators** (this is an important point, to which we shall return in later chapters).

According to your 'theory', sex appeal is a determinant of personality (because very good-looking people don't have to develop as pleasing personalities as average-looking individuals to attract members of their own and/or opposite sex). So, in your study, sex appeal would be the **independent variable** because it acts as a determinant of personality. Personality, on the other hand, would be the **dependent variable** because it is influenced by, or is an effect of sex appeal. Now, if a variable is not influenced by any other

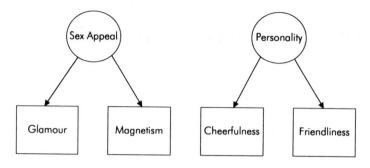

Figure 1.1   Latent and manifest variables

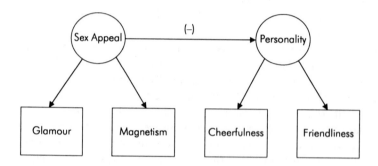

Figure 1.2   A relationship between two latent variables

variable in the model, the variable is an **exogenous variable**; exogenous variables act always as independent variables. Variables which are influenced by other variables in the model are known as **endogenous variables**. In our example, sex appeal would be an exogenous and personality an endogenous variable. Note that endogenous variables can affect other endogenous variables, i.e. they can act as both independent and dependent variables. Figure 1.2 shows the relationship between the latent variables in the model, the sign of the arrow indicating the expected direction of the link. Conceptually, the model of Figure 1.2 is very similar to a simple regression model with one predictor (i.e. independent) and one criterion (i.e. dependent) variable. The key difference is that, in the present case, the variables involved are latent, each measured by *multiple* indicators. As you might have guessed, conventional regression techniques cannot be used to estimate models such as the one depicted in Figure 1.2. It is here where LISREL and other similar methodologies – which are designed to deal with latent variables – come in handy; however, before we start telling you about LISREL, we need to briefly mention one very important concept, namely **error**.

In both Figure 1.1 and 1.2, we 'conveniently' assumed away any imperfections in our measurements and/or predictions. In Figure 1.1 we (implicitly)

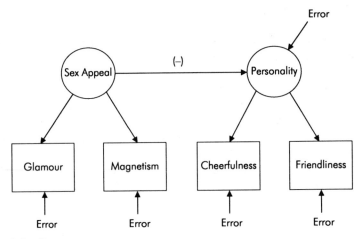

Figure 1.3 Incorporating error

assumed that our manifest variables are perfect measures of the two latent constructs, i.e. that there is no **measurement error** present. However, this is a rather unrealistic assumption as it is highly unlikely that empirical measurements will exhibit perfect validity or reliability; thus we should make allowances for the fact that we are dealing with fallible measures, i.e. imperfect representations of latent variables (particularly when subjective ratings are used, as is the case with most measures in social science research). Similarly, in Figure 1.2, there is the rather heroic assumption that personality is *solely* and *fully* determined by sex appeal, which is as realistic as saying that 'it never rains in England'. To the extent that other variables (not included in the model) have an influence on personality, then there will be **unexplained variation** of the latter; thus we need to include a **residual term** (or 'disturbance') in order to account for those influences on personality that have not been explicitly modeled.

Figure 1.3 shows a modified version of Figure 1.2, incorporating both measurement error (also known as 'error in variables') and structural error (also known as 'error in equations'). LISREL allows you to examine the relationships between latent variables (so you can test your substantive theory) as well as the relationships between the latent variables and their indicators (so that you can judge the quality of your measures). In fact, fitting a LISREL model to Figure 1.3 would tell you whether sex appeal has a negative effect on personality (as opposed to a positive or no effect); how strong that effect is (i.e. how much of the variation in personality can be 'explained' by sex appeal); and how good your measures of sex appeal and personality are (i.e. how well they are capturing the latent variables). Obviously, in order to fit a LISREL model to Figure 1.3 you need (a) some data, and (b) some knowledge on how to use LISREL. While we cannot help you with the former task (i.e. data collection), we hope to be of assistance with the latter.

A brief background

The term LISREL is an acronym for *LI*near *S*tructural *REL*ationships and, technically, LISREL is a computer program which was developed by Karl G. Jöreskog and Dag Sörbom to do **covariance structure analysis**[2] (see Appendix 1A for a brief explanation of variance and covariance). However, the program has become so closely associated with covariance structure models that such models are often referred to as LISREL models. Covariance structure models are widely used in a number of disciplines, including economics, marketing, psychology and sociology. They have been applied in investigations based on both survey and experimental data and have been used with cross-sectional as well as longitudinal research designs.[3]

Although the LISREL model remains basically the same today as when it first appeared in the early 1970s, subsequent revisions of the computer program have incorporated developments in statistical and programming technology to arrive at the current LISREL 8 version, which is the version used in this book.[4] In recent years, other software packages[5] have attempted to usurp LISREL's commanding position as the preferred software for covariance structure analysis, but LISREL has managed to defend its corner. Hence, this book focuses on doing covariance structure analysis utilizing the LISREL program; however, having mastered the principles of undertaking covariance structure analysis with LISREL, you should be able to adapt your knowledge and find little difficulty in using other similar programs.

Covariance structure analysis is a multivariate statistical technique which combines (confirmatory) factor analysis and econometric modeling for the purpose of analyzing hypothesized relationships among latent (i.e. unobserved or theoretical) variables measured by manifest (i.e. observed or empirical) indicators. A full covariance structure model is typically composed of two parts (or sub-models). The **measurement model** describes how each latent variable is measured or operationalized by corresponding manifest indicators; for example, we previously suggested that glamour and magnetism might be manifest indicators of the latent variable, sex appeal. The measurement model also provides information regarding the validities and reliabilities of the observed indicators. The **structural model**, on the other hand, describes the relationships between the latent variables themselves and indicates the amount of unexplained variance. Using our earlier example, then, the structural model would explain whether there is a significant negative relationship between sex appeal and personality, and would also indicate to what degree personality is determined by factors other than sex appeal.[6]

Covariance structure analysis is confirmatory in nature in that it seeks to confirm that the relationships you have hypothesized among the latent variables and between the latent variables and the manifest indicators are indeed consistent with the empirical data at hand. Confirmation (or lack of) is accomplished by comparing the computed covariance matrix *implied* by the hypothesized model to the *actual* covariance matrix derived from the empirical data (see Appendix 1B for an explanation of the 'implied covariance matrix'). Because this type of analysis utilizes the covariance matrix rather than the individual observations as input, covariance structure modeling is an aggregate methodology; unlike regression or ANOVA, individual cases or observations cannot be represented/predicted.

LISREL modeling has been used extensively in the United States, but appears to have found somewhat limited acceptance among researchers elsewhere. Speculation regarding as to why this may be the case can be partly attributed to the nature of the relevant literature: LISREL-related papers range from 'heavy-going' to 'completely incomprehensible' and there is no doubt that much of the literature is difficult for most mortals (professional statisticians and psychometricians excepted, of course). The LISREL manual itself does little to dispel such perceptions; although the authors state that it is 'not written for mathematical statisticians',[7] those who have actually read the manual (and lived to talk about it) recognize that this is not the most accurate of claims! Finally, researchers are often reluctant to persist with the LISREL program after encountering initial application problems (and everybody who has used LISREL has come across problems in one form or another).

The purpose of this monograph is to assist novices in the proper use of LISREL modeling. To achieve this aim, as painlessly as possible, we focus on:

- Outlining the *major steps* involved in formulating and testing a model under the LISREL framework; an appreciation of these steps and their interrelationships provides a 'blueprint' for approaching any modeling problem from a LISREL angle.
- Describing the *key decisions* associated with each step, providing practical 'tips' along the way; several important issues that may affect the success of the modeling task are discussed in a non-technical fashion and links to the relevant literature provided as required.
- Providing *examples* illustrating the practical application of the LISREL approach to familiarize the reader with the relevant terminology and assist with the interpretation of the output; again, the emphasis is on developing an understanding of the key issues involved without over-emphasizing technical details.
- Highlighting potential *problems and limitations* associated with LISREL modeling; developing a critical attitude when applying the LISREL approach, is essential to avoid 'mechanically' fitting models without careful consideration of substantive and statistical requirements.

Prior to tackling LISREL, you should become familiar with the principles of factor analysis[8] and structural equation models with observed variables.[9] Some knowledge of matrix algebra is also useful as parameter specification

under the LISREL programming language is in the form of eight parameter matrices (the program output also gives the parameter estimates in
matrix form). Knowledge of matrix algebra will also make more of the
LISREL-related literature accessible to a neophyte and, perhaps most
importantly, assist in checking one's model specification (see Chapter 4).
However, if spending your evenings learning matrix algebra doesn't appeal
to you, you will be pleased to know that LISREL 8 offers a choice of
programming languages – LISREL or SIMPLIS – and parameter specification is substantially easier in the SIMPLIS language.[10] Finally, infinite
patience and knowledge of stress management techniques will also help!

Sequential steps in LISREL modeling

Based upon our personal experience, the newcomer to LISREL will find
that it is easier to grasp the overall LISREL modeling task by focusing on
one area at a time. Consequently, we have broken down the overall process
into eight relatively distinct, but interrelated, steps (see Figure 1.4).
Although a brief overview of these steps is provided below, a full chapter is
devoted to each individual step in what follows.

The first step, **model conceptualization**, has nothing to do with statistics
(do we hear cheering?!). Model conceptualization is concerned with the
development of *theory*-based hypotheses to serve as the guide for linking
the latent variables to each other and to their corresponding indicators.[11]
In other words, the conceptualized model (i.e. the ordering of the constructs and hypothesized relationships) should be your educated perception
of the way in which the latent variables are linked together based upon
theories and evidence provided by your discipline's literature; it should also
reflect prior methodological knowledge concerning the measurement of
latent variables by means of observable indicators.

The second step, **path diagram construction**, allows you to demonstrate
your artistic ability by visually representing your substantive (theoretical)
hypotheses and measurement scheme. While this step in the process may be
omitted, we strongly recommend that it is *always* included; the need for a
path diagram will become clearer when we discuss the various steps of
Figure 1.4 in more detail (moreover you can use the construction of a path
diagram as the perfect excuse for demonstrating the extortionately expen-
sive graphics package you recently bought for your computer).

The third step of the process is **model specification** and involves describing the nature and number of parameters to be estimated; no data analysis
can be done until this step is completed. If you are opting to use the
LISREL language (instead of the SIMPLIS language option) to specify the
parameters, great care must be taken to ensure that the model is correctly
represented in mathematical form. The new SIMPLIS command language
(introduced with version 8 of the program)[12] alleviates the need for this
mathematical representation and allows you to simply name the variables

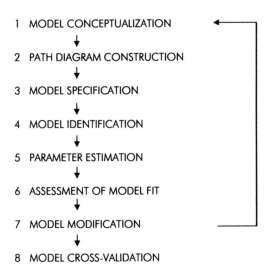

1 MODEL CONCEPTUALIZATION

2 PATH DIAGRAM CONSTRUCTION

3 MODEL SPECIFICATION

4 MODEL IDENTIFICATION

5 PARAMETER ESTIMATION

6 ASSESSMENT OF MODEL FIT

7 MODEL MODIFICATION

8 MODEL CROSS-VALIDATION

Figure 1.4   Steps in LISREL modeling

and specify their relationships using words and basic mathematical symbols, such as equality signs and arrows (you can still, however, obtain the output in LISREL language format if you so desire).

The fourth step is **model identification** (no, this does not refer to your ability to correctly identify types of automobiles or Cindy Crawford). Here, the information provided by the data is examined to determine whether it is sufficient for parameter estimation; that is, you must be able to obtain a single, unique value for every specified parameter from the observed data you have collected. If you are unable to do this, you may have to modify the model to make it identifiable before proceeding to the next step.

If the model is properly identified, then **parameter estimation** can take place. In this step, parameter estimates for the model are obtained from the data as the LISREL program attempts to generate an implied (i.e. model-based) covariance matrix that is equivalent to the observed (i.e. actual) covariance matrix. Moreover, significance tests are performed indicating whether the obtained parameters are significantly different from zero.

Step six, **assessment of model fit**, follows parameter estimation. A model fits when the covariance matrix it implies is equivalent to the covariance matrix of the observed data. You can assess this equivalence by examining various fit indices available in LISREL (there's plenty of them); these indices allow you to evaluate the quality and soundness of the measurement and structural parts of your model in terms of supporting your operationalizations and theory-based hypotheses.

Following assessment of fit, the model is examined to determine whether **model modification** is necessary in the light of the results obtained in step six. You should make sure that all alterations made to the model are based upon theory and guard against the temptation of making data-driven modifications just to get a model that fits the data better. *This is the step in LISREL modeling most likely to be misused – so beware!*

The final stage of the process, **model cross-validation**, involves fitting the model to a fresh data set (or a validation sub-sample obtained through split-sample procedures). Cross-validation is particularly important when substantial modifications have been made to the original model in step seven; under no circumstances should the *same* data set be used for both model development (i.e. calibration) and model testing (i.e. validation) purposes.

In the subsequent chapters, we will expand on each separate step of the LISREL modeling process shown in Figure 1.4, using a hypothetical model for illustration purposes and utilizing the LISREL 8 version of the program. While LISREL can be successfully used for experimental design applications as well as pure measurement models,[13] the model selected for illustration purposes involves a number of latent variables linked by a system of hypotheses and can thus be considered 'typical' of covariance structure modeling applications derived from survey data. Note that we have purposely elected to use a model that will provide an initial bad fit so as to illustrate the various concepts involved; this model is not intended to represent a good model in any substantive sense and its sole purpose is expository in nature.

Notes

1 Latent variables are also known as 'latent constructs', 'unobservables', and 'construct variables'. Observed variables are also known as 'measured variables', 'observed measures', 'items' and 'indicators'.

2 Covariance structure analysis (CSA) is also referred to in the literature as 'covariance structure modeling' (CSM), 'latent variable structural modeling' (LVSM), 'structural modeling with unobservables', 'linear structural relations', 'latent variable equation systems', 'moments structure modeling' and 'causal modeling with unobservables'. In recent years, there has been a convergence of terminology to 'structural equation models' (SEM), although strictly speaking, SEM is a broader term encompassing approaches other than the analysis of covariance structures (e.g. the PLS approach developed by Wold, 1982, 1985).

3 Annotated bibliographies on covariance structure modeling can be found in Austin and Wolfle (1991) and Austin and Caldéron (1996). Examples of journals publishing (primarily methodological) papers on covariance structure analysis include *Educational and Psychological Measurement, Multivariate Behavioral Research, Psychological Bulletin, Psychometrika, Sociological Methodology, Journal of Marketing Research, British Journal of Mathematical and Statistical Psychology* and *Quality and Quantity*. Since 1994, a dedicated journal, *Structural Equations Modeling: A Multidisciplinary Journal* has also been available (the complete contents of which can be found on the publisher's website: *http://www.erlbaum.com/journals.htm*). There is also an electronic discussion group, SEMNET, for posting questions and sharing ideas over various aspects of structural equation modeling; for information on joining SEMNET go to *http://bama.ua.edu/ archives/semnet.html* (the searchable archive facility is excellent). Last, but by no means least, there is a wealth of web-based material on structural equation modeling in general and covariance structure models in particular. The first port of call should definitely be

Ed Rigdon's homepage (*http://www.gsu.edu/~mkteer/index.html*) which, in addition to its own very useful content, provides several handy links. The *Working Group: Structural Equation Modeling* (*http://www.uni-muenster.de/SoWi/struktur*) is also worth checking out.

4 See Jöreskog and Sörbom (1996a). The first release of LISREL 8 took place in 1993; in 1998 an interactive version of the package (LISREL 8.20) was also released and updated in 1999 (LISREL 8.30). Version 8.20 is used in this book.

5 Competitors to the LISREL program include AMOS (Arbuckle, 1995), CALIS (Hartmann, 1992), COSAN (Fraser, 1988), EQS (Bentler, 1995), LISCOMP (Muthén, 1988), LINCS (Schoenberg and Arminger, 1988), MILS (Schoenberg, 1982), Mx (Neale, 1993) and SEPATH (formerly EZPATH, Steiger, 1989). For a more comprehensive listing together with links to the web sites of the distributors of these programs, see Joel West's homepage at *http://gsm.uci.edu/~joelwest/SEM/software.html*. There have been several papers comparing the strengths and weaknesses of these programs; see for example, Waller (1993), Hox (1995) and Miles (1998).

6 Some authors use the term 'structural model' to reference *all* covariance structure models including pure measurement models (i.e. they would apply the term to both Figure 1.1 and Figure 1.2). However, for exposition purposes, it is useful to distinguish models (or submodels) that simply specify the relationships between the latent variables and their indicators (i.e. measurement models) and models (or sub-models) that specify relationships between independent and dependent latent variables (i.e. structural models). Unfortunately, the terminology in the literature can be confusing, as different authors use the same term for different concepts, or address the same concept with different labels (that's what happens when statisticians, econometricians, psychometricians and behavioral scientists end up having common interests!).

7 Jöreskog and Sörbom (1989), p. ii.

8 See, for example, Harman (1976) or Kim and Mueller (1978a, 1978b). The monograph by Long (1983a) focuses specifically on confirmatory factor analysis (CFA) and is, therefore, particularly useful (if heavy-going at times).

9 A very readable introduction to structural equation models can be found in Asher (1985). For some early 'classics' in the area, see Blalock (1964), Duncan (1975) and the collection of readings by Goldberger and Duncan (1973) and Blalock (1971).

10 See Jöreskog and Sörbom (1993). Note that SIMPLIS has not been universally welcomed by LISREL 'old-timers'; for example, it has been argued that 'the absence of a general notation in SIMPLIS will seem efficient to infrequent users since they need not learn any notation, but there is a price to pay. The absence of a notation system means that there is no convenient way for SIMPLIS users to represent the standard segments of models . . . If SIMPLIS users wish to organize the discussion of their models in any way other than merely listing equation after equation, either they will have to learn LISREL notation, or struggle with long lists of variable names as they repeatedly generate the routine demarcations in each model they ever run' (Hayduk, 1996, p. xiv). We will come back to this issue in Chapters 3 and 4 where issues of model representation in graphical and mathematical terms will be discussed.

11 Note that 'theory is not the exclusive domain of academia but can be rooted in experience and practice obtained by observation of real-world behavior. Theory is often a primary objective of academic research, but practitioners may develop or propose a set of relationships that are as complex and interrelated as any academic theory' (Hair et al., 1998, pp. 589–590).

12 See Jöreskog and Sörbom (1993) for a description of the SIMPLIS language.

13 Examples of using LISREL with experimental designs can be found in Bagozzi (1977), Bagozzi and Yi (1989), and Bagozzi, Yi and Singh (1991). Measurement models are the focus of the review papers by Darden, Carlson and Hampton (1984), Hildebrandt (1984), Steenkamp and van Trijp (1991) and Homburg and Giering (1996).

APPENDIX 1A

Variance and covariance

Variance measures dispersion of the data about the mean and is, thus, a measure of variability for metric (i.e. interval and ratio) variables. By definition, variance is the average of the squared differences between each observation and the arithmetic mean (hence, variance is standard deviation squared). Each variable, X, has a variance and this is always positive (if it is zero, then we are not dealing with a variable but with a constant). Thus

$$\text{VAR} (X) = \sum (x_i - \mu)^2/N \qquad \text{(population data)}$$

$$\text{VAR} (X) = \sum (x_i - \bar{x})^2/(N - 1) \qquad \text{(sample data)}$$

where $(i = 1, 2, \ldots, N)$, N = population or sample size, μ = population mean, $\bar{x}$ = sample mean and $\sum$ = summation sign.

Covariance shows the linear relationship that exists between two variables, X and Y. If the variables have a positive linear association, the covariance will be positive; if the variables have an inverse relationship, the covariance will be negative; and if there is no linear relationship between the two variables, the covariance will be zero. Thus, a covariance can take any value between $-\infty$ and $+\infty$. Formally, a covariance is defined as follows:

$$\text{COV} (X,Y) = \sum (x_i - \mu_x)(y_i - \mu_y)/N \qquad \text{(population data)}$$

$$\text{COV} (X,Y) = \sum (x_i - \bar{x})(y_i - \bar{y})/(N - 1) \qquad \text{(sample data)}$$

In the **variance-covariance matrix** (commonly referred to as the **covariance matrix**), the variances are found on the main diagonal and each one represents the covariance of a variable with itself. The remaining (i.e. off-diagonal) parts of the matrix are made up of the covariances. For example, in the case of two variables, X and Y, the (sample) covariance matrix, **S**, would look as follows:

$$\mathbf{S} = \begin{bmatrix} \text{COV} (X,X) & \text{COV} (Y,X) \\ \text{COV} (X,Y) & \text{COV} (Y,Y) \end{bmatrix}$$

Since $\text{COV} (X,X) = \sum (x_i - \bar{x})(x_i - \bar{x})/(N - 1) = \sum (x_i - \bar{x})^2/(N - 1) = \text{VAR} (X)$

$\text{COV} (Y,Y) = \sum (y_i - \bar{y})(y_i - \bar{y})/(N - 1) = \sum (y_i - \bar{y})^2/(N - 1) = \text{VAR} (Y)$

and $\text{COV} (X,Y) = \text{COV} (Y,X)$,

the sample covariance matrix simplifies to a triangular matrix, namely

$$\mathbf{S} = \begin{bmatrix} \text{VAR} (X) & \\ \text{COV} (X,Y) & \text{VAR} (Y) \end{bmatrix}$$

The covariance matrix of the population or sample under consideration is very important to LISREL analyses and is usually the only input needed to estimate LISREL models.

Note that if the variables are standardized (i.e. have a mean of zero and a standard deviation of 1, as in z-scores), the covariance between X and Y becomes

$$\text{COV (standardized X, standardized Y)} = \text{COV } (X, Y)/s_x s_y = r_{xy}$$

where s_x and s_y are the standard deviations of X and Y respectively and r_{xy} is the familiar **correlation coefficient** between the two variables (the values of which range between -1 and $+1$). Thus, as long as we know the standard deviations, we can move back and forth from covariances to correlations by dividing (multiplying) by the product of standard deviations.

There are some simple rules for manipulating variances and covariances. Given two variables, X, Y, and two constants, a and b, then:

$$\text{VAR } (a + X) = \text{VAR } (X)$$
$$\text{VAR } (aX) = a^2 \text{VAR } (X)$$
$$\text{VAR } (X + Y) = \text{VAR } (X) + \text{VAR } (Y) + 2 \text{ COV } (X, Y)$$
$$\text{VAR } (X - Y) = \text{VAR } (X) + \text{VAR } (Y) - 2 \text{ COV } (X, Y)$$
$$\text{VAR } (aX + bY) = a^2 \text{VAR } (X) + b^2 \text{ VAR } (Y) + 2ab \text{COV } (X, Y)$$
$$\text{VAR } (aX - bY) = a^2 \text{VAR } (X) + b^2 \text{ VAR } (Y) - 2ab \text{COV } (X, Y)$$
$$\text{COV } (a, X) = 0$$
$$\text{COV } (aX, bY) = ab \text{COV } (X, Y)$$
$$\text{COV } (X, Y + Z) = \text{COV } (X, Y) + \text{COV } (X, Z)$$

APPENDIX 1B

Implied covariance matrix

Every model implies certain predictions for the variances and covariances of the variables included in the model. For example, consider a simple regression model with two variables X and Y:

$$Y = a + bX + e$$

where a and b are the regression coefficients (parameters) corresponding to the intercept and slope of the regression line respectively and e is the residual term. Now, according to this model, our expectations for the variance of Y and for the covariance between X and Y in the population are as follows:

$$\text{VAR } (Y) = \text{VAR } (a + bX + e)$$

$$\text{COV } (X, Y) = \text{COV } (X, a + bX + e)$$

Applying the rules for the manipulation of variances and covariances listed earlier in Appendix 1A, we have:

$$\text{VAR } (Y) = b^2 \text{VAR } (X) + \text{VAR } (e)$$

$$\text{COV } (X, Y) = b \text{VAR } (X)$$

Therefore, we can write the **model-based covariance matrix** as follows:

$$\Sigma(\theta) = \begin{bmatrix} b^2\text{VAR }(X) + \text{VAR }(e) & \\ b\text{VAR }(X) & \text{VAR }(X) \end{bmatrix}$$

where θ is a vector containing the model parameters. Thus $\Sigma(\theta)$ is the covariance matrix between the variables in the model expressed as a function of the model parameters. Now *if* the model were correct and *if* we knew the parameters, the population covariance matrix, Σ, would be exactly reproduced, i.e.,

$$\Sigma = \Sigma(\theta)$$

This is the fundamental equation in covariance structure modeling. However, in practice, we do not know the population variances and covariances or the parameters in (θ). Instead, we generate *estimates* of the unknown parameters, ($\hat{\theta}$), based upon the *sample* covariance matrix, S. These sample estimates are then used as predictions of the population variances and covariances and the model-based covariance matrix becomes

$$\hat{\Sigma} = \Sigma(\hat{\theta})$$

This is known as the **implied covariance matrix** and the objective of the analysis is to find estimates of parameter values such that $\hat{\Sigma}$ is as close as possible to the observed sample variances and covariances contained in S. In other words, the aim is to minimize the difference $(S - \hat{\Sigma})$. The latter is known as the **residual matrix**; ideally the elements in the residual matrix will be zeros, indicating a perfect match of $\hat{\Sigma}$ to S. In practice, of course, this is not usually achieved.

2 MODEL CONCEPTUALIZATION

You should recognize that the success of the entire LISREL modeling process depends to a very large degree on the extent to which the model is characterized by sound conceptualization. A poorly conceptualized model is unlikely to produce useful results with LISREL methodology. In this context, while LISREL can and has been used for exploratory purposes, you should bear in mind that LISREL works most effectively in a confirmatory context. Indeed, according to its authors, 'in exploratory situations with many variables and weak or non-existing substantive theory LISREL is probably not a useful tool'.[1]

Model conceptualization necessitates that two detailed tasks be undertaken. First, the hypothesized relationships between the latent variables must be specified. This stage of the model development focuses upon the structural model, and represents the theoretical framework to be tested. Here, you must clearly differentiate between the exogenous and endogenous variables in your model. Recall from Chapter 1 that exogenous variables are *always* independent variables and, thus, cannot be directionally influenced by any other variable in the model. The endogenous variables are those that are directionally influenced by other variables within the model and, consequently, are 'explained' by these variables; while an endogenous variable always acts as a dependent variable, it can also act as an independent variable for the explanation of another endogenous variable in the model. As endogenous variables are usually not perfectly and completely explained by the variables hypothesized to influence them, an error term (or residual) is also hypothesized to influence each endogenous variable in the model.

At this stage of model conceptualization, you should ensure that no important exogenous and/or endogenous variables have been omitted from the model. Such omissions may severely bias the parameter estimates derived in the LISREL analysis and bring the results of your study under question. Omitting critical variables results in **specification error**, which means that the model you propose is not a true characterization of the population and the variables under study.

Having identified relevant latent variables for inclusion in the model and differentiated between exogenous and endogenous variables, you must next decide on (a) the specific ordering of the endogenous variables and (b) the number and expected direction of the linkages between exogenous and endogenous variables and the endogenous variables themselves. Put differently, you must determine which specific exogenous and endogenous variables will influence each endogenous variable in which way (i.e. positive versus negative impact). It is here where you must make the most of previous theories, past empirical evidence and, perhaps, some exploratory research that you have conducted; this is not to say that you cannot complement the literature with some original thinking, but simply to emphasize that a sound knowledge of the substantive domain is indispensable in model conceptualization. Note that you must be in a position to theoretically defend the *absence* of linkages between variables just as convincingly as the inclusion of linkages; a hypothesis of a zero relationship between two latent variables is no more or less important than a positive or negative relationship – and, therefore, a theoretical rationale has to be provided for it.

Figure 2.1 summarizes the various issues associated with conceptualizing the structural part of the model. While this is not the place to embark on a detailed discussion of the theory construction process,[2] two points are worth emphasizing. First, it is evident from Figure 2.1 that specification error can creep into a model from various 'points of entry' (e.g. omission of important exogenous variables, inappropriate ordering of endogenous variables and inclusion of irrelevant linkages); the more familiar you are with the relevant literature, the less likely that major misspecification will occur at the model conceptualization stage (although, of course, nothing is certain in this world!). A second point concerns the focus on conceptualizing a single model. In many instances, there may be competing theories and/or contradicting evidence in your area of study and, thus, you may find it difficult to come up with a single theoretical representation that is satisfactory.[3] Under such circumstances you may posit, say, two or three different models reflecting alternative theoretical perspectives and then use LISREL to see which model is best supported by the empirical data.[4]

The second major stage in model conceptualization focuses upon the measurement model and relates to the way in which latent variables are operationalized (i.e. represented by manifest or observable variables).[5] Manifest variables in LISREL modeling usually take the form of **reflective indicators** (also known as 'effect indicators'). A reflective indicator means that one or more latent constructs are thought to 'cause' the observable variable; another way of looking at this is that observable variables are (usually imperfect) indicators of an underlying cause (i.e. a latent variable). Reflective indicators need to be distinguished from **formative indicators** (also known as 'cause' or 'causal' indicators). Whereas the former are 'caused' by the latent variable, the direction of causality is reversed with the latter, i.e. it is the indicators themselves that 'cause' the latent variable. Specifically, with formative indicators, the latent variable is defined as a combination of its indicators (plus an error term); thus, the latent variable becomes automatically endogenous (determined by its indicators) while the indicators are exogenous variables with no error terms. By default, the measurement model specification in LISREL assumes that manifest variables are reflective indicators of the latent variables; although you *can* use

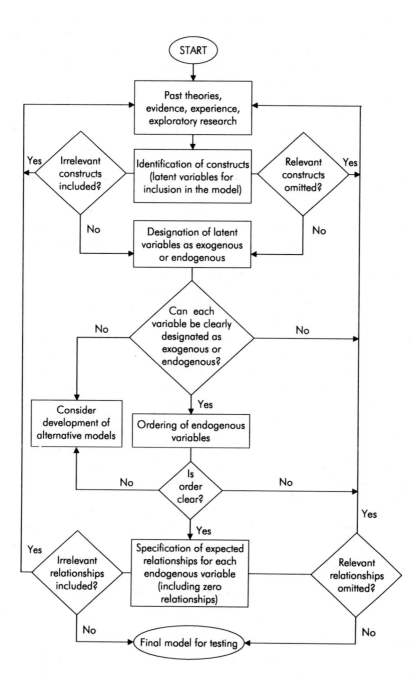

Figure 2.1   Structural model conceptualization

LISREL when formative indicators are involved, model specification and estimation can get rather complex and, thus, best suited for the advanced user. As you might be a bit confused at this stage (and who can blame you), Appendix 2A elaborates on the distinction between reflective and formative indicators and their implications for measuring latent variables.

Selecting appropriate indicators to represent latent variables is quite important and, since a single indicator usually does not adequately capture the latent variable, you should select *multiple* indicators when operationalizing both exogenous and endogenous latent variables. The best case scenario exists when several distinct observable measures (possibly also reflecting different data collection methods) are available to serve as indicators of latent constructs. However, since this is often not the case, multi-item scales may be randomly split to create multiple measures for each latent variable of interest (as we do later in this chapter). A summary of key issues relating to the conceptualization of the measurement model is given in Figure 2.2.

At this point we need to mention a practical consideration impinging upon model conceptualization, namely the *number* of latent and manifest variables to be included within a single model. While this will obviously vary according to the research topic, the researchers' modeling aims and the availability of measures, it is fair to say that the more complex the model (in terms of latent and/or manifest variables), the more likely it is that problems will be encountered with the model's fit; moreover, all other things being equal, the more variables included in one's model, the greater the sample size requirements.[6] At the same time, being overly concerned with model parsimony may lead to specification error in the structural part of the model (through the omission of important latent variables) and/or poor measurement quality (through the omission of key indicators of latent variables). Thus, you need to balance carefully the desire for conciseness against the potential for model misspecification, when deciding on the 'size' of your model. While specific guidelines on the maximum number of variables are hard to find, it has been suggested that 'without a great deal of knowledge about the number of variables under study, it is wisest to analyze relatively small data sets, say 20 variables at most';[7] this translates to about 5–6 latent variables each measured by 3–4 indicators.[8]

For illustration purposes, we are going to use a simple conceptual model with three exogenous and two endogenous variables. We will assume that we have come up with this model *after* we have immersed ourselves in the relevant literature, spoken to experts in the area, and also conducted some exploratory research in the form of in-depth interviews and focus groups (in other words, we have done our homework). We will further assume that we can actually get the necessary data to empirically test our model.

Our (hypothetical) model is concerned with salespeople's characteristics and, in particular, their Job Satisfaction (i.e. how happy they are with their job) and Customer Focus (i.e. to what extent they focus on solving customer problems rather than getting a 'quick sale'). Job Satisfaction and

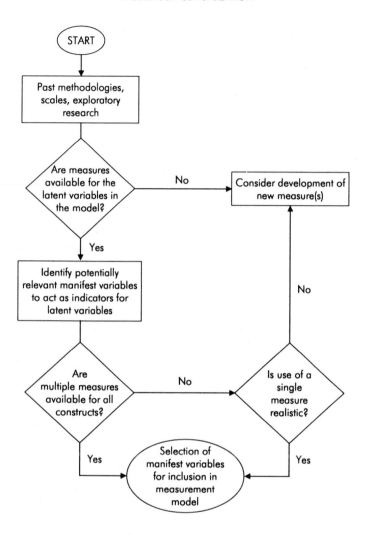

Figure 2.2   Measurement model conceptualization

Customer Focus are both seen as endogenous latent variables which are influenced by three exogenous latent variables, namely Role Ambiguity (the extent to which the salesperson feels clear about his/her job role), Role Conflict (the extent to which he/she experiences conflict with job demands) and Market Orientation (the extent to which the salesperson's organization has implemented the marketing concept). Specifically, Role Ambiguity and Role Conflict are hypothesized to have a direct negative influence on Job Satisfaction; Role Conflict is hypothesized to have a direct, negative influence on Customer Focus; Market Orientation is hypothesized to have a direct positive impact on Customer Focus; and, finally, Job Satisfaction is hypothesized to have a positive direct influence on Customer Focus. Role

Table 2.1   Expected linkages among latent variables

		Dependent variables	
		Job Satisfaction[2]	Customer Focus[2]
Independent variables	Role Ambiguity[1]	(−)	
	Role Conflict[1]	(−)	(−)
	Market Orientation[1]		(+)
	Job Satisfaction[2]		(+)

[1] Exogenous variable.
[2] Endogenous variable.

Ambiguity is not expected to directly influence Customer Focus nor is Market Orientation expected to directly impact on Job Satisfaction.

If you find the above description rather cumbersome and difficult to follow/remember, don't worry: so do we! Verbal descriptions of models, even those containing a few variables (as in our example), are not easily digested; indeed, this is a major reason why **path diagrams** are used to provide visual representations of hypothesized models. We will present such a path diagram for our example in the next chapter; for the time being, a summary of the expected linkages among the latent variables is provided in Table 2.1.

From Table 2.1 it can be seen that no reciprocal (i.e. two-way) linkages are hypothesized among the latent variables, i.e. we are dealing with what is known as a **recursive model**. While LISREL can be used for estimating **non-recursive models** (i.e. models in which two variables are both a 'cause' and an 'effect' of each other), such models are substantially more complex and, thus, better tackled after one has become familiar with using LISREL to analyze recursive models.[9]

Shifting attention to the measurement part of our model, each latent variable is assumed to be operationalized by at least two manifest variables acting as reflective indicators; Table 2.2 details the measurement scheme.

For the moment we shall assume that all manifest variables are metric (i.e. have been measured, at least, at interval level), so that we can use a covariance matrix as input in the subsequent analysis; we will further assume that this covariance matrix is based on 306 observations, reflecting responses to the manifest variables by a random sample of 306 salespeople. Note that LISREL has the capacity for handling non-metric (i.e. categorical and ordinal) variables (through a preprocessor program called PRELIS[10] or through the application of rescaling algorithms)[11] and can also accept other forms of data input (e.g. correlation and moment matrices); however, these are rather advanced options and will be discussed in Chapter 10. Moreover, the general rule in LISREL analysis is that the covariance matrix of the manifest variables should be used as input rather than the correlation matrix; indeed 'the practice of substituting correlation for covariance matrices in analysis is only rarely justified, since the associated statistics will usually be inappropriate'.[12]

Table 2.2   Measurement of latent variables

Latent variable	Manifest variables	Measure description
Job Satisfaction	Satisfaction with work content	Sum of 18 yes/no items[1]
	Satisfaction with supervision	Sum of 18 yes/no items
	Satisfaction with pay	Sum of 9 yes/no items
	Satisfaction with promotion	Sum of 9 yes/no items
Customer Focus	Selling behavior	Average of 12 9-point scales[2]
	Problem-solving behavior	Average of 12 9-point scales
Role Ambiguity	Clarity	Average of three 7-point scales[3]
	Ambiguity	Average of four 7-point scales
Role Conflict	Compatibility	Average of four 7-point scales[4]
	Conflict	Average of four 7-point scales
Market Orientation	Customer orientation	Average of six 7-point scales[5]
	Competitor orientation	Average of four 7-point scales
	Interfunctional coordination	Average of five 7-point scales

[1] Scored as 1 = yes, 0 = no; items based on Smith, Kendall and Hulin (1969).
[2] Scored as 1 = never, 9 = always; items based on Saxe and Weitz (1982).
[3] Scored as 1 = very false, 7 = very true; scale items based on Rizzo, House and Lirtzman (1970).
[4] As in 3 above.
[5] Scored as 1 = not at all, 7 = to an extreme extent; scale items based on Narver and Slater (1990).

To summarize, our full model is a five-construct, 13-indicator recursive system (see Tables 2.1 and 2.2), while our input data consist of a covariance matrix based on 306 observations.[13]

Notes

1 Jöreskog and Sörbom (1989), p. 225. The use of LISREL for exploratory purposes will be further discussed in Chapter 8 where issues relating to model modification will be considered.

2 For guidelines on model conceptualization and theory development in the context of structural equations modeling see Bagozzi (1980), James, Mulaik and Brett (1982), Saris and Stronkhorst (1984), and Davis (1985).

3 For example, in marketing, it has been noted that 'decision areas in marketing are seldom so well understood that only one reasonable model may be constructed to describe the phenomena at hand' (Rust and Schmittlein, 1985, p. 20).

4 Note that it is *not* a good idea to 'integrate' different conceptualizations within a single model; in fact, 'models in general should not be complex composites of competing conceptual views . . . models provide a greater service if they assist us in clarifying the implications of specific theoretical positions than if they precisely test poorly demarcated theoretical positions' (Hayduk, 1996, p. 3).

5 Thus, this stage focuses on what Blalock (1968) terms the 'auxiliary theory', whose function is 'to specify the relationships between the theoretical and empirical worlds or, more precisely, between abstract concepts and their indicators' (Sullivan and Feldman, 1979, p. 11).

6 Ding et al. (1995), for example, cite a number of studies agreeing that 100 to 150 subjects is the *minimum* recommended sample size when engaging in covariance structure modeling. Boomsma (1987, p. 84), on the other hand, recommends that 'the estimation of

structural equation models by maximum likelihood methods be used only when sample sizes are at least 200. Studies based on samples smaller than 100 may well lead to false inferences.'

7 Bentler and Chou (1987), p. 97.

8 Very recent research (see Marsh et al., 1998) has shown that having a large number of indicators per latent variable can have beneficial effects in terms of convergence, parameter stability and construct reliability (these concepts will be explained in latter chapters, so do not worry too much at the moment). However, these findings – which run against conventional wisdom – were obtained with simulated data and it remains to be seen whether the results will replicate on real-life data. Further research is clearly needed before firm guidelines regarding the number of indicators can be offered.

9 For an introduction to non-recursive models, see Berry (1984).

10 See Jöreskog and Sörbom (1996b) for a description of the latest version, PRELIS 2.

11 See, for example, Yadav (1992).

12 Bentler and Chou (1987), p. 90. The effects of substituting correlations for covariances are discussed at length in Cudeck (1989).

13 Note that the PRELIS program can be used to input or import raw data and then generate a covariance matrix. The latest version, which is incorporated in the interactive version of LISREL (LISREL 8.20), is very flexible and can read a variety of file formats including SPSS system files. This makes it very easy to input raw data and convert it to a matrix of one's choice (see also Chapter 10).

APPENDIX 2A

Reflective and formative indicators

The difference between reflective and formative indicators depends on the *causal priority* between the indicators and the latent variable in question. If the latent variable is viewed as an underlying construct that gives rise to something that is observed, then the indicators are reflective. For example, given a latent variable, η, and two indicators x_1 and x_2, a reflective specification implies that

$$x_1 = \beta_1 \, \eta + \varepsilon_1$$
$$x_2 = \beta_2 \, \eta + \varepsilon_2$$

where β_1, β_2 = parameters to be estimated and ε_1, ε_2 = errors of measurement.

In contrast, if the latent variable is conceived as being determined by a linear combination of observed variables, then the indicators are formative; in this case, 'the measures produce the constructs so to speak' (Bagozzi, 1994, p. 332). For our example, a formative specification implies that

$$\eta = \gamma_1 \, x_1 + \gamma_2 \, x_2 + \delta$$

where γ_1, γ_2 = parameters to be estimated and δ = residual.

The properties of formative indicators and the procedures for assessing their measurement quality are very different to those relating to reflective indicators. For full details, the reader is referred to Bollen (1984), Bollen and Lennox (1991), Fornell, Rhee and Yi (1991), and MacCallum and Browne (1993). A user-oriented introduction to measurement models based on formative indicators is provided by Diamantopoulos and Winklhofer (1999).

3 PATH DIAGRAM CONSTRUCTION

Having developed the theoretical framework of the model, the next step is to illustrate the conceptualization via a path diagram. A **path diagram** is simply a graphical representation of how the various elements of the model relate to one another; it provides an overall view of the model's structure. While the construction of a path diagram is not an essential requirement for LISREL modeling, it is too important to omit. The graphical representation assists the user in more easily comprehending the system of hypotheses contained in the model than does a verbal or mathematical representation; in fact, 'if the path diagram is drawn correctly and includes sufficient detail, it can represent exactly the corresponding algebraic equations of the model and the assumptions about the error terms in these equations'.[1] The path diagram can also decrease possibilities for specification error by highlighting omitted relationships, excluded variables, etc.; thus, the conceptualization of the model is improved. Finally, the path diagram is helpful in detecting errors in the computer program instructions given by the user, especially when the model is composed of a large number of variables linked by complex relationships. Given these benefits, it is good practice to always construct a path diagram, irrespective of the complexity of the model.

Figure 3.1 shows the path diagram for the illustrative model developed in the previous chapter. You can see that the overall model is composed of two confirmatory factor models (one for the three latent exogenous variables and one for the two latent endogenous variables) linked together by a structural model.

The confirmatory factor models depict how the latent variables have been measured; they correspond directly to the measurement scheme shown in Table 2.2 in Chapter 2. The relationships between the latent variables and their corresponding indicators (i.e. manifest variables) are represented by arrows which originate at the latent variable and end at the indicators.[2] For example, Market Orientation (Mkt Ort) has three (reflective) indicators, namely Customer Orientation (Custort), Competitor Orientation (Comport) and Interfunctional Coordination (Intcord). Note that each indicator is also associated with an error term, the latter representing 'errors in measurement' (since it is virtually impossible to perfectly measure even an observed variable).

As far as the structural model is concerned, each structural path represents a theory-based hypothesis (e.g. Role Ambiguity is hypothesized to

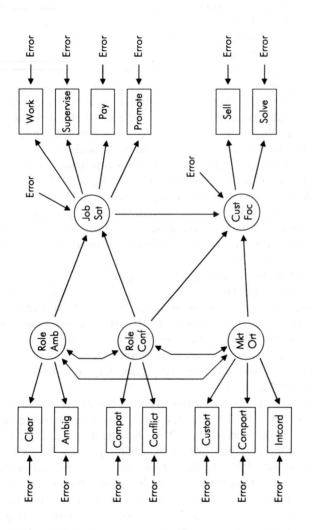

Figure 3.1   Path diagram for illustrative model

negatively influence Job Satisfaction). Consistent with our conceptualization (see Table 2.1 in Chapter 2), there are four **directional relationships** between the exogenous and endogenous latent variables and one directional relationship between the two endogenous latent variables.[3] The error terms associated with the endogenous variables represent 'errors in equations' and indicate that the dependent variables in the model are not perfectly explained by the independent variables. Finally, the curved two-way arrows connecting the three exogenous variables represent **non-directional relationships** (i.e. do not distinguish between a dependent and an independent variable); they simply indicate that the exogenous variables are thought to be intercorrelated.

A point worth noting from Figure 3.1 is that the absence of an arrow implies the absence of a relationship. For example, the absence of a path from Role Ambiguity (Role Amb) to Customer Focus (Cust Foc) indicates that the former variable is not expected to have a **direct effect** on the latter. This does not mean that Role Ambiguity does not have any influence on Customer Focus; rather its impact is captured by an **indirect effect** (i.e. via Job Satisfaction). Note also that certain **model assumptions** are reflected in the absence of paths. Thus, the lack of an arrow between the exogenous variables and the error terms of the endogenous variables states that residual influences are assumed to be uncorrelated to the independent variables included in the model.[4] Similarly, the absence of paths between measurement errors (both within-constructs and between-constructs) reflects the assumption of uncorrelated measurement errors.[5]

One problem with the path diagram in Figure 3.1 is that it is *model-specific*, i.e. it lacks a standard notation for referencing the various elements of the model. Thus, in describing our path diagram we had to make reference to Tables 2.1 and 2.2 in order to describe the links between the latent variables and the measures used to operationalize them. An alternative, and more efficient approach, is to use conventional LISREL notation and standard construction rules (see Appendix 3A). The resulting path diagram is shown in Figure 3.2.

In LISREL notation, an exogenous latent variable is called a KSI (denoted by the Greek letter ξ); thus the three exogenous variables in our model are KSI-1 (ξ_1), representing Role Ambiguity, KSI-2 (ξ_2), representing Role Conflict and KSI-3 (ξ_3), representing Market Orientation. The fact that these variables are thought to be intercorrelated is shown by PHI (ϕ) and the corresponding subscripts. Endogenous latent variables are known as ETA's (denoted by the Greek letter η); thus the two endogenous variables in the model are ETA-1 (η_1), representing Job Satisfaction and ETA-2 (η_2), representing Customer Focus. There are four directional relationships between the exogenous and endogenous latent variables, which are identified by GAMMA (γ) and the appropriate subscripts. There is also a single directional relationship between the endogenous variables, which is identified by BETA (β) and the corresponding subscripts. Finally, 'errors in equations' (random disturbances)

$\gamma = \{$ standardized regression (when use correlation matrix)
$\quad\quad$ coefficients
$\beta = \}$

measurement   structure   measurement

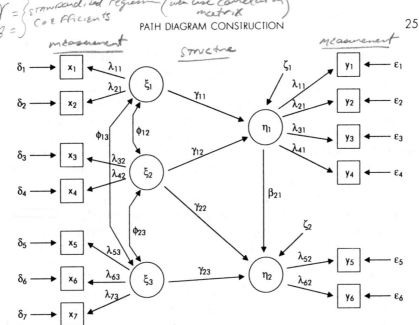

Figure 3.2   Path diagram for illustrative model in LISREL notation

are identified by ZETA (ζ) and the appropriate subscripts for the endogenous variables involved.

With regards to the measurement sub-model, indicators for exogenous latent variables are represented by the x's and indicators for endogenous latent variables by the y's. The relationship between the latent variables and their indicators are captured by LAMBDA (λ) and the relevant subscripts. Measurement errors for indicators of exogenous variables are denoted by DELTA (δ) and for indicators of endogenous variables as EPSILON (ε).

One potential source of confusion when using LISREL notation is the order of the subscripts associated with the various linkages. For directional paths (i.e. those represented by the β, γ and λ parameters), the general rule is that the first subscript references the target variable (i.e. the 'effect') and the second subscript references the source variable (i.e. the 'cause'). For instance, γ_{23} tells us that the second endogenous variable, η_2, is directly influenced by the third exogenous variable, ξ_3; similarly, λ_{31} implies that y_3 is an indicator of the first endogenous latent variable, η_1. What this rule implies is that the order of subscripts *matters* when directional linkages are involved; reversing the subscripts implies a different link altogether (e.g. $\beta_{12} \neq \beta_{21}$). In contrast, with non-directional linkages (e.g. those represented by the (ϕ's), subscript order is not important; for example, in Figure 3.1, we could replace ϕ_{12}, ϕ_{13} and ϕ_{23} with ϕ_{21}, ϕ_{31} and ϕ_{32}.

Although LISREL notation takes some time to get used to (yes, we know it's all Greek to you), it offers several benefits, making the effort to become familiar with it worthwhile. First, LISREL notation allows you to express *any* model (however complex) using standard terminology and provides a common language for communicating with other researchers. Second, and related to the first point, most LISREL-related literature uses this standard notational scheme and, unless you are familiar with it, you will find the literature very difficult to follow. Third, the program output, under the LISREL option, is based on the notational conventions just discussed (and summarized in Appendix 3A); if you do not understand these conventions, you will find the output as instructive as a mainframe computer manual written in Albanian! Fourth, the standard LISREL notation used to construct a path diagram translates *directly* to the **mathematical specification** of the model (see Chapter 4); what this means is that if the path diagram is correctly constructed, 'a reader should be able to ascertain precisely the statistical model to be tested from the observed indicators, latent variables, and the presence and absence of paths depicted in the diagram'.[6] Lastly, conventional notation allows you to express your hypotheses very clearly and succinctly; for example, the hypothesis that Role Ambiguity has a negative influence on Job Satisfaction can be stated simply as: $\gamma_{11} < 0$.

As a final point, you may be pleased to know that the interactive versions of LISREL 8 (versions 8.20 and 8.30) allow you to build a path diagram interactively. While the steps involved are easy to follow, the whole process is somewhat long-winded. In our view, it is best to first specify the model in SIMPLIS or LISREL language and then ask for a path diagram as part of the program output (see Chapter 4).[7]

Notes

1 Jöreskog and Sörbom (1989), p. 5.
2 Note that the direction of the arrows linking latent variables to manifest variables is consistent with the 'reflective indicator' mode of measurement as discussed in Appendix 2A.
3 We use the term 'directional relationship' in preference to 'causal relationship' because 'SEM does nothing more than test the relations among variables as they were assessed . . . Directional arrows in path diagrams typically used to depict relations in structural equation models should not be taken to indicate hypotheses of causal direction unless explicitly designated as such' (Hoyle, 1995, pp. 10–11) and 'the conditions for establishing causality . . . are no different when data are analyzed when using SEM than when they are analyzed using correlation, multiple regression, or analysis of variance' (Hoyle and Panter, 1995, pp. 174–175). For a discussion of causality issues in the context of structural equation modeling, see James, Mulaik and Brett (1982), Cliff (1983), Martin (1987), Freedman (1987), Hoyle and Smith (1994), Mulaik (1986, 1987, 1993), and Mulaik and James (1995).
4 This assumption corresponds to the familiar regression assumption that predictors are uncorrelated with the error term (e.g. see Achen, 1992).
5 Another assumption is that 'errors in measurement' and 'errors in equations' are uncorrelated; this is also reflected in the absence of paths in Figure 3.1.

6 Hoyle and Panter (1995), p. 160.
7 For details on how to build a path diagram interactively, fire up the program, click on 'Help', click on 'LISREL 8.20 Tutorial' and, finally, click on 'Creating model input from a path diagram'. Then make yourself a cup of coffee and go through the sequence described.

APPENDIX 3A

Path diagram construction for a LISREL model

1   An *endogenous* latent (unobservable) variable is positioned in a circle and designated by η (read as: eta).

2   An *exogenous* latent (unobservable) variable is positioned in a circle and designated by ξ (read as: ksi).

3   A *manifest* (observable) variable used as an indicator of a latent *endogenous* variable is positioned in a box and designated by *y*.

4   A *manifest* (observable) variable used as an indicator of a latent *exogenous* variable is positioned in a box and designated by *x*.

5   The *error* (residual) term for a latent *endogenous* variable is designated by ζ (read as: zeta); the error term represents 'error in equations' (i.e. random disturbances).

6   The *error* (residual) term for an *indicator y* of a latent *endogenous* variable is designated by ε (read as: epsilon) and for an *indicator x* of a latent *exogenous* variable is designated by δ (read as: delta); these error terms represent 'errors in measurement'.

7   A *directional ('causal') relationship* between two variables is represented by a *one-way* straight arrow starting from the hypothesized 'cause' and pointing to the hypothesized 'effect'. Each hypothesized relationship is referenced by a small Greek letter (see no. 8 and 9 below), and two subscripts, the first subscript indicates the target of an arrow (the 'effect') and the second subscript indicates the origin of the arrow (the 'cause'). No one-way arrow can point to an exogenous latent variable.

8   A *directional ('causal') relationship* between two *endogenous latent variables* is signified by β (read as: beta); a *directional ('causal') relationship* between an *exogenous* and an *endogenous latent variable* is signified by γ (read as: gamma).

9   The relationships between *latent variables* and their *reflective indicators* (i.e. the manifest variables) are indicated by one-way straight arrows originating from the latent variables and designated by λ (read as: lambda).

10 The influence of *residual terms* is represented by one-way arrows originating from the error variable ζ (read as: zeta), ε (read as: epsilon), and δ (read as: delta), and pointing to the corresponding latent or manifest variables (i.e. η, *y* and *x* respectively).

11 A *non-directional relationship* between two exogenous variables is depicted by a curved line with *double arrows* and designated by φ (read as: phi). These relationships are permissible only between exogenous latent variables (i.e. ξ) and between error terms of endogenous latent variables (i.e. ζ). When the relationship is between error terms, it is designated by ψ (read as: psi).

12 The measurement model for the exogenous latent variables, stipulating the relationship between the exogenous latent variables (ξ) and corresponding manifest variables (*x*) is always positioned to the *left side* of the path diagram.

13 The measurement model for the endogenous latent variables, stipulating the relationships between the endogenous latent variables (η) and corresponding manifest variables (*y*) is always positioned to the *right side* of the path diagram.

14 The structural model, stipulating the relationships between the exogenous (ξ) and endogenous (η) latent variables is always positioned in the *center* of the path diagram.

LX = Lambda X

LY = Lambda Y

BE = Beta

GA = Gamma

PH = Phi

PS = Psi

TD = Theta-Delta

TE = Theta - Epsilon

ME = means

SD = STD. Deviation

SE = Select.

FI = fixed

FR = free

L

TV = t values

CM = covariance matrix

KM = correlation matrix

LA = LABel

SY = symmetrical

FU = full (all elements in the matrix)

LE = latent Endogenous

LK = Latent Exogenous.

VA = values

ST = start value.

NY = # of observed Endogen. variable

NX = # of observed Exogen. variables

NE = # of latent Endogenous variables

NK = # of latent Exogen.

4 MODEL SPECIFICATION

The relationships depicted in the path diagrams in Chapter 3 must now be translated into a **system of linear equations**. This step is necessary for identification (see Chapter 5) and estimation purposes (see Chapter 6) and ensures that correct instructions are entered into the input file of the LISREL program.

At a basic level, the formal specification of our illustrative model can be represented by the following sets of equations:

Structural equations

Job Satisfaction = f(Role Ambiguity, Role Conflict, Error)
Customer Focus = f(Role Conflict, Market Orientation, Job
                Satisfaction, Error)

Measurement equations for endogenous variables

Satisfaction with Work = f(Job Satisfaction, Error)
Satisfaction with Supervision = f(Job Satisfaction, Error)
Satisfaction with Pay = f(Job Satisfaction, Error)
Satisfaction with Promotion = f(Job Satisfaction, Error)

Selling Behavior = f(Customer Focus, Error)
Problem-Solving Behavior = f(Customer Focus, Error)

Measurement equations for exogenous variables

Clarity = f(Role Ambiguity, Error)
Ambiguity = f(Role Ambiguity, Error)

Compatibility = f(Role Conflict, Error)
Conflict = f(Role Conflict, Error)

Customer Orientation = f(Market Orientation, Error)
Competitor Orientation = f(Market Orientation, Error)
Interfunctional Coordination = f(Market Orientation, Error)

where f indicates a *linear* function. This latter property is important since, in general, in LISREL it is assumed that 'the equations are *linear in the variables and linear in the parameters*'.[1] While it is sometimes possible to use LISREL to estimate models that are nonlinear in the variables but linear in the parameters (as in regression analysis), the procedures involved are much too complex to be considered here.[2]

Sticking with a linear specification, let us illustrate more precisely the nature of equations in our model by looking at the first structural equation relating to Job Satisfaction. Since Job Satisfaction is modeled as a linear function of Role Ambiguity and Role Conflict (plus an error term), we can write:

Job Satisfaction = $w_1 \cdot$ (Role Ambiguity) + $w_2 \cdot$ (Role Conflict) + Error   (1)

where w_1, w_2 = parameters to be estimated.

The other equations in the model can be represented in a similar manner, for example, the measurement equation linking Compatibility and Role Conflict is

Compatibility = $w \cdot$ (Role Conflict) + Error   (2)

You will have noticed that the above equations are very similar to conventional regression equations, the only difference being that they contain no intercept terms. The reason for this is that 'there is seldom any interest in the mean values of latent variables and intercept terms in equations';[3] consequently, it is usually assumed that all variables (latent as well as manifest) are measured as deviations from their means (i.e. the data are mean-centered).[4]

You may have also noticed that the derivation of the model equations is based *directly* on the path diagram of Figure 3.1; there is a one-to-one correspondence between each equation in the model and each set of one-way arrows pointed to a dependent variable. For example, Job Satisfaction has three one-way arrows pointing to it (one from Role Ambiguity, one from Role Conflict and one from residual influences (error)); the equation for Job Satisfaction reflects this *exactly* (see Equation 1 above).

Finally, you cannot have failed to notice that trying to derive the mathematical specification of the illustrative model using the terminology of Figure 3.1 is rather tedious and long-winded. We can do much better if we use the standard LISREL notation introduced in Chapter 3 and derive the formal specification of our model from Figure 3.2 instead of Figure 3.1. This results in the following three sets of equations:

Structural equations

$$\eta_1 = \gamma_{11}\xi_1 + \gamma_{12}\xi_2 + \zeta_1$$
$$\eta_2 = \beta_{21}\eta_1 + \gamma_{22}\xi_2 + \gamma_{23}\xi_3 + \zeta_2$$

Measurement equations for the endogenous variables

$$y_1 = \lambda_{11}\eta_1 + \varepsilon_1$$
$$y_2 = \lambda_{21}\eta_1 + \varepsilon_2$$
$$y_3 = \lambda_{31}\eta_1 + \varepsilon_3$$
$$y_4 = \lambda_{41}\eta_1 + \varepsilon_4$$
$$y_5 = \lambda_{52}\eta_2 + \varepsilon_5$$
$$y_6 = \lambda_{62}\eta_2 + \varepsilon_6$$

Measurement equations for the exogenous variables

$$x_1 = \lambda_{11}\xi_1 + \delta_1$$
$$x_2 = \lambda_{21}\xi_2 + \delta_2$$
$$x_3 = \lambda_{32}\xi_2 + \delta_3$$
$$x_4 = \lambda_{42}\xi_2 + \delta_4$$
$$x_5 = \lambda_{53}\xi_3 + \delta_5$$
$$x_6 = \lambda_{63}\xi_3 + \delta_6$$
$$x_7 = \lambda_{73}\xi_3 + \delta_7$$

If you are somewhat unsure of how the above equations were developed, trace each equation back to the path diagram in Figure 3.2 and have a look at Table 4.1.

We are now ready to construct the input file to instruct the LISREL program to illustrate our model. Table 4.2 shows this input file using SIMPLIS language.

The first line is an optional title line. If you have a really long title, you can use as many title lines as you need, as long as the lines do not begin with the words Observed Variables, Labels, or DA (these words or letters indicate the start of the LISREL command line). To avoid these problems completely, you can place an exclamation mark (!) at the beginning of each title line and place any words on the lines you wish. Although the title line is optional, it is good practice to include it in an input file (if only to remind you what the model is all about!).

The second and third lines provide the labels (names) for the manifest (observed) variables. Here are a few tips regarding variable names. First, notice that the variable names entered in the input file cannot be longer than eight characters; hence, Ambiguity becomes Ambig, Compatibility becomes Compat and so on. Second, if you need to place a space in a variable name, the variable name must be placed inside apostrophes so that the LISREL program will read it as *one* variable rather than two. Note that a space within a variable name counts as one of the allowable eight characters; for example, the variable Job Satisfaction becomes 'Job Sat' in the input file. If the variable name has more than eight characters (including spaces), the program truncates the name down to the first eight characters; thus 'Role Conf' will be referred to as 'Role Con' in the output.

Table 4.1   Mathematical specification for a LISREL model in standard notation

1   Each dependent variable (one to which a one-way arrow points, i.e. x-, y- and η-variables) can be mathematically described by a *single* linear equation.
2   Dependent variables are positioned to the *left* of the equal sign (=); independent variables (from which one-way arrows originate) are positioned to the *right* of the equal sign (=). Remember that exogenous variables (ξ) can never be dependent variables, but endogenous variables (η) can be dependent in some equations and independent in others.
3   The linkages (arrows in the path diagram) between the variables in the model are represented by coefficients (the λ's, γ's and β's). The signs and magnitudes of the coefficients reflect the nature (positive or negative) and strength of the hypothesized relationships.
4   When a number of independent variables affect a dependent variable, the effect to the independent variables is considered to be *additive*, so the number of terms on the right side of the equation is equal to the number of one-way arrows pointing to the dependent variable concerned.
5   Error terms (ζ, δ and ε) are assumed to be mutually uncorrelated; ζ and δ are assumed to be uncorrelated with ξ-variables; ε is assumed to be uncorrelated with η-variables.

Table 4.2   SIMPLIS input file for illustrative model

```
!ILLUSTRATIVE MODEL OF JOB SATISFACTION AND CUSTOMER FOCUS
Observed Variables: Work Supervise Pay Promote Sell Solve Clear Ambig
Compat Conflict Custort Comport Intcord
Covariance Matrix from File ex1.cov
Sample Size: 306
Latent Variables: 'Job Sat' 'Cust Foc' 'Role Amb' 'Role Conf' 'Mkt Ort'
Relationships:
'Job Sat' = 'Role Amb' 'Role Conf'
'Cust Foc' = 'Role Conf' 'Mkt Ort' 'Job Sat'
Clear = 1*'Role Amb'
Ambig = 'Role Amb'
Compat = 1*'Role Conf'
Conflict = 'Role Conf'
Custort = 1*'Mkt Ort'
Comport Intcord = 'Mkt Ort'
Work = 1*'Job Sat'
Supervise - Promote = 'Job Sat'
Sell = 1*'Cust Foc'
Solve = 'Cust Foc'
Options: ND=3
Path Diagram
End of Problem
```

Third, *observed variables must be entered in the order in which they are found in the associated covariance matrix* (see Appendix 4A). In our example, the first variable in the covariance matrix is Work, so Work is the first variable name listed on the Observed Variables line. Finally, LISREL is case-sensitive. That means that you must be consistent with your use of upper and lower case characters when entering the variable names. For example, if you enter Clear on the Observed Variables line and used CLEAR when specifying the relationships, the program will not recognize CLEAR as a defined variable because it does not match the description found on the Observed Variables line.

The fourth line tells the LISREL program the location of the covariance matrix we are using as input. In this case, the covariance matrix is located in a separate file called ex1.cov. Recall from Chapter 1 (see Appendix 1B) that the covariance matrix yielded by the empirical data is denoted as **S**. Well, this covariance matrix which contains the variances and covariances among the manifest variable *is* **S**; it is reproduced in Appendix 4A. Since we have thirteen manifest variables in our model, we have thirteen lines in the covariance matrix.[5] Note that if you supply the covariance matrix in a separate file (as we did) you cannot have any variable names, formatting, etc, included: *only* the numbers showing the variances and covariances should be contained in the data file, otherwise the LISREL program will respond with an error message. Thus, while we have included the variable names in Appendix 4A to show the order of the variables for our model, we did *not* include these names in the ex1.cov file. An alternative approach to providing the input covariance matrix in a separate file, is to enter it directly into the SIMPLIS input file. Appendix 4B shows how this is done.

The fifth line, 'Sample Size: 306' tells the LISREL program how many observations make up the data set you are using. In this case, it is stated that the covariance matrix is based on 306 observations.

In line six, we have specified the labels or names of the latent variables in our model. The same tips regarding the names of manifest variables apply to latent variables (see discussion relating to the second and third lines of the input file).

In lines 7–19 (under 'Relationships') we specify the hypothesized relationships among the latent variables as well as the relationships between the latent variables and their indicators (i.e. the manifest variables). Because latent variables are unobservable and, therefore, have no scales of their own, their origin and unit of measurement have to be defined. The origin is fixed by assuming that the mean of each latent variable is zero, while the unit of measurement is fixed either by assuming that it is a standardized variable (with variance fixed to 1) or by defining the unit of each latent variable in relation to one of its observed indicators. It is the latter approach we have followed in our example. Specifically, for each latent variable, we have fixed one of the coefficients (known as **loadings**) in the relevant measurement equations to unity. Thus, Role Ambiguity (Role Amb) has been scaled by using Clarity (Clear) as a **reference variable**, Role Conflict (Role Conf) by using Compatibility (Compat) as a reference variable and so on. Given that there are five latent variables in our model, five of the manifest variables act as reference variables. In selecting reference variables, it is recommended that 'one should choose the fixed value for the observed variable, which, in some sense, best represents the latent variable'.[6] Note that when designating a manifest variable as a reference variable, the reference variable does *not* make the manifest and the latent variables the same unless the reference variable's error variance is also fixed to 0.[7] In this context it has been argued that 'with multiple indicators there is no need to fix residual variances to zero; fixing the residual to zero makes the latent and observed variable the same, which ignores important information about reliability of the reference indicator'.[8] Note also that the selection of a reference variable will affect the variance of the latent variable and thus the *unstandardized* paths from and to the latent variable; however, the *standardized* results would be the same no matter which manifest variable is used as a reference variable. Assigning a reference variable to each latent variable is the customary method of scaling latent variables; however, if a reference variable is not specified for a latent variable, the LISREL 8 program will automatically standardize the latent variable.

In specifying the model relationships in a SIMPLIS input file one can use either equations (as done in Table 4.2) or arrows. For examples, the following are perfectly equivalent ways of specifying the impact of Role Ambiguity and Role Conflict on Job Satisfaction:

```
'Job Sat' = 'Role Amb' 'Role Conf'
'Role Amb' 'Role Conf' -> 'Job Sat'
```

Notice that when using equal signs to express relationships, the 'target' variable appears on the left side of the equation, while the 'source' variable appears to the right. The opposite holds true when utilizing arrows. Notice also that when several adjacent variables are involved in a relationship (either as independent or dependent variables), one can include them in a single equation by referencing only the first and last variable involved. For example, the equation

```
Supervise - Promote = 'Job Sat'
```

is really a summary expression for three equations, namely

```
Supervise = 'Job Sat'
Pay = 'Job Sat'
Promote = 'Job Sat'
```

As far as relationships between exogenous latent variables are concerned, by default, LISREL 8 assumes that they are freely correlated; therefore, the relationships between these variables do not have to be explicitly specified in the SIMPLIS input file.

In line 20, we use one of the Options offered by the program regarding the printed output. Specifically, LISREL 8 only prints to two decimal places unless instructed to do otherwise; we would like to have the results in three decimal places, so we have specified Number of Decimals (ND) = 3. Other options available include: Print Residuals (all residuals are printed instead of in summary form); Wide Print (default is 80 characters per line; can be set to up to 132 characters per line); Method of Estimation (default is Maximum Likelihood (ML); there is a choice of six other methods); Admissibility Check (can be turned off or set to a higher number of iterations than the default (20)); Iterations (default is 20; can be set to any number); and Save Sigma in File filename (saves the *fitted* covariance matrix, $\hat{\Sigma}$, to a file). All these options can be included in a single command line as follows:[9]

```
Options: ND = 3, RS, WP, ME = GLS, AD = OFF, IT = 100,
SI = fit.cov
```

Here, we are asking for three decimal places, all residuals, output in wide print form, Generalized Least Squares (GLS) as the estimation method, no admissibility check, a maximum of 100 iterations and the fitted covariance matrix saved in a file called fit.cov.

Line 21 requests that a path diagram of an estimated model be produced. If you include this command line, the path diagram will pop up on the screen when the LISREL program runs successfully. The path diagram is a very nice feature as it allows you to see the parameter estimates and other important information (to be discussed in subsequent chapters) on-screen.

The interactivity of versions 8.20 and 8.30 of the LISREL program also enables you to add/delete paths and re-estimate the model on-screen; this is particularly useful when contemplating modifications to the original model (see Chapter 8).

The last line, 'End of Problem', is optional and is used to notify the program that the input file is complete.

The SIMPLIS input file in Table 4.2 will produce approximately six pages of output. Initially, the input file will be reproduced, followed by the covariance matrix used as data; this portion of the output is shown in Appendix 4C (the remainder of the output file will be presented and discussed in subsequent chapters).

As mentioned briefly in Chapter 1, it is also possible to construct the input file in SIMPLIS language but request that the output is provided in LISREL format; unlike SIMPLIS, the LISREL language is based on the standard notational conventions we established in Chapter 3 and presents the parameter specifications (and subsequent estimates) in *matrix* form. Thus, whereas in SIMPLIS format, the estimated model is given in the form of equations, in LISREL format the model is described in terms of parameter matrices. To request LISREL output, simply insert the command line LISREL output before the Path Diagram command. One important reason for wishing to obtain the output in LISREL format (other than to impress your friends with your incredible knowledge of matrix algebra) is that it provides *additional* information not available in the SIMPLIS output; these include comprehensive residual analysis (RS), modification indices (MI), standardized (SS) and completely standardized (SC) solutions, and effect decomposition (EF).[10] These options will be discussed in subsequent chapters and can all be specified on one line as follows:

LISREL Output: RS MI SS SC EF

If we were to request LISREL output, in addition to the information contained in Appendix 4C (i.e. reproduction of the input file and associated covariance matrix), we would also obtain a detailed listing of all **parameter specifications** of our model; this is shown in Table 4.3.

Table 4.3 Parameter specifications for illustrative model

```
!ILLUSTRATIVE MODEL OF JOB SATISFACTION AND CUSTOMER FOCUS
Parameter Specifications
```

LAMBDA-Y — *endogenous*

	Job Sat	Cust Foc
Work	0	0
Supervis	1	0
Pay	2	0
Promote	3	0
Sell	0	0
Solve	0	4

LAMBDA-X — *exogenous*

	Role Amb	Role Con	Mkt Ort
Clear	0	0	0
Ambig	5	0	0
Compat	0	0	0
Conflict	0	6	0
Custort	0	0	0
Comport	0	0	7
Intcord	0	0	8

BETA

	Job Sat	Cust Foc
Job Sat	0	0
Cust Foc	9	0

GAMMA

	Role Amb	Role Con	Mkt Ort
Job Sat	10	11	0
Cust Foc	0	12	13

PHI

	Role Amb	Role Con	Mkt Ort
Role Amb	14		
Role Con	15	16	
Mkt Ort	17	18	19

PSI
Note: This matrix is diagonal.

Job Sat	Cust Foc
20	21

THETA-EPS

Work	Supervis	Pay	Promote	Sell	Solve
22	23	24	25	26	27

THETA-DELTA

Clear	Ambig	Compat	Conflict	Custort	Comport
28	29	30	31	32	33

THETA-DELTA

Intcord
34

A total of 34 independent parameters are to be estimated according to the model specification. These are allocated to eight parameter matrices and are sequentially numbered (from 1 to 34). Parameters to be estimated are known as **free parameters**, whereas parameters which have been given *a-priori* fixed values are known as **fixed parameters**.[11] One example of fixed parameters are parameters associated with reference variables; as already noted, such parameters are fixed in order to set the unit of measurement of the latent variables. Fixed parameters can also reflect the absence of paths between two variables; for example, the parameter value of the path between Role Ambiguity and Customer Focus is (implicitly) set to zero, since no direct relationship between the two variables was hypothesized when conceptualizing the model (see Chapter 3). In Table 4.3 fixed parameters are identified by zeros; this does not mean that their values are necessarily zero. For example, the values of parameters relating to reference values are equal to unity (see Table 4.2 earlier) while, as just noted, parameters reflecting the absence of a direct link between two variables are given zero values. An important point to note at this stage is that it is the *specific* pattern of free and fixed parameters that reflects the formal specification of a LISREL model; any change in the parameters implies a changed model.

The parameter matrices in Table 4.3 are formally defined in Appendix 4D, while Appendix 4E provides a general description of our illustrative model in matrix form, using standard LISREL notation. You should study these Appendices carefully as this will help your understanding of the program output in LISREL format. Here, we give a brief description of each matrix in Table 4.3 to provide you with an initial idea of what is going on.

The first matrix printed is the LAMBDA-Y matrix. This matrix links the endogenous variables to their corresponding indicators. Because these latent endogenous variables do not have definite scales, we have scaled them by fixing the first indicator of each endogenous variable to 1 (see earlier discussion). In this example, Work is the first indicator of Job Satisfaction and Selling is the first indicator of Customer Focus, hence the relevant parameters are designated by zeros. The remaining indicators of Job Satisfaction are numbered sequentially 1 through 3, and the remaining indicator of Customer Focus (solve) is numbered 4.

The second matrix is the LAMBDA-X matrix which specifies the links between the exogenous variables and their indicators. The parameter specifications of the two indicators of Role Ambiguity are numbered 0 and 5, the two indicators of Role Conflict are numbered 0 and 6, and the three indicators of Market Orientation are numbered 0, 7 and 8; again, those indicators identified by zeros are those serving as reference variables (see Table 4.2 earlier).

The third matrix (BETA) describes the relationship(s) between the endogenous variables. Here we have hypothesized a single directional relationship from Job Satisfaction to Customer Focus; the parameter specification depicting this relationship is numbered 9. The absence of a path from Customer Focus to Job Satisfaction is reflected in the zero entry in the relevant parameter specification.

The fourth matrix (GAMMA) describes the relationships between the exogenous variables and the endogenous variables. In our example, Role Ambiguity and Role Conflict are hypothesized to influence Job Satisfaction; the parameter specifications depicting these hypotheses are numbered 10 and 11, respectively. Similarly, Role Conflict and Market Orientation are hypothesized to influence Customer Focus; the corresponding parameter specifications are numbered 12 and 13. Again, the zeros in this matrix reflect absence of paths between the variables involved.

The PHI matrix shows the relationships of the exogenous variables with each other. In our illustrative model, the exogenous variables are expected to be intercorrelated; the parameter specifications for these intercorrelations are numbered 14–19.

The PSI, THETA-EPS, and THETA-DELTA matrices respectively contain parameter specifications for the error terms of the endogenous variables, the error terms of the indicators of endogenous variables, and the error terms of the indicators of exogenous variables. The parameters to be estimated are numbered 20–34. Note that all these matrices are *diagonal* matrices: they contain the error variances of the relevant variables but no error covariances. This reflects an assumption of error independence both within and between latent variables (see also assumption 5 in Table 4.1).

We are now ready to proceed with the estimation of our model. Well, *almost* ready, as we first have to make sure that we have enough information to enable us to estimate each of the 34 free parameters contained in the eight matrices in Table 4.3. This raises the issue of model identification and is the subject of the next chapter.

Notes

1 Bollen (1989), p. 12.
2 For dealing with non-linearities in LISREL, see Busemeyer and Jones (1983), Kenny and Judd (1984), Heise (1986), Hayduk (1987), Ping (1995, 1996), Jaccard and Wan (1996), Jöreskog and Yang (1996) and Bollen and Paxton (1998).
3 Jöreskog and Sörbom (1989), p. 3.
4 Note that it *is* possible in LISREL to estimate models containing intercepts and latent variable means. Such parameters are of particular interest in multi-sample problems and when changes over time are studied (as in growth curve estimation). See Sörbom (1974, 1976, 1982), Hayduk (1987) and Bollen (1989).
5 The thirteen values in the diagonal of the covariance matrix are the variances of the manifest variables, while the off-diagonal elements represent covariances. See Chapter 1, Appendix 1A for a refresher on the structure of a covariance matrix.
6 Jöreskog and Sörbom (1989), p. 4.
7 Recently, Hayduk (1996) recommended fixing not only the coefficient for the reference variable but also its error variance (to a value reflecting the reference variable's unreliability); the latter step is accomplished by 'making a personal judgement of the percent (proportion) of the indicator's variance that is error, and then multiplying the real

variance of the indicator by the specified percent (proportion) to determine the specific numeric value at which [the error variance] is fixed' (Hayduk, 1996, p. 34). However, the practice of fixing both the coefficients (loadings) *and* the error variances of reference variables is currently not widespread.

8 Maruyama (1998), p. 183.

9 Alternatively, each of the chosen options can be placed on a separate command line in the SIMPLIS input file, e.g. Number of Decimals = 3.

10 Further options (usually used only by hard-core LISRELites) include printing of variances and covariances for the latent variables (VA), factor score regression (FS), correlations of parameter estimates (PC) and technical information (PT).

11 Yet other types of parameters are **constrained parameters** (also known as restricted parameters). These come about when we constrain one parameter to have the same estimated value as another coefficient (e.g. we may have a theory that says that two independent latent variables are supposed to have equally strong effects on a dependent latent variable and we want to test this hypothesis). Note that, with constrained parameters it is only necessary to actually estimate *one* of them (as this automatically determines the value of the other parameter); thus, in the parameter specifications in Table 4.3, constrained parameters would be given the *same* number and thus, would not be counted as separate free parameters.

APPENDIX 4A

Covariance matrix to be analyzed

	Work	Supervise	Pay	Promote	Sell	Solve	Clear	Ambig	Compat	Conflict	Custort	Comport	Intcord
Work	0.160												
Supervise	0.089	0.372											
Pay	0.123	0.157	0.491										
Promote	0.138	0.249	0.272	0.915									
Sell	0.227	0.378	0.439	0.532	1.681								
Solve	0.149	0.221	0.306	0.317	0.950	0.899							
Clear	-0.139	-0.236	-0.217	-0.211	-0.525	-0.290	1.013						
Ambig	-0.168	-0.445	-0.351	-0.447	-0.939	-0.502	0.993	2.077					
Compat	-0.161	-0.342	-0.209	-0.372	-0.721	-0.243	0.461	0.840	1.771				
Conflict	-0.168	-0.357	-0.177	-0.363	-0.753	-0.291	0.442	0.848	1.495	2.051			
Custort	0.190	0.309	0.285	0.353	0.918	0.569	-0.482	-0.837	-0.537	-0.526	1.153		
Comport	0.167	0.294	0.336	0.450	0.764	0.434	-0.370	-0.708	-0.473	-0.489	0.786	1.237	
Intcord	0.168	0.291	0.228	0.327	0.708	0.431	-0.367	-0.658	-0.371	-0.399	0.823	0.715	1.086

APPENDIX 4B

Direct entry of covariance matrix into the SIMPLIS input file

To include the sample covariance matrix in the SIMPLIS input file (rather than supplying it as a separate file), simply enter the command line

```
Covariance Matrix:
```

and follow it immediately with the actual numbers representing the variances and covariances of the manifest variables *in the order listed in the* 'Observed Variables' *command line*. For example, the first three lines of the covariance matrix for our illustrative model would be entered as

```
Covariance Matrix:
0.160
0.089   0.372
0.123   0.157  0.491
```

It is not necessary to provide the variances and covariances in a triangular matrix form; you can also sequentially list them as long as you preserve the order of the manifest variables. Thus, the following format is perfectly acceptable:

```
Covariance Matrix:
0.0160  0.089  0.372  0.123  0.157  0.491
```

Whichever format you opt for, make sure that each variance/covariance is separated from its neighbors by a space or two. Also make sure that (a) all variances/covariances have been entered (if you have k manifest variables, then you should have $k(k+1)/2$ variances and covariances), and (b) that they have been entered in the *correct order*. Omission of an element of the covariance matrix and/or an incorrect order will either result in an error message or, worse, fit the model to the wrong set of data. Errors of this nature *do* happen – particularly when the covariance matrix is large – and it is worth double-checking to ensure that all is well at this early stage.

In general, it is recommended to keep the data and command files separate; indeed the authors of LISREL recommend that 'all data be read from external files. *Do not put the data in the command file*' (Jöreskog and Sörbom, 1996a, p. 322, emphasis in the original). You have been warned!

APPENDIX 4C

Selected output from SIMPLIS input file for illustrative model

DATE: 4/28/99
TIME: 10:44

L I S R E L 8.20

BY

Karl G. Jöreskog & Dag Sörbom

This program is published exclusively by
Scientific Software International, Inc.
7383 N. Lincoln Avenue, Suite 100
Chicago, IL 60646-1704, U.S.A.
Phone: (800)247-6113, (847)675-0720, Fax: (847)675-2140
Copyright by Scientific Software International, Inc., 1981-98
Use of this program is subject to the terms specified in the
Universal Copyright Convention.

Website: www.ssicentral.com

The following lines were read from file
C:\MYDOCU~1\LISREL~1\EXAMPL~1\EXAMPLE1.SPL:

```
!ILLUSTRATIVE MODEL OF JOB SATISFACTION AND CUSTOMER FOCUS
Observed Variables: Work Supervise Pay Promote Sell Solve Clear Ambig
Compat Conflict Custort Comport Intcord
Covariance Matrix from File ex1.cov
Sample Size: 306
Latent Variables: 'Job Sat' 'Cust Foc' 'Role Amb' 'Role Conf' 'Mkt Ort'
Relationships:
'Job Sat' = 'Role Amb' 'Role Conf'
'Cust Foc' = 'Role Conf' 'Mkt Ort' 'Job Sat'
Clear = 1*'Role Amb'
Ambig = 'Role Amb'
Compat = 1*'Role Conf'
Conflict = 'Role Conf'
Custort = 1*'Mkt Ort'
Comport Intcord = 'Mkt Ort'
Work = 1*'Job Sat'
Supervise - Promote = 'Job Sat'
Sell = 1*'Cust Foc'
Solve = 'Cust Foc'
Options: ND=3
Path Diagram
End of Program
```

Sample Size = 306

!ILLUSTRATIVE MODEL OF JOB SATISFACTION AND CUSTOMER FOCUS

Covariance Matrix to be Analyzed

	Work	Supervis	Pay	Promote	Sell	Solve
Work	0.160					
Supervis	0.089	0.372				
Pay	0.123	0.157	0.491			
Promote	0.138	0.249	0.272	0.915		
Sell	0.227	0.378	0.439	0.532	1.681	
Solve	0.149	0.221	0.306	0.317	0.950	0.899
Clear	-0.139	-0.236	-0.217	-0.211	-0.525	-0.290
Ambig	-0.168	-0.445	-0.351	-0.447	-0.939	-0.502
Compat	-0.161	-0.342	-0.209	-0.372	-0.721	-0.243
Conflict	-0.168	-0.357	-0.177	-0.363	-0.753	-0.291
Custort	0.190	0.309	0.285	0.353	0.918	0.569
Comport	0.167	0.294	0.336	0.450	0.764	0.434
Intcord	0.168	0.291	0.228	0.372	0.708	0.431

Covariance Matrix to be Analyzed

	Clear	Ambig	Compat	Conflict	Custort	Comport
Clear	1.013					
Ambig	0.993	2.077				
Compat	0.461	0.840	1.771			
Conflict	0.442	0.848	1.495	2.051		
Custort	-0.482	-0.837	-0.537	-0.526	1.353	
Comport	-0.370	-0.708	-0.473	-0.489	0.786	1.237
Intcord	-0.367	-0.658	-0.371	-0.399	0.823	0.715

Covariance Matrix to be Analyzed

	Intcord
Intcord	1.086

APPENDIX 4D

Parameter matrices of a comprehensive LISREL model

Matrix name	Mathematical notation	LISREL abbreviation	Matrix description
LAMBDA-Y	$\mathbf{\Lambda}_y$	LY	a ($p \times m$) matrix containing the coefficients linking the y- to the η-variables
LAMBDA-X	$\mathbf{\Lambda}_x$	LX	a ($q \times n$) matrix containing the coefficients linking the x- to the ξ-variables
BETA	$\mathbf{B}$	BE	a ($m \times m$) matrix containing the coefficients representing directional links between η-variables
GAMMA	$\mathbf{\Gamma}$	GA	a ($m \times n$) matrix containing the coefficients representing directional links between ξ- and η-variables
PHI	$\mathbf{\Phi}$	PH	a ($n \times n$) matrix containing the covariances between the ξ-variables
PSI	$\mathbf{\Psi}$	PS	a ($m \times m$) matrix containing the covariances between the ζ-variables (error terms of the latent endogenous variables)
THETA-EPSILON	$\mathbf{\Theta}_\varepsilon$	TE	a ($p \times p$) matrix containing the covariances between the ε-variables (error terms of the y-indicators)
THETA-DELTA	$\mathbf{\Theta}_\delta$	TD	a ($q \times q$) matrix containing the covariances between the δ-variables (error terms of the x-indicators)

where p, q, m and n is the number of y-, x-, η- and ξ-variables, respectively.

APPENDIX 4E

Illustrative model in matrix form

We can represent the structural and measurement equations for our model as follows (using the standard notation introduced in Chapter 3):

Structural equations

$$\begin{bmatrix} \eta_1 \\ \eta_2 \end{bmatrix} = \begin{bmatrix} 0 & 0 \\ \beta_{21} & 0 \end{bmatrix} \times \begin{bmatrix} \eta_1 \\ \eta_2 \end{bmatrix} + \begin{bmatrix} \gamma_{11} & \gamma_{12} & 0 \\ 0 & \gamma_{22} & \gamma_{23} \end{bmatrix} \times \begin{bmatrix} \xi_1 \\ \xi_2 \\ \xi_3 \end{bmatrix} + \begin{bmatrix} \zeta_1 \\ \zeta_2 \end{bmatrix}$$

Measurement equations for the endogenous variables

$$\begin{bmatrix} y_1 \\ y_2 \\ y_3 \\ y_4 \\ y_5 \\ y_6 \end{bmatrix} = \begin{bmatrix} 1 & 0 \\ \gamma_{21} & 0 \\ \gamma_{31} & 0 \\ \gamma_{41} & 0 \\ 0 & 1 \\ 0 & \gamma_{62} \end{bmatrix} \times \begin{bmatrix} \eta_1 \\ \eta_2 \end{bmatrix} + \begin{bmatrix} \varepsilon_1 \\ \varepsilon_2 \\ \varepsilon_3 \\ \varepsilon_4 \\ \varepsilon_5 \\ \varepsilon_6 \end{bmatrix}$$

Measurement equations for the exogenous variables

$$\begin{bmatrix} x_1 \\ x_2 \\ x_3 \\ x_4 \\ x_5 \\ x_6 \\ x_7 \end{bmatrix} = \begin{bmatrix} 1 & 0 & 0 \\ \gamma_{21} & 0 & 0 \\ 0 & 1 & 0 \\ 0 & \gamma_{42} & 0 \\ 0 & 0 & 1 \\ 0 & 0 & \gamma_{63} \\ 0 & 0 & \gamma_{73} \end{bmatrix} \times \begin{bmatrix} \xi_1 \\ \xi_2 \\ \xi_3 \end{bmatrix} + \begin{bmatrix} \delta_1 \\ \delta_2 \\ \delta_3 \\ \delta_4 \\ \delta_5 \\ \delta_6 \\ \delta_7 \end{bmatrix}$$

The matrix equations shown above correspond directly to the equations developed earlier in the text based upon the path diagram in Figure 3.2 and the rules in Table 4.1. These matrix equations can be also represented in summary form as follows (using the parameter matrices defined in Appendix 4D).

Structural model

$$\eta = \mathbf{B}\eta + \mathbf{\Gamma}\xi + \zeta \tag{1}$$

Measurement model for the endogenous latent variables

$$y = \mathbf{\Lambda}_y\eta + \varepsilon \tag{2}$$

Measurement model for the exogenous latent variables

$$x = \Lambda_x \xi + \delta \tag{3}$$

These three equations provide the most general description of *any* LISREL model (the specific form of the model being determined by the particular pattern of free and fixed parameters contained in the relevant matrices). We can thus summarize the formal specification of a LISREL model as follows:

- Three matrix equations can be used to describe the measurement model for η-variables, the measurement model for the ξ-variables, and the structural model for any particular LISREL model.
- The matrix equation for the measurement model of the endogenous latent variables links the vector of y-variables to the vector of η-variables via the Λ_y matrix (which contains the λ_y parameters) and the vector of error terms, ε.
- The matrix equation for the measurement model of the exogenous latent variables links the vector of x-variables to the vector of ξ-variables via the Λ_x matrix (which contains the λ_x parameters) and the vector of error terms, δ.
- The matrix equation for the structural model links two vectors of η-variables together by means of the **B** matrix (which contains the β parameters). It also links the vector of η-variables to the vector of ξ-variables by means of the Γ matrix (which contains the γ parameters). Finally, the η-variables are connected to the vector of residuals, ζ.
- The row and column positions for each coefficient in the above matrices correspond *directly* to the subscripts of each coefficient path diagram. For example, the path between ξ_2 and η_1 is represented by γ_{12}, which therefore appears in the first row of the second column of the Γ matrix. When no relationship is hypothesized between variables, a zero in the corresponding position in the matrices is used to denote that absence.

5 MODEL IDENTIFICATION

Broadly speaking, the problem of identification revolves around the question of whether one has sufficient information to obtain a *unique* solution for the parameters to be estimated in the model. If a model is not identified, then it is not possible to determine unique values for the model coefficients; instead, there can be any number of acceptable parameter estimates and the selection of one set of values over another becomes entirely arbitrary.

To illustrate this problem, what would you do if you were asked to find a unique solution to the equation $A \cdot B = 40$? While you could eliminate some pairs of numbers (e.g. 2, 25; 4, 5; 9, 7; etc.) as not fitting the equation, you would also find that many pairs of numbers solve the equation equally well. Thus, you would be in a quandary as to which specific pair of numbers (1, 40; 2, 20; 4, 10; 5, 8) you should select as the correct solution; you have what is known as an **identification problem**.

Similar problems can occur in LISREL modeling when the information provided by the empirical data (e.g. variances and covariances of the manifest variables) is not sufficient to allow for a unique solution to be derived for the model parameters. In such a case, the LISREL program finds it can generate numerous solutions to the system of equations linking the variances and covariances of the observed variables to the model parameters and consequently, can fit any number of covariance matrices ($\hat{\Sigma}$) to the model. When this occurs, the model is said to be **unidentified** or **underidentified**; thus 'it is the failure of the combined model and data constraints to identify (locate or determine) unique estimates that results in . . . "the identification problem"'.[1]

Given that a system of equations can only be solved if the number of equations is at least equal to the number of unknowns, to obtain a unique solution of the parameters in a LISREL model, it is necessary 'that the number of independent parameters being estimated is less than or equal to the number of non-redundant elements of S, the sample matrix of covariances among the observed variables'.[2] To determine if your model meets this minimum requirement for identification, you can use the following formula:

$$t \leq s/2$$

where: t = the number of parameters to be estimated
        s = the number of variances and covariances amongst the manifest (observable) variables, calculated as $(p+q)(p+q+1)$
        p = the number of y-variables
        q = the number of x-variables

If $t > s/2$, then your model is unidentified.[3] To correct this problem, you must further constrain the model. In our previous example, we noted that you could find many solutions to the equation $A \cdot B = 40$, but what if we had told you that $B = 5$? You could then easily find a unique solution to the equation. Similarly, you can apply constraints to a LISREL model (a) by including more manifest variables (i.e. indicators) in the model, (b) by fixing additional parameters to zero (this is the most commonly used method), or (c) by setting parameters equal to each other. Essentially what you are doing is trying to ensure that each free parameter can be expressed as a function of the sample variances and covariances. A word of caution: any changes you make in the model by using the above options should be *theoretically* justified; you should never randomly add constraints to the model simply to achieve identification. Indeed, 'it is better to be known for having developed the correct model (even if you could not get estimates of its coefficients) than for having identified and estimated the wrong model'.[4]

If $t = s/2$, the model is said to be **just-identified**; therefore, a single, unique solution can be obtained for the parameter estimates. Going back to our example, assume that not only do you know that $A \cdot B = 40$, but also that $A + 2B = 18$. Utilizing both equations, you can derive a unique solution for A and B of 8 and 5, respectively. Unfortunately, in a just-identified model, all the information made available through the specification of the model is used to derive the parameter estimates, so no information remains to *test* the model (in other words, the degrees of freedom are zero).

If $t < s/2$, the model is **overidentified**. In this case, more than one estimate of each parameter can be obtained (because the equations available outnumber the number of parameters to be estimated); the degrees of freedom are positive and equal to $s/2 - t$. While this situation may initially appear contradictory to the desire to find a unique solution for the system of parameter equations, it is not. An overidentified model offers the opportunity to use one set of estimates to test the model. To illustrate this point, assume that besides the two equations ($A \cdot B = 40$ and $A + 2B = 18$), you are also given a third equation: $2A + B = 24$. Now you can derive two sets of estimates for A and B. Using the first two equations you get $A = 8$ and $B = 5$; using the second and third equations you get $A = 10$ and $B = 4$. In this context, the availability of two estimates for at least one of the parameters provides the possibility of using the second estimate to 'test the model. If the two estimates differ significantly, this outcome provides evidence that the model is false in some respect.'[5]

Now that you have a rough idea what identification is all about, let us look at a specific LISREL model to illustrate the key issues in more detail. Figure 5.1 shows a very simple model consisting of a single latent variable, ξ, measured by two indicators x_1 and x_2.

The question is: is this model identified? To answer this question let us formally specify the model (using the standard LISREL notation introduced in Chapter 4) so that we can determine how many (and which)

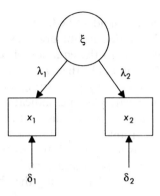

Figure 5.1   An unidentified LISREL model

parameters need to be estimated. One way of specifying the model is to fix the variance of the latent variable to unity (i.e. $\phi = 1$) and let the loadings of both indicators free (see Chapter 4). The relevant model equations would then read as follows:

$$x_1 = \lambda_1 \xi + \delta_1$$
$$x_2 = \lambda_2 \xi + \delta_2$$

Thus, we have two loadings (λ_1, λ_2) and two error variances ($VAR(\delta_1)$ and $VAR(\delta_2)$) to estimate (i.e. $t = 4$).

Alternatively, we could use one of the indicators as a reference variable to scale the construct and let the construct variance be freely estimated. If, say, we choose x_1, as the reference variable, then we would set $\lambda_1 = 1$ and the model specification would read as

$$x_1 = \xi + \delta_1$$
$$x_2 = \lambda_2 \xi + \delta_2$$

Again we have four parameters to estimate ($t = 4$), namely one loading (λ_2), two error variances ($VAR(\delta_1)$ and $VAR(\delta_2)$) and one construct variance (ϕ). Thus, irrespective of whether we standardize the latent variable or scale it in relation to one of its indicators, the number of parameters to be estimated is the same.[6]

Having determined that $t = 4$, let us look at the information that we have available in the sample covariance matrix **S**. Given that we only have two indicators, **S** is comprised of $VAR(x_1)$, $VAR(x_2)$ and $COV(x_1, x_2)$.[7] Thus, we only have *three* bits of information from which to estimate *four* parameters. Therefore, despite its simplicity, the model in Figure 5.1 is not identified.

Note that we could have arrived at the same conclusion by applying the formula for checking the minimum condition for identification, i.e. $t \leq s/2$. Here, $t = 4$ and $s = 2 \cdot 3 = 6$ (hence $s/2 = 3$); thus, $t > s/2$. In fact, what this formula does is calculate the number of non-redundant (i.e. distinct)

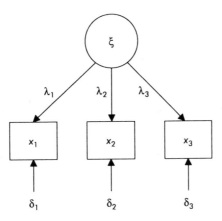

Figure 5.2 A just-identified LISREL model

elements in the sample covariance matrix, **S** (i.e. the number of variances and covariances of the indicators) and compare it to the number of free parameters based upon the specification of the model. Given that for a parameter 'it is necessary that at least one algebraic expression be obtainable expressing that free parameter as a function sample variances/covariances',[8] unless the number of available sample variances and covariances is at least equal to the number of parameters in need of estimation, the model will not be identified.

So, what can we do to achieve identification for the model in Figure 5.1? One option is to try and reduce the number of parameters, t, to be estimated. If, for example, we are willing to assume that the latent variable ξ, will influence the two indicators x_1 and x_2 to the same extent, then we can introduce the **equality constraint** $\lambda_1 = \lambda_2$. This means that each indicator loading will be estimated so that its value is equal to that of the other indicator's loading. In other words, we would only have to estimate a single value for both loadings, which brings the number of parameters to be estimated down to three (i.e. $t = 3$). If we do this, given that $s/2 = 3$, then the model would be just-identified (since $t = s/2$) and thus we could proceed with parameter estimation.

An alternative route would be to try and introduce more information in the sample covariance matrix **S** (which would increase $s/2$). For example, if we introduced a third indicator, x_3, then the model would be respecified as follows (see also Figure 5.2):

$$x_1 = \lambda_1 \xi + \delta_1$$
$$x_2 = \lambda_2 \xi + \delta_2$$
$$x_3 = \lambda_3 \xi + \delta_3$$
$$\phi = 1$$

While there are now six parameters to be estimated instead of four (three loadings and three error variances), the sample covariance matrix, **S**, now

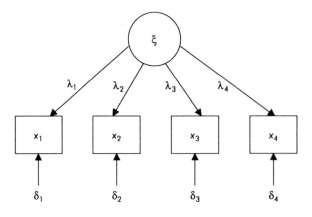

Figure 5.3 An overidentified LISREL model

also contains six non-redundant elements ($VAR(x_1)$, $VAR(x_2)$, $VAR(x_3)$, $COV(x_1, x_2)$, $COV(x_1, x_3)$, $COV(x_2, x_3)$)); thus $t = s/2$ and, therefore the model in Figure 5.2 is just-identified.

Finally, if a fourth indicator x_4, were to be introduced, we would end up with excess information and thus an overidentified model (Figure 5.3). This is because $t = 8$ (four loadings plus four error variances, assuming standardization of the construct variance, i.e. $\phi = 1$) and $s = 4 \cdot 5 = 20$ (hence $s/2 = 10$). Thus $t < s/2$ and the model has 2 degrees of freedom. From a scientific point of view the four-indicator model (Figure 5.3) is preferable to the three-indicator model (Figure 5.2) because 'just-identified models always have a perfect fit to data. But such good fits are tautological and trivial, and in no way indicate the scientific usefulness of a model'.[9] In contrast, 'models containing over-identified parameters generally will not fit the data exactly, thus creating the critically important possibility that a model could be found to fit observed data poorly. Only when this possibility exists is a finding of good fit meaningful'.[10]

Sometimes, it is also possible to estimate the parameters of an unidentified model by making the latter part of a larger model which is identified. For example, consider, the two-construct, four-indicator model in Figure 5.4. This consists of two models like the one in Figure 5.1. While on its own, each of these models would be unidentified (for reasons already discussed), putting them together results in an overidentified model with one degree of freedom.[11]

Now for the bad news: the fact that your model satisfies the condition $t \leq s/2$ does not *guarantee* that your model is identified. While this condition is necessary, it is not sufficient for identification; in fact, 'no easily applicable sufficient, or necessary and sufficient conditions for the full covariance structure model are available'[12] and 'the most effective way to demonstrate that a model is identified is to show that through algebraic manipulations of the model's covariance equations each of the parameters

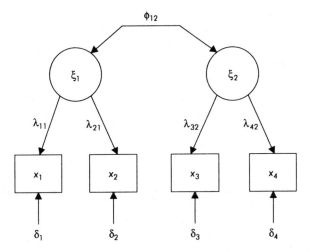

Figure 5.4 A two-construct, four-indicator LISREL model

can be solved in terms of the population variances and covariances of the observed variables'.[13] Unfortunately, in most cases this is easier said than done as, even with moderately complex models, trying to set up and solve the relevant expressions is a mammoth task (best left to people who like spending their holidays by attending mathematics workshops). As luck would have it, however, there are few steps that mere mortals can take to make reasonably sure that a model is indeed identified.

The first step is to ensure that all latent variables in the model have been assigned a defined scale (either via standardization or by the use of reference indicators); often problems of identification arise because of inappropriate specifications at this stage.[14] The second step is to check that $t \leq s/2$. The third step is to see whether your model falls into a category of models for which identification has already been proven; several authors discuss identification conditions for particular types of models (e.g. confirmatory factor analysis models) and it is a good idea to consult such sources.[15] Finally, you can rely on the LISREL program itself which has a very handy diagnostic facility for detecting identification problems.[16] If such problems are found, the program provides warning messages of the form:

```
W_A_R_N_I_N_G: parameter so-and-so may not be
              identified. Standard error estimates,
              T-values, Modification Indices and
              Standardized residuals cannot be
              computed.
```

LISREL's diagnostic facility is particularly useful because it can handle **empirical underidentification** problems as well. Such problems occur because although a model is identified *in principle* it may not be so *in practice*. For example, while it may be possible to express all free parameters as functions of the sample variances and covariances, some of the resulting expressions may involve division of covariances. If the latter happen to be zero (or very near zero) in the particular sample being analyzed, the calculation of the parameter's value will fail because division by zero is not algebraically defined. Empirical underidentification problems may also be encountered if perfect or near perfect (about ± 0.90) correlations exist among the observed variables.[17]

For our illustrative model – shown earlier in the path diagram in Figure 3.2 and formally specified in Chapter 4 – we have $t = 34$ (see Table 4.3), $p = 6$ and $q = 7$. Thus $s/2 = [(6+7)\cdot(6+7+1)]/2 = 91$. Because the number of (non-redundant) variances and covariances available exceeds the number of parameters to be estimated, our model is overidentified with $91-34 = 57$ degrees of freedom. Furthermore, the LISREL program did not issue any identification warnings; although LISREL's warning facility is not infallible, 'experience dictates that it is nearly so'.[18] Thus, we can proceed with parameter estimation.

Notes

1 Hayduk (1987), p. 140.
2 Long (1983b), p. 66.
3 Note that t reflects the number of *independent* parameters; thus constrained parameters (see note 11 in Chapter 4) should only be counted once.
4 Hayduk (1987), p. 147.
5 Aaker and Bagozzi (1979), p. 153.
6 This should not surprise you because the two approaches of giving a latent variable a unit of measurement are equivalent (see Chapter 4).
7 Recall that $COV(x_1, x_2) = COV(x_2, x_1)$; see Appendix 1A.
8 MacCallum (1995), p. 28.
9 James, Mulaik and Brett (1982), p. 135.
10 MacCallum (1995), p. 28.
11 By now you should be able to work out for yourself that $t = 9$ and $s/2 = 10$.
12 Long (1983b), p. 66.
13 Long (1983a), p. 44.
14 A typical error among novices is to set *both* the construct variance to unity *and* fix the loading of an indicator to unity; another error is to let all loadings free and the construct variance also free. Both these errors will result in unidentification. Note that, by default, LISREL 8 automatically standardizes all latent variables if no reference variables are specified; thus the above problems will only occur if the default settings are over-written by the user.
15 See, in particular, Hayduk (1987), Bollen (1989), Rigdon (1995), Maruyama (1998) and references given therein.
16 This is based upon an assessment of what is known as the **information matrix**; specifically, 'if the model is identified, the information matrix is almost certainly positive definite. If the information matrix is singular, the model is not identified' (Jöreskog and Sörbom, 1989, p. 17). Note that there are several other diagnostic procedures for checking identification; for details, see, for example, Hayduk (1987) and Bollen (1989).
17 Empirical unidentification issues are further discussed in Kenny (1979) and Rindskopf (1984).
18 Jöreskog and Sörbom (1989), p. 18.

6 PARAMETER ESTIMATION

The purpose of estimation is to generate numerical values for the free (and constrained) parameters in one's model. More specifically, the goal of estimation is to minimize the differences between each element found in S (the sample covariance matrix) and the corresponding element in $\hat{\Sigma}$ (the implied covariance matrix). You should recall from Chapter 1 (see, in particular, Appendix 1B) that every LISREL model implies certain predictions about the variances and covariances of the variables included in the model. These predictions 'can be compared to the variances and covariances calculated from the data on the observed indicators'.[1] In other words, you want an estimated covariance matrix, $\hat{\Sigma}$, generated by your model that is as close as possible to the covariance matrix, S, you originally inputted as data.[2] A function that measures how close is $\hat{\Sigma}$ to S is called a **fitting function**; different estimation methods have different fitting functions.[3]

In LISREL 8, seven methods can be used to estimate the parameters of a model: Instrumental Variables (IV), Two-Stage Least Squares (TSLS), Unweighted Least Squares (ULS), Generalized Least Squares (GLS), Maximum Likelihood (ML), Generally Weighted Least Squares (WLS) and Diagonally Weighted Least Squares (DWLS). Assuming that the model is correct (i.e. there is no specification error) and that you have a large sample size, all of these methods will produce estimates that are close to the 'true' parameter values. While a detailed description of the characteristics of the various methods is outside the scope of this book,[4] the following are some key differences.

IV and TSLS are fast, non-iterative, **limited-information techniques**. They estimate each parameter equation separately (i.e. without using information from other equations in the model). Consequently, they are relatively robust against misspecification. At the same time, they are statistically less efficient than **full-information techniques** which estimate the entire system of equations simultaneously and have the advantage that 'the estimation of each parameter utilizes the information provided by the entire system'.[5] IV and TSLS are primarily used to compute **starting values** for the other methods (see below). However, they can also be used in their own right, especially when the model is tentative and, therefore, model specification is uncertain.[6] The remaining estimation procedures (ULS, GLS, ML, WLS and DWLS) are full-information techniques and, thus, more statistically efficient than limited-information methods. However, they are also more susceptible to specification errors, because 'since the estimation of each parameter is dependent upon every other parameter in the model, estimates of each parameter are affected by misspecification in any equation of the model'.[7]

ULS, GLS, ML, WLS and DWLS are all **iterative procedures**, whereby final parameter estimates are obtained through a numerical search process which minimizes the value of the fitting function by successively improving the estimates.[8] Iterative estimation requires an initial choice of preliminary (i.e. tentative) estimates of the free parameters in the model. These are known as **starting values** and are automatically supplied by the LISREL program (using IV or TSLS methods)[9] unless the user chooses to provide his/her own set of starting values. On the basis of these starting values, the program computes an implied covariance matrix, $\hat{\Sigma}_0$, which is then compared to the sample covariance matrix, S. This comparison results in the **residual matrix** $(S - \hat{\Sigma}_0)$, whose elements comprise the differences between the values in S and $\hat{\Sigma}_0$. Next, the program computes a new improved set of provisional estimates which, in turn, generates a new implied covariance matrix, $\hat{\Sigma}_1$, which is again compared to the sample covariance matrix, S, and so on. The iteration process continues until it is no longer possible to update the parameter estimates and produce an implied covariance matrix, $\hat{\Sigma}_i$, which is any closer to the sample covariance matrix, S. Likewise, at this stage, the values of the elements in the residual matrix $(S - \hat{\Sigma}_i)$ will be as low as they are going to get. When an iterative estimation procedure has found as close a match as possible between $\hat{\Sigma}$ (the implied covariance matrix) and S (the sample covariance matrix), **convergence** has been reached.

In general, if the model and the data are compatible, the LISREL program is effective in providing good starting values and converging after a few iterations to an **admissible solution**.[10] Indeed, 'when the model fits the data well, the starting values produced by the program are often so close to the iterated solution that only a few iterations are necessary to compute these solutions. For some models, the estimated starting values are identical to ML and other estimates'.[11] Unfortunately, things can go wrong, resulting in non-convergence or non-admissible solutions; Appendix 6A discusses some common estimation problems and potential remedies.

The default estimation method in LISREL 8 is maximum likelihood (ML). It is also the more widely used method in practice.[12] ML provides consistently efficient estimation under the assumption of multivariate normality and is relatively robust against moderate departures from the latter.[13] Moreover, ML estimation is accompanied by a whole range of statistics which can be used to assess the extent to which one's model is in fact consistent with the data (see Chapter 7). Although ML is not the most appropriate estimation method under all circumstances, the general recommendation is 'that authors routinely report results from ML estimation. If characteristics of the data raise questions as to the appropriateness of ML, then the results of alternative estimation procedures might be reported in summary form if they contradict ML results or in a footnote if they corroborate them'.[14]

Table 6.1   SIMPLIS input file for illustrative model

```
!ILLUSTRATIVE MODEL OF JOB SATISFACTION AND CUSTOMER FOCUS
Observed Variables: Work Supervise Pay Promote Sell Solve Clear Ambig
Compat Conflict Custort Comport Intcord
Covariance Matrix from File ex1.cov
Sample Size: 306
Latent Variables: 'Job Sat' 'Cust Foc' 'Role Amb' 'Role Conf' 'Mkt Ort'
Relationships:
'Job Sat' = 'Role Amb' 'Role Conf'
'Cust Foc' = 'Role Conf' 'Mkt Ort' 'Job Sat'
Clear = 1*'Role Amb'
Ambig = 'Role Amb'
Compat = 1*'Role Conf'
Conflict = 'Role Conf'
Custort = 1*'Mkt Ort'
Comport Intcord = 'Mkt Ort'
Work = 1*'Job Sat'
Supervise - Promote = 'Job Sat'
Sell = 1*'Cust Foc'
Solve = 'Cust Foc'
Options: ND=3
Path Diagram
End of Problem
```

With regards to the remaining methods, GLS provides similar results to ML when the multivariate normality assumption holds and is also relatively robust against violations in the latter. ULS is the only **scale-dependent method** which means that changes in the scale of one or more observed variables result in changes in estimates that do not simply reflect the scale transformation. In contrast, with **scale-free methods** (such as ML and GLS), 'the parameter estimates would change, but only to reflect the change in the scale of the observed variables being analyzed'.[15] Thus, ULS estimation is only justified when all observed variables are measured in the same units. Finally, the WLS and DWLS methods have the advantage that they make no assumptions concerning the distribution of the observed variables (i.e. they fall into the category of **asymptotic distribution-free (ADF) estimators;**[16] however, to function properly, they require *very* large sample sizes (1000 plus) and are computationally very demanding. Moreover, even under conditions of non-normality, 'the question of whether or not this approach is superior to one that uses maximum likelihood (ML) or general least squares (GLS) estimation is still open to conjecture'.[17]

Bearing the above in mind, we opted for ML estimation for our illustrative model.[18] In what follows, we first discuss the output produced in SIMPLIS format and follow this by a discussion of the output in LISREL format. Both outputs were generated by running the input file shown in Table 4.2 in Chapter 4 and reproduced for convenience in Table 6.1.

Reading the program output: SIMPLIS format

The parameter estimates produced by the program are shown in Table 6.2. Let us first concentrate on the part of output titled LISREL Estimates.

Table 6.2 Parameter estimates: SIMPLIS output

!ILLUSTRATIVE MODEL OF JOB SATISFACTION AND CUSTOMER FOCUS

Number of Iterations = 40

LISREL Estimates (Maximum Likelihood)

```
    Work = 1.000*Job Sat, Errorvar.= 0.104   , R² = 0.351
                                    (0.00973)
                                     10.666

 Supervis = 1.783*Job Sat, Errorvar.= 0.193   , R² = 0.480
           (0.205)                  (0.0205)
            8.697                    9.431

      Pay = 1.823*Job Sat, Errorvar.= 0.304   , R² = 0.380
           (0.226)                  (0.0292)
            8.081                    10.436

  Promote = 2.417*Job Sat, Errorvar.= 0.587   , R² = 0.359
           (0.305)                  (0.0553)
            7.920                    10.609

     Sell = 1.000*Cust Foc, Errorvar.= 0.0477 , R² = 0.971
                                     (0.0729)
                                      0.653

    Solve = 0.582*Cust Foc, Errorvar.= 0.346  , R² = 0.606
           (0.0381)                  (0.0373)
            15.256                    9.279

    Clear = 1.000*Role Amb, Errorvar.= 0.440  , R² = 0.565
                                     (0.0481)
                                      9.147

    Ambig = 1.667*Role Amb, Errorvar.= 0.486  , R² = 0.766
           (0.128)                   (0.0956)
            13.038                    5.089

   Compat = 1.000*Role Con, Errorvar.= 0.300  , R² = 0.831
                                     (0.0970)
                                      3.090

 Conflict = 1.015*Role Con, Errorvar.= 0.534 , R² = 0.739
           (0.0764)                  (0.106)
            13.295                    5.042

   Custort = 1.000*Mkt Ort, Errorvar.= 0.374  , R² = 0.724
                                     (0.0518)
                                      7.222

  Comport = 0.834*Mkt Ort, Errorvar.= 0.556   , R² = 0.551
           (0.0604)                  (0.0558)
            13.802                    9.965

  Intcord = 0.838*Mkt Ort, Errorvar.= 0.398   , R² = 0.633
           (0.0561)                  (0.0447)
            14.941                    8.907

  Job Sat = - 0.189*Role Amb - 0.0464*Role Con, Errorvar.= 0.0241  ,
           (0.0292)            (0.0148)                   (0.00562)
            -6.473             -3.130                      4.289

            R² = 0.571

  Cust Foc = 2.212*Job Sat - 0.0587*Role Con + 0.534*Mkt Ort, Errorvar.= 0.656
            (0.419)           (0.0619)            (0.0768)                (0.0965)
             5.282            -0.948               6.961                   6.795

            R² = 0.584
```

Table 6.2 (continued)

Covariance Matrix of Independent Variables

	Role Amb	Role Con	Mkt Ort
Role Amb	0.573		
	(0.081)		
	7.100		
Role Con	0.486	1.471	
	(0.074)	(0.170)	
	6.568	8.672	
Mkt Ort	-0.513	-0.527	0.979
	(0.067)	(0.088)	(0.113)
	-7.650	-6.014	8.636

Covariance Matrix of Latent Variables

	Job Sat	Cust Foc	Role Amb	Role Con	Mkt Ort
Job Sat	0.056				
Cust Foc	0.199	1.577			
Role Amb	-0.131	-0.592	0.573		
Role Con	-0.160	-0.722	0.486	1.471	
Mkt Ort	0.121	0.822	-0.513	-0.527	0.979

These are presented in equation form, whereby (a) each manifest variable (i.e. indicator) is expressed as a linear function of its underlying latent variable, and (b) each dependent latent variable is expressed as a linear function of the relevant independent latent variables. More specifically, the first thirteen equations describe the measurement part of the model and are presented in the order of the manifest variables listed in the Observed Variables command line (see Table 6.1). The last two equations describe the structural part of the model and are listed in the order of the *endogenous* latent variables in the Latent Variables command line.

For each *free* parameter in each equation, three pieces of information are given, namely (a) the **unstandardized parameter estimate**, (b) its **standard error**, and (c) the relevant ***t*-value**. For example, in the equation linking Solve (Problem-Solving Behavior) to Cust Foc (Customer Focus), 0.582 is the unstandardized estimate, 0.0381 is the standard error and 15.256 is the *t*-value. As far as *fixed* parameters are concerned, only the pre-specified values are reproduced. For example, Sell (Selling Behavior) was used as a reference variable to scale Cust Foc (see Chapter 4). This is evident from the SIMPLIS input file specification where the relevant parameter value has been fixed to 1 (see Table 6.1). This value is indeed reproduced in the relevant equation in the output (i.e. Sell = 1.000 · Cust Foc) and, being a fixed parameter, is not accompanied by a standard error or *t*-value.

The interpretation of the unstandardized parameter estimates is straightforward. Their magnitudes show the resulting change in a dependent variable from a unit change in an independent variable, with all other independent variables being held constant. The direction of the change is captured by the sign of the relevant parameter (i.e. positive signs signify an increase in the value of the dependent variable and negative signs a decrease). For example, the equation Job Sat = -0.189·Role Amb - 0.0464·Role Con tells us that changing Role Amb (Role Ambiguity) by one unit results in a 0.189 unit decrease in Job Sat (Job Satisfaction). Thus, the interpretation of unstandardized parameter estimates is akin to that of regression coefficients in conventional regression analysis. Since unstandardized estimates are computed with all variables in their original metric, they 'describe the effect that variables have in an absolute sense, and can be used to compare similar models in other populations. However, these estimates are tied to the measurement units of the variables they represent. Any change in the measurement unit for earlier independent or dependent variable changes the value and, hence, comparability of parameters across populations'.[19]

Below each parameter estimate is its standard error. This shows how precisely the value of the parameter has been estimated: the smaller the standard error, the better the estimation. However, an excessively small standard error (i.e. approaching zero) spells trouble, since the test statistic (i.e. the *t*-value as discussed below) of the parameter cannot be defined. Equally, an excessively large standard error indicates that the parameter cannot be reasonably determined by the data at hand.[20] From a statistical perspective, standard errors under ML estimation are correct under assumptions of multivariate normality but otherwise need to be interpreted with caution.

If the value of a parameter is divided by its standard error, the *t*-value is obtained. For example, looking at the equation linking Comport (Competitor Orientation) to Mkt Ort (Market Orientation), the *t*-value comes to 13.802 which is equal to the ratio between the unstandardized parameter estimates and the associated standard error (i.e. 0.834/0.0604).[21] With a large sample size, *t*-values are approximately normally distributed;[22] despite their designation, they do *not* follow a *t*-distribution. The *t*-values are used to determine whether a particular parameter is significantly different from zero in the population; *t*-values between −1.96 and 1.96 indicate that the corresponding parameter is not significantly different from zero (at the 5% significance level).[23]

Two further pieces of information accompany the equations in Table 6.2. First, the **error variances** are shown; these reflect errors in measurement (for the measurement part of the model) and residual terms (for the structural part of the model).[24] Being free parameters, estimates of error variances are accompanied by their standard errors and *t*-values. Secondly, the **squared multiple correlation**, R^2, is displayed for each equation. This value is analogous to the R^2 obtained in the conventional regression analysis and shows the amount of variance in the dependent variable accounted for by the independent variable(s) in the equation. For example, the R^2 of 0.571 in the Job Sat (Job Satisfaction) equation tells us that 57.1% of the variance in Job Sat is jointly 'explained' by Role Amb (Role Ambiguity) and Role Con (Role Conflict).

The next part of the output is titled Covariance Matrix of Independent Variables and shows the estimates of the variances and covariances among the exogenous latent variables in the model;[25] again, each estimate is accompanied by its standard error and t-value. For example, the covariance between Role Con (Role Conflict) and Role Amb (Role Ambiguity) is 0.486, the standard error is 0.074 and the t-value 6.568.

Finally, the Covariance Matrix of Latent Variables is shown. This contains the variances and covariances of *all* latent variables; note that there is a degree of redundancy between this matrix and the Covariance Matrix of Independent Variables as the variance/covariance estimates of the latter (but not their standard errors or t-values) are again reproduced here.

So, what does all this output actually tell us about our model? First, the very fact that we were able to estimate our model without encountering any warnings is in itself a positive sign; not infrequently, the process of estimation is plagued by the sort of problems discussed in Appendix 6A. Second, an inspection of parameter values reveals the absence of any 'improper' (i.e. unreasonable) estimates; for example, none of the error variances are negative and the same applies to the variances of the latent variables.[26] Third, the vast majority of the parameter estimates (32 out of 34) are significantly different from zero (as indicated by t-values greater than |1.96|; the only nonsignificant parameters are the error variance of Sell (Selling Behaviour) and the coefficient of the hypothesized path from Role Con (Role Conflict) to Cust Foc (Customer Focus). Fourth, the signs of the parameter estimates are consistent with the hypothesized relationships among the latent variables (see Chapter 2); thus both Role Amb (Role Ambiguity) and Role Con (Role Conflict) have a negative influence on Job Sat (Job Satisfaction), while Job Sat and Mkt Ort (Market Orientation) have positive influences on Cust Foc (Customer Focus).[27] Fifth, the squared multiple correlations of the manifest variables are indicative of the degree to which the indicators are free from measurement error (the closer to 1, the better the manifest variable acts as an indicator of the corresponding latent variable); here, the R^2 values are moderate to high (ranging between 0.351 and 0.971), suggesting that the manifest variables are reasonably successful as measures of the latent variables in the model. Sixth, the squared multiple, R^2, correlations of both endogenous latent variables are substantial (greater than 0.5); this indicates that independent latent variables explain a considerable portion of the variance in the endogenous latent variables. Finally, the covariances among the independent latent variables tell us that Role Amb (Role Ambiguity) and Role Con (Role Conflict) are positively related to one another but negatively related to Mkt Ort (Market Orientation); moreover, all these relationships are significant, as indicated by the relevant t-values.[28]

At this point it should be noted that the SIMPLIS output file contains additional information not included in Table 6.2. This includes a variety of fit statistics, residual analysis, and diagnostics for modifying the model. These parts of the output will be discussed in Chapters 7 and 8, dealing with the assessment of model fit and model modification respectively.

Reading the program output: LISREL format

Table 6.3 shows the program output for the illustrative model but in LISREL format this time. To obtain the output file in this format we simply inserted LISREL Output: RS SS SC EF before the Path Diagram command in the input file (see Table 6.1). It will be recalled from Chapter 4 that, in LISREL format, a model is described in terms of eight parameter matrices (see, in particular, Appendix 4D). The parameter specifications for our illustrative model across these matrices were given earlier in Table 4.3 of Chapter 4; reference to this table should facilitate the interpretation of the LISREL output file as should reference to the model's path diagram (see Figure 3.2 in Chapter 3).

The first two parameter matrices (LAMBDA-Y and LAMBDA-X) show the values of the estimates, the standard errors, and the t-values for the y- and x-variables respectively (i.e. the indicators of the endogenous and exogenous latent variables). The information they provide is identical to that of the first thirteen equations in the SIMPLIS output file in Table 6.2.

The third matrix (BETA) shows the parameter estimates, standard errors and t-values for the relationships between the η-variables (i.e. endogenous latent variables). Similarly, the fourth matrix (GAMMA) shows the parameter estimates, standard errors and t-values for the relationships between the ξ-variables (i.e. exogenous latent variables) and the η-variables. Thus, the information contained in the BETA and GAMMA matrices is identical to that provided in the last two equations in the SIMPLIS output file in Table 6.2.

The next part of the output titled Covariance Matrix of ETA and KSI is identical to the Covariance Matrix of Latent Variables in Table 6.2 and does not need to be discussed any further. The same applies to the next matrix (PHI) which contains identical information as the Covariance Matrix of Independent Variables in the SIMPLIS output file. The PSI matrix contains the error variance estimates, standard errors and t-values relating to the residual terms of the structural part of the model; thus the information it contains is the same as the Job Sat (Job Satisfaction) and Cust Foc (Customer Focus) equations in Table 6.2. Similarly, the R^2 values for these equations are listed under Squared Multiple Correlations for Structural Equations.

The THETA-EPS and THETA-DELTA matrices contain the error variance estimates, standard errors and t-values for the y- and x-variables respectively; these are identical to the error variance information in the first thirteen equations in Table 6.2. Similarly the R^2 values for these equations are now denoted as Squared Multiple Correlations for

Table 6.3   Parameter estimates: LISREL output

```
!ILLUSTRATIVE MODEL OF JOB SATISFACTION AND CUSTOMER FOCUS

Number of Iterations = 40

LISREL Estimates (Maximum Likelihood)
```

LAMBDA-Y

	Job Sat	Cust Foc
Work	1.000	- -
Supervis	1.783	- -
	(0.205)	
	8.697	
Pay	1.823	- -
	(0.226)	
	8.081	
Promote	2.417	- -
	(0.305)	
	7.920	
Sell	- -	1.000
Solve	- -	0.582
		(0.038)
		15.256

of company for what? (handwritten annotation)

LAMBDA-X

	Role Amb	Role Con	Mkt Ort
Clear	1.000	- -	- -
Ambig	1.667	- -	- -
	(0.128)		
	13.038		
Compat	- -	- -	1.000
Conflict	- -	- -	1.015
			(0.076)
			13.295
Custort	- -	- -	1.000
Comport	- -	- -	0.834
			(0.060)
			13.802
Intcord	- -		0.838
			(0.056)
			14.941

BETA

	Job Sat	Cust Foc
Job Sat	- -	- -
Cust Foc	2.212	- -
	(0.419)	
	5.282	

GAMMA

	Role Amb	Role Con	Mkt Ort
Job Sat	-0.189	-0.046	- -
	(0.029)	(0.015)	
	-6.473	-3.130	
Cust Foc	- -	-0.059	0.534
		(0.062)	(0.077)
		-0.948	6.961

Covariance Matrix of ETA and KSI

	Job Sat	Cust Foc	Role Amb	Role Con	Mkt Ort
Job Sat	0.056				
Cust Foc	0.199	1.577			
Role Amb	-0.131	-0.592	0.573		
Role Con	-0.160	-0.722	0.486	1.471	
Mkt Ort	0.121	0.822	-0.513	-0.527	0.979

Table 6.3 (continued)

```
      PHI

          Role Amb    Role Con    Mkt Ort
          --------    --------    --------
Role Amb    0.573
           (0.081)
            7.100
Role Con    0.486       1.471
           (0.074)     (0.170)
            6.568       8.672
 Mkt Ort   -0.513      -0.527       0.979
           (0.067)     (0.088)     (0.113)
           -7.650      -6.014       8.636

      PSI
      Note: This matrix is diagonal.

          Job Sat     Cust Foc
          --------    --------
            0.024       0.656
           (0.006)     (0.097)
            4.289       6.795

      Squared Multiple Correlations for Structural Equations

          Job Sat     Cust Foc
          --------    --------
            0.571       0.584

      THETA-EPS

             Work    Supervis         Pay     Promote        Sell       Solve
          --------    --------    --------    --------    --------    --------
            0.104       0.193       0.304       0.587       0.048       0.346
           (0.010)     (0.021)     (0.029)     (0.055)     (0.073)     (0.037)
           10.666       9.431      10.436      10.609       0.653       9.279

      Squared Multiple Correlations for Y - Variables

             Work    Supervis         Pay     Promote        Sell       Solve
          --------    --------    --------    --------    --------    --------
            0.351       0.480       0.380       0.359       0.971       0.606

      THETA-DELTA

            Clear       Ambig      Compat    Conflict     Custort     Comport
          --------    --------    --------    --------    --------    --------
            0.440       0.486       0.300       0.534       0.374       0.556
           (0.048)     (0.096)     (0.097)     (0.106)     (0.052)     (0.056)
            9.147       5.089       3.090       5.042       7.222       9.965

      THETA-DELTA

          Intcord
          --------
            0.398
           (0.045)
            8.907

      Squared Multiple Correlations for X - Variables

            Clear       Ambig      Compat    Conflict     Custort     Comport
          --------    --------    --------    --------    --------    --------
            0.565       0.766       0.831       0.739       0.724       0.551

      Squared Multiple Correlations for X - Variables

          Intcord
          --------
            0.633
```

`Y-Variables` and `Squared Multiple Correlations for X-Variables` respectively.

In summary, other than a change in format, there is hardly any difference between the SIMPLIS output in Table 6.2 and the LISREL output in Table 6.3. However, as already mentioned in Chapter 4, the LISREL output option enables the user to obtain *additional* information not available under SIMPLIS. Note that this additional output can only be generated by specifying particular *keywords* in the `LISREL Output` command line; if no such keywords are specified then the same information will be obtained as with SIMPLIS output.

Table 6.4 shows selected portions of the LISREL output resulting from including the `RS` (residual analysis) keyword in the `LISREL Output` line.

The elements of the `Fitted Covariance Matrix` are the estimated variances and covariances of the manifest variables based upon the model. Thus, this matrix is nothing but the implied covariance matrix, $\hat{\Sigma}$, which is compared to the sample covariance matrix, S.[29] The results of this comparison are listed under `Fitted Residuals` which forms the **residual matrix**, $(S - \hat{\Sigma})$. For example, the residual between Comport (Competitor Orientation) and Solve (Problem-Solving Behavior) is 0.035; this value represents the difference between the sample covariance of 0.434 (see Appendix 4A in Chapter 4) and the fitted (i.e. model-implied) covariance of 0.399 (see Table 6.4). Here we have a case of **underfitting** since the model underestimates the magnitude of the covariance involved. In contrast, the negative residual between, say, Clear (Role Clarity) and Work (Satisfaction with Work) is an instance of **overfitting** since the actual covariance has been overestimated. We shall have more to say about residuals in Chapter 7 when the role of residual analysis in evaluating model fit is discussed in detail.

If the keywords `SS` and `SC` are included in the `LISREL Output` line, then the program produces two types of **standardized solutions** (Table 6.5). In the `Standardized Solution` *only* latent variables are standardized, whereas manifest variables are left in their original metric. In the `Completely Standardized Solution`, on the other hand, *both* latent *and* manifest variables are standardized. For directional linkages, a standardized parameter estimate shows the resulting change in a dependent variable from a standard deviation change in an independent variable.[30] For non-directional linkages (i.e. covariances), standardized parameter estimates reflect simply the correlations between the variables involved (see Appendix 1A in Chapter 1).

Comparing the two types of standardized solutions, the only difference that can be detected is in the LAMBDA-Y and LAMBDA-X matrices. This difference simply reflects the fact that y- and x-variables are standardized in the `Completely Standardized Solution` but not in the `Standardized Solution`.

One advantage of standardization is that it makes the interpretation of the bivariate relationships between the latent variables easier to grasp. As

Table 6.4 Fitted covariance matrix and fitted residuals for illustrative model

!ILLUSTRATIVE MODEL OF JOB SATISFACTION AND CUSTOMER FOCUS

Fitted Covariance Matrix

	Work	Supervis	Pay	Promote	Sell	Solve
Work	0.160					
Supervis	0.100	0.372				
Pay	0.102	0.183	0.491			
Promote	0.136	0.242	0.248	0.915		
Sell	0.199	0.354	0.362	0.480	1.625	
Solve	0.115	0.206	0.211	0.279	0.917	0.880
Clear	-0.131	-0.233	-0.238	-0.316	-0.592	-0.344
Ambig	-0.218	-0.388	-0.397	-0.526	-0.986	-0.574
Compat	-0.160	-0.285	-0.292	-0.387	-0.722	-0.420
Conflict	-0.162	-0.290	-0.296	-0.392	-0.733	-0.426
Custort	0.121	0.216	0.221	0.293	0.822	0.478
Comport	0.101	0.181	0.185	0.245	0.686	0.399
Intcord	0.102	0.181	0.185	0.246	0.689	0.401

Fitted Covariance Matrix

	Clear	Ambig	Compat	Conflict	Custort	Comport
Clear	1.013					
Ambig	0.954	2.077				
Compat	0.486	0.809	1.771			
Conflict	0.493	0.822	1.494	2.051		
Custort	-0.513	-0.856	-0.527	-0.535	1.353	
Comport	-0.428	-0.714	-0.439	-0.446	0.817	1.237
Intcord	-0.430	-0.717	-0.442	-0.448	0.821	0.685

Fitted Covariance Matrix

	Intcord
Intcord	1.086

Fitted Residuals

	Work	Supervis	Pay	Promote	Sell	Solve
Work	0.000					
Supervis	-0.011	0.000				
Pay	0.021	-0.026	0.000			
Promote	0.002	0.007	0.024	0.000		
Sell	0.028	0.024	0.077	0.052	0.056	
Solve	0.034	0.015	0.095	0.038	0.033	0.019
Clear	-0.008	-0.003	0.021	0.105	0.067	0.054
Ambig	0.050	-0.057	0.046	0.079	0.047	0.072
Compat	-0.001	-0.057	0.083	0.015	0.001	0.177
Conflict	-0.006	-0.067	0.119	0.029	-0.020	0.135
Custort	0.069	0.093	0.064	0.060	0.096	0.091
Comport	0.066	0.113	0.151	0.205	0.078	0.035
Intcord	0.066	0.110	0.043	0.126	0.019	0.030

Fitted Residuals

	Clear	Ambig	Compat	Conflict	Custort	Comport
Clear	0.000					
Ambig	0.039	0.000				
Compat	-0.025	0.031	0.000			
Conflict	-0.051	0.026	0.001	0.000		
Custort	0.031	0.019	-0.010	0.009	0.000	
Comport	0.058	0.006	-0.034	-0.043	-0.031	0.000
Intcord	0.063	0.059	0.071	0.049	0.002	0.030

Fitted Residuals

	Intcord
Intcord	0.000

Table 6.5 Standardized and completely standardized solutions for illustrative model

```
!ILLUSTRATIVE MODEL OF JOB SATISFACTION AND CUSTOMER FOCUS
```

Standardized Solution

LAMBDA-Y

	Job Sat	Cust Foc
Work	0.237	- -
Supervis	0.423	- -
Pay	0.432	- -
Promote	0.573	- -
Sell	- -	1.256
Solve	- -	0.730

LAMBDA-X

	Role Amb	Role Con	Mkt Ort
Clear	0.757	- -	- -
Ambig	1.261	- -	- -
Compat	- -	1.213	- -
Conflict	- -	1.231	- -
Custort	- -	- -	0.989
Comport	- -	- -	0.825
Intcord	- -	- -	0.829

BETA

	Job Sat	Cust Foc
Job Sat	- -	- -
Cust Foc	0.418	- -

GAMMA

	Role Amb	Role Con	Mkt Ort
Job Sat	-0.603	-0.237	- -
Cust Foc	- -	-0.057	0.421

Correlation Matrix of ETA and KSI

	Job Sat	Cust Foc	Role Amb	Role Con	Mkt Ort
Job Sat	1.000				
Cust Foc	0.667	1.000			
Role Amb	-0.728	-0.623	1.000		
Role Con	-0.556	-0.474	0.529	1.000	
Mkt Ort	0.518	0.662	-0.686	-0.439	1.000

PSI
Note: This matrix is diagonal.

	Job Sat	Cust Foc
	0.429	0.416

Regression Matrix ETA on KSI (Standardized)

	Role Amb	Role Con	Mkt Ort
Job Sat	-0.603	-0.237	- -
Cust Foc	-0.252	-0.156	0.421

Table 6.5 (continued)

!ILLUSTRATIVE MODEL OF JOB SATISFACTION AND CUSTOMER FOCUS

Completely Standardized Solution

LAMBDA-Y

	Job Sat	Cust Foc
Work	0.593	- -
Supervis	0.693	- -
Pay	0.617	- -
Promote	0.599	- -
Sell	- -	0.985
Solve	- -	0.779

LAMBDA-X

	Role Amb	Role Con	Mkt Ort
Clear	0.752	- -	- -
Ambig	0.875	- -	- -
Compat	- -	0.912	- -
Conflict	- -	0.860	- -
Custort	- -	- -	0.851
Comport	- -	- -	0.742
Intcord	- -	- -	0.796

BETA

	Job Sat	Cust Foc
Job Sat	- -	- -
Cust Foc	0.418	- -

GAMMA

	Role Amb	Role Con	Mkt Ort
Job Sat	-0.603	-0.237	- -
Cust Foc	- -	-0.057	0.421

Correlation Matrix of ETA and KSI

	Job Sat	Cust Foc	Role Amb	Role Con	Mkt Ort
Job Sat	1.000				
Cust Foc	0.667	1.000			
Role Amb	-0.728	-0.623	1.000		
Role Con	-0.556	-0.474	0.529	1.000	
Mkt Ort	0.518	0.662	-0.686	-0.439	1.000

PSI
Note: This matrix is diagonal.

Job Sat	Cust Foc
0.429	0.416

THETA-EPS

Work	Supervis	Pay	Promote	Sell	Solve
0.649	0.520	0.620	0.641	0.029	0.394

Table 6.5 (continued)

THETA-DELTA

Clear	Ambig	Compat	Conflict	Custort	Comport
0.435	0.234	0.169	0.261	0.276	0.449

THETA-DELTA

Intcord
0.367

Regression Matrix ETA on KSI (Standardized)

	Role Amb	Role Con	Mkt Ort
Job Sat	-0.603	-0.237	- -
Cust Foc	-0.252	-0.156	0.421

these relationships are now cast in correlation rather than in covariance terms, their relative magnitudes become much clearer. For example, looking at the Correlation Matrix of ETA and KSI, one can see that the strongest bivariate relationship is between Role Amb (Role Ambiguity) and Job Sat (Job Satisfaction) while the weakest is between Role Con (Role Conflict) and Mkt Ort (Market Orientation).

A second advantage of standardization is that it helps identify the relative contribution of independent latent variables in influencing the endogenous latent variables. For example, inspection of the Regression Matrix ETA on KSI shows that Role Amb (Role Ambiguity) has a greater impact on Job Sat (Job Satisfaction) than does Role Con (Role Conflict) and that Mkt Ort (Market Orientation) is, by far, the strongest predictor of Cust Foc (Customer Focus).

A final advantage of standardization is that it facilitates the detection of 'improper' estimates; for example, correlations greater than 1.00 are easier to detect than are covariances taking on unreasonable values.

Having said all this, it should be appreciated that if the original metric used to scale a variable 'has some natural meaning, then all is lost by standardization'.[31] However, in social science applications the metrics of variables are usually arbitrary (e.g. rating scale points) so this is unlikely to pose a major problem. A more critical issue is the use of standardized estimates when more than one sample or population is involved. Here, there should be no doubt that 'standardized parameters are appropriate only when one desires to compare the relative contributions of a number of independent variables on the same dependent variable and for the same sample of observations. They are not appropriate and can lead to erroneous inferences when one wishes to make comparisons across populations or samples.'[32]

Finally, if the keyword EF is included in the LISREL Output line, the program provides an **effect decomposition** via the calculation of total and indirect effects. Indirect effects represent the influence of an independent variable on a dependent variable as mediated by one or more intervening variables. For example, looking at the path diagram in Figure 3.1 of Chapter 3, it can be seen that, in addition to its direct effect on Cust Foc (Customer Focus), Role Conf (Role Conflict) is expected to also have an indirect effect on Cust Foc via Job Sat (Job Satisfaction). Moreover, the path diagram shows that Role Amb (Role Ambiguity) is not hypothesized to directly impact on Cust Foc; its full impact is expected to be channeled through the Job Sat variable. In contrast, Mkt Ort (Market Orientation) is expected to impact on Cust Foc only directly; no indirect effects are modeled for this variable.

Indirect effects are derived by multiplying the unstandardized parameter estimates of the intervening variables. For example, the indirect effect of Role Conf on Cust Foc (-0.103 in Table 6.6) is obtained by multiplying the parameter estimate linking Role Conf to Job Sat (-0.046) by the parameter estimate linking Job Sat to Cust Foc (2.212); the latter two estimates can be found in the GAMMA and BETA matrices of Table 6.3.[33]

As you might have suspected, total effects are computed by adding the indirect effect of a variable to its direct effect. Thus, the total effect of Role Conf on Cust Foc (-0.161) is equal to its direct effect of -0.059 (see GAMMA matrix in Table 6.3) plus its indirect effect of -0.103 (as calculated above). Needless to say that for independent variables that do not have an indirect effect on the dependent variables under consideration, the total effect will equal the direct effect (this is the case for Mkt Ort in our example); similarly, for variables for which no direct effects are postulated, their total effect will equal their calculated indirect effects (this is the case for Role Amb in our example).

For each indirect and total effect, the program output also shows an estimated standard error and an accompanying t-value. However, these statistics need to be interpreted with caution because 'when nonsignificant variables (whose confidence intervals include zero and possibly estimates of the opposite sign) are included in the multiplicative computation of indirect paths . . . results can be particularly misleading'.[34]

As Table 6.6 shows, the presentation of total and indirect effects in the LISREL output file is split into four distinct parts. First, the way in which each exogenous latent variable impacts upon the endogenous latent variables is shown under Total Effects of KSI on ETA and Indirect Effects of KSI on ETA; the examples given earlier to illustrate the calculation of indirect and total effects referred to this part of the output. Next, the total effects among the endogenous latent variables are shown under Total Effects of ETA on ETA; given that only two endogenous latent variables are included in our illustrative model there cannot be any indirect effects and the total effect of Job Sat (Job Satisfaction) on Cust Foc (Customer Focus) is equal to the direct effect as captured by the relevant path (see BETA matrix in Table 6.3 earlier). The next part of the output shows the way in which the endogenous latent variables impact upon their indicators and is titled Total Effects of

Table 6.6 Indirect and total effects for illustrative model

!ILLUSTRATIVE MODEL OF JOB SATISFACTION AND CUSTOMER FOCUS

Total and Indirect Effects

Total Effects of KSI on ETA

	Role Amb	Role Con	Mkt Ort
Job Sat	-0.189	-0.046	- -
	(0.029)	(0.015)	
	-6.473	-3.130	
Cust Foc	-0.418	-0.161	0.534
	(0.086)	(0.058)	(0.077)
	-4.831	-2.788	6.961

Indirect Effects of KSI on ETA

	Role Amb	Role Con	Mkt Ort
Job Sat	- -	- -	- -
Cust Foc	-0.418	-0.103	- -
	(0.086)	(0.037)	
	-4.831	-2.763	

Total Effects of ETA on ETA

	Job Sat	Cust Foc
Job Sat	- -	- -
Cust Foc	2.212	- -
	(0.419)	
	5.282	

Largest Eigenvalue of B*B' (Stability Index) is 4.895

Total Effects of ETA on Y

	Job Sat	Cust Foc
Work	1.000	- -
Supervis	1.783	- -
	(0.205)	
	8.697	
Pay	1.823	- -
	(0.226)	
	8.081	
Promote	2.417	- -
	(0.305)	
	7.920	
Sell	2.212	1.000
	(0.419)	
	5.282	
Solve	1.287	0.582
	(0.257)	(0.038)
	5.015	15.256

Table 6.6   (continued)

Indirect Effects of ETA on Y

	Job Sat	Cust Foc
	--------	--------
Work	- -	- -
Supervis	- -	- -
Pay	- -	- -
Promote	- -	- -
Sell	2.212 (0.419) 5.282	- -
Solve	1.287 (0.257) 5.015	- -

Total Effects of KSI on Y

	Role Amb	Role Con	Mkt Ort
	--------	--------	--------
Work	-0.189 (0.029) -6.473	-0.046 (0.015) -3.130	- -
Supervis	-0.337 (0.048) -6.955	-0.083 (0.026) -3.181	- -
Pay	-0.344 (0.052) -6.598	-0.085 (0.027) -3.144	- -
Promote	-0.456 (0.070) -6.506	-0.112 (0.036) -3.133	- -
Sell	-0.418 (0.086) -4.831	-0.161 (0.058) -2.788	0.534 (0.077) 6.961
Solve	-0.243 (0.053) -4.624	-0.094 (0.034) -2.747	0.311 (0.049) 6.382

ETA on Y and Indirect Effects of ETA on Y. Here, it is noteworthy that Job Sat indirectly affects the indicators of Cust Foc; for example, the indirect effect of Job Sat on Solve (Problem Solving Behavior) is computed by multiplying the path coefficient linking Job Sat and Cust Foc (2.212) by the loading linking Cust Foc and Solve (0.582). Finally, under Total Effects of KSI on Y, the impact of the exogenous latent variables on the indicators of the endogenous latent variables is described. This impact is always of an indirect nature as an exogenous latent variable can never be directly linked to the indicators of an endogenous latent variable (see conventions for specifying a LISREL model in Chapter 4). For example, the effect of Role Amb (Role Ambiguity) on Solve (Problem Solving

Behavior) is equal to the path coefficient linking Role Ambiguity to Job Sat (Job Satisfaction) times the path coefficient linking Job Sat to Cust Foc (Customer Focus) times the loading linking Cust Foc to Solve; this comes to $-0.189 \times 2.212 \times 0.582 = -0.243$.

The discussion on direct, indirect and total effects serves to highlight the importance of setting up a path diagram for one's model (see Chapter 3). Without such a diagram, it is very easy to lose track of how each latent or manifest variable is directly and/or indirectly affected by other variables in the model. Looking at Table 6.6 in conjunction with Figure 3.1 should facilitate the interpretation of the various types of effects associated with a LISREL model. Even better, with LISREL 8, the user has the option to get a path diagram on screen and thus move back and forth between the path diagram and the output file at the click of a mouse. Moreover, it is possible to select what sort of information appears on the path diagram (e.g. parameter estimates vs. *t*-values) as well as edit and modify the path diagram on screen. Appendix 6B shows the path diagram with the estimates of the illustrated model as produced by the program; further details on this facility of LISREL are contained in the SIMPLIS manual.[35]

As a final point it is worth noting that if the EF *and* the SS and/or SC keywords are included in the LISREL Output command line, then, in addition to the effect decomposition based on the unstandardized parameter estimates in Table 6.6, the program will print total and indirect effects based upon the standardized and/or completely standardized solutions; the relevant output is shown in Appendix 6C (just in case you were dying to see it).[36]

Having estimated our model, we are now ready to assess its fit. This is what Chapter 7 is all about.

Notes

1 Hayduk (1987), p. 97.
2 Thus 'estimation involves finding values . . . that generate an estimated covariance matrix $\hat{\Sigma}$ that is as close as possible to the sample covariance matrix S' (Long, 1983b, p. 44). Strictly speaking, the specification of a LISREL model implies certain predictions about the *population* variances and covariances of the observed variables. Thus, the comparison should be between the model-based covariance matrix Σ (θ) and the actual population covariance matrix Σ, where θ is a vector containing the model parameters (see Bollen (1989) and Appendix 1B). In practice, however, we usually work with sample data and thus Σ is replaced with S and Σ (θ) with $\hat{\Sigma}$, where $\hat{\Sigma} = \Sigma$ ($\hat{\theta}$); the latter is the implied covariance matrix, namely 'the covariance matrix that would result if values of fixed parameters and estimates of free parameters were substituted into the structural equations, which then were used to derive a covariance matrix' (Hoyle, 1995, p. 5).
3 Fitting functions are also known as 'discrepancy functions' or 'loss functions'.
4 For details on different estimation procedures, see Long (1983a, 1983b), Jöreskog and Sörbom (1989, 1996a), Bollen (1989) and references given therein.
5 Long (1983b), p. 43.
6 Note that LISREL 8 does not provide fit statistics (see Chapter 7) for models estimated

by TSLS or IV and only version 8.30 of the program provides standard errors for TSLS estimates.

7 Long (1983b), p. 43.

8 Note that, with iterative procedures, there is the possibility that the search process may locate what is known as a **local minimum** in the fitting function, i.e. 'a value of the fitting function that appears to be the smallest when there are other smaller values' (Long, 1983b, p. 46). However, in practice, this seems to happen very rarely (Jöreskog and Sörbom, 1989).

9 Specifically, IV is used to provide starting values for the ULS method and TSLS for the GLS, ML, WLS and DWLS methods.

10 A **non-admissible (or improper) solution** is one which results in parameters which are 'unreasonable', i.e. fall outside a feasible range. Typical examples are correlations greater than ±1.00, negative variances (known as 'Heywood cases') and covariance or correlation matrices that are not positive-definite; for a discussion see Rindskopf (1984), Gerbing and Anderson (1987) and Dillon, Kumar and Mulani (1987). Note that the LISREL program has a built-in admissibility check which is described in Appendix 6A (see also, Jöreskog and Sörbom, 1989, 1996a).

11 Jöreskog and Sörbom (1989), p. 25.

12 Note, however, that 'the reason for this preference for maximum likelihood techniques seems to be that it is the default method in most computer packages' (Baumgartner and Homburg, 1996, p. 149).

13 The assumption of multivariate normality can be tested using the PRELIS 2 program; see Chapter 12.

14 Hoyle and Panter (1995), p. 164.

15 Long (1983a), p. 58.

16 For a technical discussion of ADF estimation methods see Browne (1984) – if you really must!

17 Byrne (1995), p. 147.

18 Note that since ML is the default estimation method in LISREL 8, we did not have to explicitly request this in the SIMPLIS input file (see Table 6.1). Had we wished to specify an alternative estimation method, say GLS, we would have had to add ME = GLS on the Options command line. Alternatively, we could have inserted an additional command line as follows: Method of Estimation = Generalized Least Squares.

19 Bagozzi (1977), p. 217.

20 Note, however, that 'what is small or large depends on the units of measurement in observed and/or latent variables and the magnitude of the parameter estimate itself. In practice t-values are often used, which are independent of the units of measurement' (Jöreskog and Sörbom, 1989, p. 41).

21 Note that this calculation is only approximate since all figures have been rounded off to three decimal points.

22 In other words, they behave as standard normal deviates (i.e. z-statistics).

23 If departures from multivariate normality are substantial, 't-values should be considerably greater than |2.0| before it can be concluded with confidence that a coefficient is significant' (Steenkamp and van Trijp, 1991, p. 286). Moreover, 'the t-statistic tests the hypothesis that a *single* parameter is equal to zero. The use of t-tests on parameters understates the overall Type I error rate and multiple comparison procedures must be used' (Fornell and Larcker, 1981, p. 40, emphasis in the original).

24 These are the 'errors in variables' and 'errors in equations' introduced in Chapter 1 and subsequently displayed in the path diagram in Figure 3.1 of Chapter 3.

25 You may have noticed that the title of this matrix is somewhat misleading because endogenous variables (such as Job Sat in our example) can also function as independent variables in some equations (such as the Cust Foc equation in our example). See also Chapter 1 on this issue.

26 Since a variance is the covariance of a variable with itself, it should always be non-

negative (see Chapter 1, Appendix 1A). If a variance is zero, then we are dealing with a constant, not a variable.

27 Inspection of the standard errors paints a similar picture; most are small in relation to their corresponding parameters, with the exception of the error variance of Sell and the path coefficient from Role Con to Cust Foc. Note that the nonsignificant error variance of Sell is somewhat worrying because 'nonsignificant error variances usually suggest specification errors, since it is unreasonable to expect the absence of random error in most managerial and social science contexts . . . . However, nonsignificant error variances sometimes arise between two or more measures of a latent construct correlate so highly . . . . that little random error does in fact exist' (Bagozzi and Yi, 1988, p. 77). We shall return to this issue when we discuss the fit of the model (Chapter 7) and consider possible modifications (Chapter 8). As far as the nonsignificant path between Role Con and Cust Foc is concerned, this raises questions of statistical power which, again, will be addressed in Chapters 7 and 8.

28 The sign of the coefficient linking Role Con and Cust Foc is also consistent with expectations (i.e. shows a negative impact) but, as noted, the relevant estimate failed to reach significance.

29 See the earlier discussion of the estimation process in this chapter and also Appendix 1B in Chapter 1.

30 A standardized parameter equals the value of the raw (i.e. unstandardized) parameter times the ratio of the standard deviations of the independent to the dependent variable.

31 Kenny (1979), p. 256.

32 Bagozzi (1980), p. 187. For discussions of the relative merits of standardized vs. unstandardized coefficients see, for example, Blalock (1967), Wright (1960) and Kim and Mueller (1976).

33 Again, in these computations (as well as those relating to total effects), allowances must be made for rounding off.

34 Howell (1987), p. 124.

35 See Jöreskog and Sörbom (1993).

36 As was the case with the SIMPLIS output, the LISREL output contains additional information on residuals, model fit and model modification; these portions of the output will be discussed in Chapters 7 and 8 (and thus have been excluded from Tables 6.3 to 6.6).

APPENDIX 6A

Estimation problems

Problems in estimating LISREL models arise due to (a) syntax errors in the input file, (b) errors in the data file, or (c) incompatibility between data and model (i.e. the data are inadequate for the specified model or the model is wrong for the data).

Syntax errors in the input file include the use of keywords not recognized by the program, missing required command lines (e.g. the `Observed Variables` or `Sample Size` lines), logical errors on command lines (e.g. referring to latent variables in the `Relationships` command which have not been defined in the `Latent Variables` command line), and invalid command line names. While one may think that these are really only minor glitches, it has been noted that 'in general, most LISREL problems tend to result from typographical or syntactical errors' (Byrne, 1998, p. 66). While LISREL 8 will detect most syntax problems in the input file (and print an appropriate error message), it is worthwhile to spend some time checking the input file against the model specification and/or path diagram to ensure that all is well at this stage.

Errors in the data file (typically containing the covariance matrix, S) are much harder to detect. On the positive side, LISREL 8 will spot whether S has too few elements (given the number of variables listed under the `Observed Variables` command) or whether there are any illegal characters in the data (e.g. a letter or symbol instead of a number). On the negative side, LISREL 8 will *not* detect whether S has too many elements or whether there are any unreasonable (but still legal) values (e.g. a variance of 3800 relating to a variable scored from 1 to 5). Again, the advice is to check and double-check the entries (and the order of entries) in S against the list of observed variables. Recall that given k variables, the covariance matrix should contain $k(k + 1)/2$ non-redundant elements. Moreover, the listing of the elements should follow *exactly* the variable order specified in the `Observed Variables` line (see Chapter 4). Any mistake here and you are in for a lot of trouble.

A particularly nasty data-related problem is faced when the sample covariance matrix, S, is not **positive definite**. A non-positive definite (or 'singular') matrix has a determinant of zero and cannot be inverted (i.e. its inverse does not exist). Under these conditions various bits of statistical information related to the matrix cannot be computed or trusted. Since a requirement of several estimation procedures (including maximum likelihood) is that S is positive definite, if the input matrix does not have this property, the LISREL program may respond with the following depressing message:

    F_A_T_A_L E_R_R_O_R: Matrix to be analyzed is not positive definite.

Typical reasons for S not being positive definite is pairwise deletion of missing data or collinearity (i.e. linear dependency) among the observed variables. Pairwise deletion may result in a covariance matrix that is different to the one that would have been generated had the complete data set been used; in this context 'pairwise deletion implies strict (and often unreasonable assumptions) about the missing data generating process' (Wothke, 1993, p. 266). An obvious solution is to use listwise deletion of missing cases (assuming, of course, that one has a large sample and only a few cases with missing data). Other, more complex, solutions (based on imputation methods) are discussed in Wothke (1993).

Collinearities among the observed variables come about as a result of outliers in the data, a sample size that is less than the number of observed variables, or the inclusion of a composite variable defined as the sum of two or more component variables which are also independently included in the covariance matrix. Solutions to the collinearity problem include the removal of the offending outliers (see Bollen, 1989, for details on outlier detection), reducing the number of observed variables, or removing the redundant variables.

Two further options for dealing with a non-positive definite **S** is to use an estimation method that does not assume that **S** is positive definite (such as ULS) or employ a **smoothing procedure**. The latter involves making subtle alterations to **S** so that it becomes positive definite. Such a procedure is available in LISREL 8 under the Ridge option, whereby a small constant times the diagonal values of **S** is added to the elements in **S**. The constant can be automatically determined by the program or set by the researcher and is progressively increased until **S** becomes positive definitive (for details, see Jöreskog and Sörbom, 1989, 1996). In fact, faced with a non-positive definite **S**, the LISREL program often responds with the following message (the actual value of the ridge constant will differ from situation to situation):

```
W_A_R_N_I_N_G: Matrix to be analyzed is not positive definite, ridge
               option taken with ridge constant - 1.000.
```

Apart from syntax data-related errors, problems may still be encountered because of model-related problems. One such problem is when the estimated covariance matrix constructed from the model (i.e. the implied covariance matrix, $\hat{\Sigma}$) is not positive definite. This is typically due to poor starting values (see Chapter 6) which can be so bad that iteration cannot even begin. When this happens, the following message is produced by the LISREL program:

```
F_A_T_A_L E_R_R_O_R: Unable to start iterations because matrix SIGMA
                     is not positive definite.
                     Provide better starting values.
```

To resolve this problem, one can provide one's own starting values or use ULS estimation initially and use the resulting estimates as starting values; both strategies are discussed in detail in Wothke (1993).

Assuming that iterations *can* begin, further problems may be detected when the LISREL program conducts what is known as an **admissibility test**. With LISREL 8, this happens at the 20th iteration and involves a check on the viability of the solution (i.e. to make sure that no rows of only zeros are included in the LAMBDA-Y and LAMBDA-X matrices and the PHI, PSI, THETA-EPS and THETA-DELTA are all positive definite). If the solution is found to be non-admissible, then the following error message is printed:

```
F_A_T_A_L E_R_R_O_R: Admissibility test failed.
```

When this happens one should carefully check one's model and data to see whether they are as intended. It is recommended that one should '*not set the admissibility check off unless the model has fixed zero diagonal elements in Φ, Ψ, Θ_ε or Θ_δ by intention* . . . Although there may be exceptions, our experience suggests that if a solution is not admissible after 10 iterations, it will remain non-admissible if the program is allowed to continue to iterate' (Jöreskog and Sörbom, 1989, p. 278, emphasis in the original).

Even if the admissibility test is passed, the solution may still fail to converge. Specifically, 'an infinite or arbitrary lengthy iterative process may occur if the change in parameter estimates is always large compared to the convergence criterion. This may occur if the model is very nonlinear (e.g. a non-recursive model), if the model is extremely bad for the data to be modeled, . . ., if the start values for the parameters are very poor, if unreasonable equality constraints are being imposed, or if critical parameters are underidentified' (Bentler and Chou, 1987, p. 100). If the solution has not converged after the default number of iterations (three times the number of free parameters in the model), the LISREL program stops iterating and prints out one of the following messages:

```
W_A_R_N_I_N_G:  The number of iterations exceeded XX.
```

where XX = default number of iterations, or

```
W_A_R_N_I_N_G:  Serious problems were encountered during
                minimization. Check your model and data.
```

Faced with the first message, one should try setting the number of iterations to a higher number (assuming, of course, that one is satisfied with the model specification and the data). This can be done by inserting IT = XX in the Options command line of the SIMPLIS input file and often solves the problem.

The second message is typically indicative of empirical unidentification (see Chapter 5) in the sense that the information matrix is nearly singular (i.e. almost non-positive definite). This can be checked by asking the program to print the correlations of the parameters estimates (using the keyword PC on the Options command line); very large correlations suggest that 'it is impossible to obtain sufficiently good parameter estimates' (Jöreskog and Sörbom, 1989, p. 278).

In addition to empirical unidentification, non-convergence problems may occur due to too little information provided by the data, presence of outliers and non-normalities, too many model parameters and model misspecification. Solutions to these problems include 'collecting more observations, estimating fewer parameters, using an estimation procedure that is less restrictive in terms of normality (e.g. GLS), removing outliers, using a smoothing procedure, . . ., properly specifying the model, or imposing constraints on the variances and/or covariances in order to yield reasonable estimates' (Schumacker and Lomax, 1996, p. 27).

In conclusion, a variety of problems may have to be resolved when estimating a LISREL model in order to ensure that a viable solution is obtained. Given the range of these problems, the reader is advised to consult Bentler and Chou (1987) and Wothke (1993) to obtain additional guidance on how to overcome them.

APPENDIX 6B

Path diagram as produced by LISREL 8 program

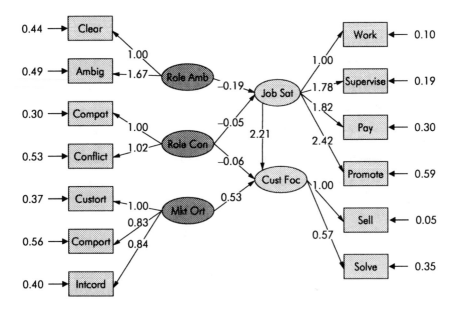

APPENDIX 6C

Standardized and completely standardized indirect and total effects

```
!ILLUSTRATIVE MODEL OF JOB SATISFACTION AND CUSTOMER FOCUS

Standardized Total and Indirect Effects

          Standardized Total Effects of KSI on ETA

              Role Amb    Role Con    Mkt Ort
              --------    --------    --------
  Job Sat      -0.603      -0.237       - -
  Cust Foc     -0.252      -0.156      0.421

          Standardized Indirect Effects of KSI on ETA

              Role Amb    Role Con    Mkt Ort
              --------    --------    --------
  Job Sat       - -         - -         - -
  Cust Foc     -0.252      -0.099       - -

          Standardized Total Effects of ETA on ETA

              Job Sat     Cust Foc
              --------    --------
  Job Sat       - -         - -
  Cust Foc     0.418        - -

          Standardized Total Effects of ETA on Y

              Job Sat     Cust Foc
              --------    --------
     Work      0.237        - -
 Supervis      0.423        - -
      Pay      0.432        - -
  Promote      0.573        - -
     Sell      0.524       1.256
    Solve      0.305       0.730

     Completely Standardized Total Effects of ETA on Y

              Job Sat     Cust Foc
              --------    --------
     Work      0.593        - -
 Supervis      0.693        - -
      Pay      0.617        - -
  Promote      0.599        - -
     Sell      0.411       0.985
    Solve      0.325       0.779
```

Standardized Indirect Effects of ETA on Y

	Job Sat	Cust Foc
Work	- -	- -
Supervis	- -	- -
Pay	- -	- -
Promote	- -	- -
Sell	0.524	- -
Solve	0.305	- -

Completely Standardized Indirect Effects of ETA on Y

	Job Sat	Cust Foc
Work	- -	- -
Supervis	- -	- -
Pay	- -	- -
Promote	- -	- -
Sell	0.411	- -
Solve	0.325	- -

Standardized Total Effects of KSI on Y

	Role Amb	Role Con	Mkt Ort
Work	-0.143	-0.056	- -
Supervis	-0.255	-0.100	- -
Pay	-0.260	-0.103	- -
Promote	-0.345	-0.136	- -
Sell	-0.316	-0.196	0.529
Solve	-0.184	-0.114	0.307

Completely Standardized Total Effects of KSI on Y

	Role Amb	Role Con	Mkt Ort
Work	-0.357	-0.141	- -
Supervis	-0.418	-0.165	- -
Pay	-0.372	-0.146	- -
Promote	-0.361	-0.142	- -
Sell	-0.248	-0.154	0.415
Solve	-0.196	-0.121	0.328

7 ASSESSMENT OF MODEL FIT

When we talk about a model's 'fit', we refer to the extent to which a hypothesized model is consistent with the data. As we saw in Chapter 6, the process of estimation results in an implied covariance matrix $\hat{\Sigma}$ which is as close as possible to sample covariance matrix S: the closer $\hat{\Sigma}$ is to S, the better the fit of the model.[1] In this context, 'virtually all measures of overall fit involve functions of S and $\hat{\Sigma}$. These fit indices gauge the 'closeness' of S to $\hat{\Sigma}$, although this closeness is measured in different ways'.[2]

Before embarking on a detailed discussion of fit criteria, several words of caution are in order: First, 'fit indices provide no guarantee whatsoever that a model is useful . . . Fit indices yield information bearing only on the model's lack of fit . . . they can in no way reflect the extent to which the model is plausible; this judgement rests squarely on the shoulders of the researcher.'[3] Second, 'a good fit for a model proves nothing. There are conceivably many models that could fit as well – or in some cases – better. In fact, a poor fit would tell you more; this would be more conclusive evidence that the model is not supported by the data.'[4] Third, 'evaluation of model fit should derive from a variety of sources and be based on several criteria that can assess model fit from a diversity of perspectives'.[5] Fourth, 'most real world applications of structural equation models with latent variables are bound to exhibit a certain amount of ambiguity in the sense that some criteria will point to acceptance of a model whereas others may be equivocal or even suggest rejection'.[6] Finally, and most importantly, 'we cannot evaluate and interpret results as if they were divorced from the theory driving one's study or from other conceptual and philosophical issues that bear upon the findings';[7] indeed, 'scientific progress could be impeded if fit coefficients . . . are used as the primary criterion for judging the adequacy of a model'.[8]

With these caveats in mind, we now proceed to evaluate the fit of our illustrated model that was estimated in Chapter 6. We do this in three stages, involving (a) the assessment of the model's 'global', i.e. overall fit, (b) the assessment of the measurement part of the model, and (c) the assessment of the structural part of the model.

Overall fit assessment

The purpose of assessing a model's overall fit is to determine the degree to which the model *as a whole* is consistent with the empirical data at hand. Over the years, a wide range of **goodness-of-fit indices** have been developed that can be used as summary measures of a model's overall fit.[9] Unfortunately, none of them is unequivocally superior to the rest in all circumstances, because 'particular indices have been shown to operate somewhat differently given the sample size, estimation procedure, model complexity, violation of the underlying assumptions of multivariate normality and variable independence, or any combination thereof'.[10] To make matters worse, there is a lack of 'a clear notion of precisely what it is that is to be summarized about a model by any fit index, and . . . any agreement on the characteristics that such an index should have'.[11] As a result, different authors tend to favor different indices, often leading to direct conflicts when recommending which indices should (or should not) be relied upon.[12]

As getting involved in the controversy surrounding fit indices is bound to put you off LISREL forever, we have decided to follow a more pragmatic approach when discussing the fit indices generated by the LISREL program. This involves (a) a brief description of each index in non-technical terms and, (b) a recommendation regarding the extent it should be relied upon as an indicator of a model's fit; the latter is based on what the methodological literature says, on balance, about the fit index concerned.[13]

Table 7.1 shows the range of fit indices (labeled as Goodness of Fit Statistics) produced by the LISREL program. Note that this information is given in this form, irrespective of whether or not LISREL Output has been specified in the SIMPLIS input file.

The first fit measure included in the output is the **chi-square statistic** (denoted as Minimum Fit Function Chi-Square). Its value is computed as $(N-1) F_{min}$ where N is the sample size and F_{min} is the value of the fitting function (e.g. ML or GLS) at convergence (see Chapter 6); F_{min} is shown in Table 7.1 as Minimum Fit Function Value. The chi-square statistic is the traditional measure for evaluating overall model fit in covariance structure models and provides 'a test of perfect fit in which the null hypothesis is that the model fits the population data perfectly. A statistically significant chi-square causes rejection of the null hypothesis, implying imperfect model fit and possible rejection of the model'.[14] Thus, the null hypothesis tested by the chi-square test is H_0: $\Sigma = \Sigma(\theta)$, and in contrast to conventional hypothesis testing procedures, the aim is *not* to reject H_0.[15] In using the chi-square statistic, the relevant degrees of freedom are calculated as $\frac{1}{2}k(k + 1) - t$, where k = number of observed variables and t = number of parameters to be estimated.[16]

For our illustrative model the Minimum Fit Function Chi-Square value comes to 165.572; with 57 degrees of freedom this yields a highly significant result ($p < 0.01$), implying that our model is not adequate. The same picture is painted by the Normal Theory Weighted Least Squares Chi-Square which uses a slightly more complicated formula to calculate the test statistic; its substantive interpretation remains the same.[17]

Although at first sight the chi-square seems to be an attractive measure of a model's fit (not least because it provides a formal significance test of the covariance structure hypothesis), caution needs to be exercised in its

Table 7.1   Overall fit indices for illustrative model

```
!ILLUSTRATIVE MODEL OF JOB SATISFACTION AND CUSTOMER FOCUS

                    Goodness of Fit Statistics

                    Degrees of Freedom = 57
          Minimum Fit Function Chi-Square = 165.572 (P = 0.00)
   Normal Theory Weighted Least Squares Chi-Square = 168.310 (P = 0.00)
          Estimated Non-centrality Parameter (NCP) = 111.310

                 Minimum Fit Function Value = 0.543
        Population Discrepancy Function Value (F0) = 0.365
     Root Mean Square Error of Approximation (RMSEA) = 0.0800

            Expected Cross-Validation Index (ECVI) = 0.775
                ECVI for saturated Model = 0.597
                ECVI for Independence Model = 6.826

 Chi-Square for Independence Model with 78 Degrees of Freedom = 2056.035
                 Independence AIC = 2082.035
                    Model AIC = 236.310
                   Saturated AIC = 182.000
                 Independence CAIC = 2143.441
                   Model CAIC = 396.912
                   Saturated CAIC = 611.846

            Root Mean Square Residual (RMR) = 0.0614
                 Standardized RMR = 0.0699
            Goodness of Fit Index (GFI) = 0.922
        Adjusted Goodness of Fit Index (AGFI) = 0.875
        Parsimony Goodness of Fit Index (PGFI) = 0.577

            Normed Fit Index (NFI) = 0.919
           Non-Normed Fit Index (NNFI) = 0.925
        Parsimony Normed Fit Index (PNFI) = 0.672
           Comparative Fit Index (CFI) = 0.945
           Incremental Fit Index (IFI) = 0.946
            Relative Fit Index (RFI) = 0.890

                  Critical N (CN) = 157.088

 CONFIDENCE LIMITS COULD NOT BE COMPUTED DUE TO TOO SMALL P-VALUE FOR CHI-SQUARE
```

application. The chi-square statistic is sensitive to departures from multivariate normality (particularly excessive kurtosis), sample size,[18] and also assumes that the model fits perfectly in the population. For these reasons it has been suggested that 'instead of regarding χ^2 as a test statistic, one should regard it as a goodness (or badness)-of-fit measure in the sense that large χ^2-values correspond to bad fit and small χ^2-values to good fit. The degrees of freedom serve as a standard by which to judge whether χ^2 is large or small'.[19]

The assumption of the chi-square statistic that the model fits perfectly in the population (i.e. that $\Sigma = \Sigma(\theta)$ is highly restrictive because it is implausible that *any* model that we use is anything more than an approximation to reality. Indeed, 'since a null hypothesis that a model fits exactly in some population is known *a priori* to be false, it seems pointless even to try and test whether it is true . . . Rather than trying to ask whether a model is correct, or fits the population covariance matrix exactly, it is sensible to assess the degree of lack of fit of the model'.[20] This is what the **non-centrality parameter** (denoted as Estimated Non-Centrality Parameter (NCP) in Table 7.1) seeks to do. Specifically, if the hypothesized model is only an approximation to reality (as most models are), then $\Sigma \neq \Sigma(\theta)$. In these circumstances, the test statistic will not be χ^2-distributed but will follow a non-central χ^2-distribution with non-centrality parameter, λ.[21] The latter reflects the discrepancy between Σ and $\Sigma(\theta)$ and an estimate of λ is obtained by subtracting the degrees of freedom from the chi-square statistic.[22] The larger the λ, the farther apart is the true alternative hypothesis from the null hypothesis.

For our illustrative model, NCP = 111.31 which is very high. In fact, normally the LISREL program output provides a 90% confidence interval for the NCP;[23] the fact that no such interval is included in Table 7.1 is indicative of the size of the estimated discrepancy between Σ and $\Sigma(\theta)$.

The next measure to consider is the **root mean square error of approximation** (RMSEA) which, like the NCP, also focuses on the discrepancy between Σ and $\Sigma(\theta)$ but *per degree of freedom* this time (hence taking model complexity into account). The RMSEA is generally regarded as one of the most informative fit indices and is calculated as $(F_0/DF)^{1/2}$, where F_0 is the Population Discrepancy Function Value (i.e. the estimated value of the fitting function when a model is fitted to the *population* covariance matrix, Σ) and *DF* are the degrees of freedom.[24] The RMSEA shows 'how well would the model, with unknown but optimally chosen parameter values, fit the population covariance matrix if it were available'.[25] Values less than 0.05 are indicative of good fit, between 0.05 and under 0.08 of reasonable fit, between 0.08 and 0.10 of mediocre fit and >0.10 of poor fit.[26]

For our illustrative model, RMSEA = 0.08 which suggests mediocre fit. Note that the LISREL program normally also performs a test of the closeness of fit (testing the hypothesis H_0: RMSEA <0.05) and provides a 90% confidence interval for the RMSEA. The absence of these parts of the output from Table 7.1 is, again, due to the fact that the discrepancy between Σ and $\Sigma(\theta)$ is so large that no confidence intervals can be computed.

Whereas both the NCP and the RMSEA focus on **error due to approximation** (i.e. the discrepancy between Σ and $\Sigma(\theta)$), the **expected cross-validation index** (ECVI) focuses on **overall error** (i.e. the discrepancy between Σ and $\hat{\Sigma}$, namely the difference between the *population* covariance matrix and the model fitted to the *sample*). Appendix 7A shows the various types of error involved in fitting a model based on discrepancies among different matrices and frequent reference to it should aid your understanding of the various fit indices. With regards to the ECVI, this measure assesses whether a model is likely to cross-validate across samples of the same size from the same population; specifically, 'it measures the discrepancy between the fitted covariance matrix in the analyzed sample, and the expected covariance matrix that would be obtained in another sample of equivalent size'.[27] Thus, the ECVI is a useful indicator of a model's overall fit.

For our illustrative model, ECVI = 0.775. However, this value is not informative in itself as there is no 'appropriate' range of values for the ECVI coefficient. To assess the model's ECVI, the latter must be compared against the ECVI values of other models; the model with the smallest ECVI value is then chosen as representing the greatest potential for replication. In practice, the 'other' models used for comparison purposes are the **independence model** and the **saturated model**. The former is a model of complete independence among all variables (i.e. all observed variables are uncorrelated) and is the most restricted model. This model (also known as the 'null' model) has k parameters and $k(k-1)/2$ degrees of freedom, where k is the number of observed variables. Note from Table 7.1 that the program output also lists the chi-square value for this model under Chi-Square for Independence Model (with 78 degrees of freedom in this instance); this chi-square value is used in the computation of other fit indices (e.g. NFI and NNFI) to be considered shortly.

The saturated model, on the other hand, is one in which the number of parameters to be estimated is exactly equal to the number of variances and covariances among the observed variables; it has $k(k+1)/2$ parameters and zero degrees of freedom (i.e. it is just-identified). Thus, a hypothesized model can be viewed as falling between the independence model at one extreme and the saturated model at the other extreme and its ECVI can be compared with the ECVI for Independence Model and the ECVI for Saturated Model. In our example, whereas the ECVI value is much lower than that of the independence model, it is larger than the ECVI value for the saturated model. The latter is yet another sign of the model's problematic fit.

The next set of fit measures comprises what are known as **information criteria** and, as was the case with the ECVI, these are used to compare models. Information criteria attempt to incorporate the issue of **model parsimony** in the assessment of model fit by taking the number of estimated parameters into account. LISREL 8 computes two such criteria namely **Akaike's information criterion** (AIC) and what is known as the **consistent version of AIC** (CAIC) which adjusts the AIC for sample size effects. Smaller values for the AIC and CAIC represent a better fit of the hypothesized model (denoted as Model AIC (CAIC) in Table 7.1). As was the case with the ECVI, the independence and saturated models are used for comparison purposes (denoted as Independence AIC (CAIC) and Saturated AIC (CAIC) respectively). Note that information criteria require a sample size of at least 200 to make their application reliable and are substantially affected by departures from multivariate normality.

For our illustrative model, AIC = 236.310 and CAIC = 396.912. While the CAIC value is lower than both those for the independence and saturated models, the AIC value is higher than that for the saturated model; thus a conflicting picture of fit is painted by the two information criteria in this instance.

Moving down to the next two measures of fit, these are directly based on the information provided by the residual matrix $(S - \hat{\Sigma})$ which was introduced in Chapter 6 (see Table 6.4). A **fitted residual** is simply the difference between a sample covariance (variance) and a fitted (i.e. model-implied) covariance (variance); if the model fit is good, the fitted residuals should be small in comparison to the magnitude of the elements in S. A summary measure of fitted residuals is the **root mean square residual** (RMR) which represents the average value of the elements in $(S - \hat{\Sigma})$. A problem with interpreting fitted residuals (and, therefore, the RMR statistic) is that their size varies with the unit of measurement and the latter can vary from variable to variable. This problem can be avoided by concentration on the **standardized residuals** which are the fitted residuals divided by their estimated standard errors. Each standardized residual 'can be interpreted as standard normal deviate and considered "large" if it exceeds the value of 2.58 in absolute value'.[28] A summary measure of standardized residuals is the **standardized** RMR; values below 0.05 are indicative of acceptable fit.

In our illustrative model, the values of RMR and standardized RMR come to 0.0614 and 0.0699 respectively; as the latter value exceeds the 0.05 threshold, it raises further doubts regarding the model's fit. Note that LISREL 8 also provides a detailed listing of fitted and standardized residuals enabling the researcher to identify not only how many but *which* particular residuals are excessively high. This part of the program output will be discussed in Chapter 8 as it offers a useful diagnostic facility for model modification purposes.

The next three measures of fit are **absolute fit indices** in that they directly assess 'how well the covariances predicted from the parameter estimates reproduce the sample covariances'.[29] Their computation does not depend on a relative comparison with a 'baseline' model; in contrast, **relative fit indices** (also known as 'incremental' or 'comparative' fit indices) measure the 'proportionate improvement in fit by comparing a target model with a more restricted, nested baseline model . . . A null model in which all the observed variables are uncorrelated is the most typically used baseline model'.[30] The **goodness-of-fit index** (GFI) is an indicator of the relevant amount of variances and covariances accounted for by the model and thus shows how closely the model comes to perfectly reproducing the observed covariance matrix. The **adjusted goodness-of-fit index** (AGFI) is simply the GFI adjusted for the degrees of freedom in the model, while the **parsimony goodness-of-fit index** (PGFI) makes a different type of adjustment to take into account model complexity. Values of the GFI and AGFI should range between 0 and 1 and values >0.90 are usually taken as reflecting acceptable fits.[31] Acceptable values for the PGFI are typically much lower and 'it is not inconceivable to have acceptable models with nonsignificant chi-squares, goodness-of-fit indices in the 0.90s and parsimonious fit indices in the 0.50s'.[32] For reasons too technical to explain here, out of the three indices, the GFI is generally recommended as the most reliable measure of absolute fit in most circumstances.

For our illustrative model, GFI = 0.922, AGFI = 0.875 and PGFI = 0.577; thus the picture painted by these indices is not as negative as that painted by, say, the chi-square, RMSEA and ECVI measures.

The next set of fit measures in the program output is comprised of relative fit indices which show 'how much *better* the model fits compared to a baseline model, usually the independence model'.[33] With the exception of the **non-normed fit index** (NNFI), all the indices in this group have a range between 0 and 1 with values close to 1 representing good fit (the NNFI can take values greater than 1). However, as was the case with the PGFI, lower values of the PNFI are to be expected in relation to its non-parsimonious counterpart (i.e. the NFI). Again, for reasons that need not concern us here, the literature recommends that the NNFI and the **comparative fit index** (CFI) ought to be relied upon for fit assessment.[34]

For our illustrative model, NNFI = 0.925, CFI = 0.945 and RFI = 0.890; with the exception of the RFI, these indices indicate a reasonable relative fit of the model (over the independence model).

The final measure of fit included in Table 7.1 is the **critical N** (CN) statistic. This differs conceptually from the previous fit measures in that it shows 'the size that a sample must reach in order to accept the fit of a given model on a statistical basis'.[35] A rule of thumb indicating that a model is an adequate representation of the data is CN > 200.

For our illustrative model, CN = 157.088, which falls well short of the suggested threshold. Note, however, that both the value of the CN statistic itself and the suggested cut-off point have been challenged in the literature and, thus, the CN measure needs to be used with caution.[36]

From the above discussion it becomes obvious that different fit indices assess fit in different ways and that to reach a judgement concerning the overall fit of a model, one has to rely on multiple criteria; indeed, '*no one* index serves as a definite criterion for testing a hypothesized model. An "ideal" fit index just does not exist'.[37] For practical purposes, the results of the chi-square test used in conjunction with the RMSEA, ECVI, standardized RMR, GFI and CFI indices should be more than sufficient to reach an informed decision concerning the model's overall fit.

The assessment of a model's overall fit needs to be accompanied by a detailed assessment of the measurement and structural parts of the model. This is necessary because 'it is possible that global measures of fit will indicate a satisfactory model but certain parameters corresponding to hypothesized relations may be nonsignificant and/or measures low in reliability may exist'.[38] Moreover, if as was the case with our illustrative model, the overall fit criteria paint a picture of unsatisfactory fit, further analysis is necessary to determine the causes of poor fit. Measures of overall fit may alert us that something is wrong with the model but do not tell us 'what is wrong with the model or which part of the model is wrong'.[39]

Assessment of measurement model

In evaluating the measurement part of the model, we focus on the relationships between the latent variables and their indicators (i.e. the manifest variables). The aim is to determine the **validity** and **reliability** of the measures used to represent the constructs of interest. Validity reflects the extent to which an indicator actually measures what it is supposed to measure, while reliability refers to the consistency of measurement (i.e. the extent to which an indicator is free of random error).[40] Clearly, unless we can trust the quality of our measures, then any assessment of the substantive relations of interest (i.e. the links among the latent variables themselves) will be problematic. Thus, an evaluation of the measurement part of the model should precede the detailed evaluation of the structural part of the model. Focusing initially on the validity of the indicators, this can be readily assessed by examining the magnitude and significance of the paths between each latent variable and its indicators. If, say, x is supposed to be a valid measure of, say, ξ, then clearly the direct relation between x and ξ should be substantial (and certainly significantly different from zero). This direct relation is captured by the loading, λ, in the measurement equation below:

$$x = \lambda \xi + \delta \qquad (1)$$

where δ = measurement error.

Now, as you know from Chapter 6, the program output lists the unstandardized parameter estimates for all the equations in a model, together with their standard errors and t-values. This information is presented in equation form in the SIMPLIS output format (see Table 6.2) and matrix form in the LISREL output format (see Table 6.3); in the latter case the parameters of interests are the unstandardized loadings in the LAMBDA-X and LAMBDA-Y matrices.

For our illustrative model, all indicator loadings are significant (at $p < 0.05$ or better), as indicated by t-values well in excess of 1.96 in absolute terms (see Tables 6.2 and 6.3). This provides validity evidence in favor of the indicators used to represent the constructs of interest. Having said that, the output also shows that the error variance of one of the indicators of Cust Foc (Customer Focus), namely the one relating to Sell (Selling Behavior) is not significant.[41] This is somewhat worrying because it implies that there is no measurement error whatsoever for this indicator. In this context, although one is clearly interested in *minimizing* measurement error, *zero* measurement error is a cause for concern, because 'it is unreasonable to expect the absence of random error in most managerial and social science contexts'.[42] Thus a nonsignificant error variance may be indicative of specification error, an issue to be further explored in Chapter 8.

One problem with relying on unstandardized loadings and associated t-values is that it may be difficult to compare the validity of different indicators measuring a particular construct. This problem arises because indicators of the same construct may be measured on very different scales; if this is the case, then direct comparisons of the magnitudes of the loadings are clearly inappropriate. In addition, bearing in mind that each latent variable has to be assigned a scale by fixing the loading of one of its indicators to unity (see Chapter 4), the loadings of the other indicators for that latent variable are only interpretable relative to the unit of the reference indicator. Clearly, if a different indicator is used as the reference variable, the magnitudes of the loadings will change.[43] For these reasons, it is recommended that the magnitudes of the *standardized* loadings are also inspected; this can be done by examining the Completely Standardized Solution (see Table 6.5) which is easily obtainable as part of the program output.[44] In our illustrative model, inspection of the standardized loadings reveals that Compat (Compatibility) is the most valid indicator for Role Con (Role Conflict), while Work (Satisfaction with Work) is the least valid indicator for Job Sat (Job Satisfaction); similar inferences can be drawn with regards to the indicators of the other latent variables in the model.[45]

Shifting attention to the reliability of the indicators, the latter can be examined by looking at the squared multiple correlations (R^2) of the indicators. These have already been discussed in Chapter 6 (see Tables 6.2 and 6.3) and they show the proportion of variance in an indicator that is explained by its underlying latent variable (the rest is due to measurement error). A high multiple squared correlation value denotes high reliability for the indicator concerned.[46] In our illustrative example, the most reliable indicator for Mkt Ort (Market Orientation) is Custort (Customer Orientation) and the least reliable is Comport (Competitor Orientation); again, similar inferences can be drawn for the indicators of the other latent variables.

In addition to assessing the reliability of the individual indicators, it is possible to calculate a **composite reliability** value for each latent variable (also known as 'construct reliability'). To do this, we use the information on the indicator loadings and error variances from the Completely Standardized Solution and apply the following formula (yes, we do have to do this manually as LISREL does not automatically compute composite reliabilities):

$$\rho_c = (\textstyle\sum \lambda)^2 / \left[(\textstyle\sum \lambda)^2 + \textstyle\sum (\theta) \right] \qquad (2)$$

where ρ_c = composite reliability
λ = indicator loadings
θ = indicator error variances (i.e. variances of the δ's or ε's)
$\textstyle\sum$ = summation over the indicators of the latent variable

For example, the composite reliability of Mkt Ort (Market Orientation) is calculated as follows (using the information on the standardized loadings and error variances in Table 6.5):

$$\rho_c = (0.851 + 0.742 + 0.796)^2/[(0.851 + 0.742 + 0.796)^2$$
$$+ (0.276 + 0.449 + 0.367)]$$
$$= 5.707/(5.707 + 1.092)$$
$$= 0.853$$

Since ρ_c values greater than 0.6 are desirable,[47] we can conclude that *as a set* the three indicators of Market Orientation provide reliable measurement of the construct.

A complementary measure to composite reliability is the **average variance extracted**, ρ_v. This shows directly 'the amount of variance that is captured by the construct in relation to the amount of variance due to measurement error';[48] ρ_v values less than 0.50 indicate that measurement error accounts for a greater amount of variance in the indicators than does the underlying latent variable (and hence doubts can be raised regarding the soundness of the indicators and/or the latent variable itself).

Again, the LISREL program does not provide ρ_v values as a matter of course (yes, you should complain to the program vendors!) and one has to calculate these manually. Fortunately, the information needed is identical to that required for the computation of composite reliabilities, only the formula changes slightly:[49]

$$\rho_v = \left(\sum \lambda^2\right)/\left[\sum \lambda^2 + \sum(\theta)\right] \tag{3}$$

where λ, θ, and $\sum$ are defined as above.

Sticking to the Mkt Ort (Market Orientation) example, the average variance extracted comes to:

$$\rho_v = [(0.851)^2 + (0.742)^2 + (0.796)^2]/[(0.851)^2 + (0.742)^2 + (0.796)^2$$
$$+ (0.276 + 0.449 + 0.367)]$$
$$= 1.908/(1.908 + 1.092)$$
$$= 0.636$$

Since $\rho_v > 0.50$, we can conclude that a substantially higher amount of variance in the indicators is captured by the construct compared to that accounted for measurement error. This provides additional confidence in our operationalization of Market Orientation.

Table 7.2 shows the composite reliability and average variance extracted for all five latent variables included in our illustrative model. It can be seen that all composite reliabilities comfortably exceed the 0.60 threshold and, with one exception, the average variance extracted exceeds 0.50. The exception in question is the Job Sat (Job Satisfaction) variable for which $\rho_v = 0.393$. The reason for this low ρ_v value is the fact that the variance accounted for by Job Satisfaction with regards to each of its indicators is relatively low; indeed, inspection of Tables 6.2 and 6.3 shows that the squared multiple correlations of the four indicators of Job Satisfaction are quite low (ranging from 0.351 to 0.480) and much lower than the squared multiple correlations of the indicators of all other latent variables. Clearly, if a construct cannot account for a substantial amount of variance in the

Table 7.2   Composite reliabilities and average variance extracted
for illustrative model

Latent variable	Composite reliability (ρ_c)	Average variance extracted (ρ_v)
Role Ambiguity	0.798	0.666
Role Conflict	0.879	0.786
Market Orientation	0.853	0.636
Job Satisfaction	0.720	0.393
Customer Focus	0.880	0.789

individual indicators, it cannot possibly capture a substantial amount of variance in the set of indicators. The Job Satisfaction case illustrates the importance of complementing composite reliability calculations with assessments of the average variance extracted for each latent variable in a model.

In summary, the assessment of the measurement part of our illustrative model revealed good evidence of validity and reliability for the operationalizations of most of the latent variables. Although an instance of a nonsignificant error variance and a case of low variance extracted were observed, on the whole, the assessment of the measurement part of the model did not reveal any crucial deficiencies. We now turn to the evaluation of the structural part of the model.

Assessment of structural model

In evaluating the structural part of the model, we focus on the substantive relationships of interest (i.e. the linkages between the various endogenous and exogenous latent variables). The aim here is to determine whether the theoretical relationships specified at the conceptualization stage (see Chapter 2) are indeed supported by the data. Three issues are of relevance here. First, the signs of the parameters representing the paths between the latent variables indicate whether the direction of the hypothesized relationships is as hypothesized (i.e. positive or negative). Second, the magnitudes of the estimated parameters provide important information on the strength of the hypothesized relationships; at the very least these parameters should be significant (as indicated by t-values in excess of $|1.96|$).[50] Third, the squared multiple correlations (R^2) for the structural equations indicate the amount of variance in each endogenous latent variable that is accounted for by the independent latent variables that are expected to impact upon it; clearly, the higher the squared multiple correlation, the greater the joint explanatory power of the hypothesized antecedents.

All the above information is provided as part of the program output either in equation form (if SIMPLIS output format is used – see Table 6.2) or in matrix form (if LISREL format is specified – see Table 6.3); in the latter case, the parameters of interest are the elements of the GAMMA, BETA and PSI matrices.

For our illustrative model, the signs of all parameters are consistent with the hypothesized relationships among the latent variables (see Table 2.1 in Chapter 2). Moreover, all but one of the parameter estimates are significant (at $p < 0.05$ or better). Finally, the squared multiple correlations for the two endogenous variables in the model are quite respectable; for Job Sat (Job Satisfaction), $R^2 = 0.571$ and for Cust Foc (Customer Focus), $R^2 = 0.584$.

Additional insights into the *relative* impact of each independent variable on each endogenous variable can be gained by looking at the standardized parameter estimates relating to the structural equations (see Table 6.5).[51] These are not affected by differences in the unit of measurement of the independent variables (see Chapter 6) and, therefore, can be compared within equations. In our example, Role Amb (Role Ambiguity) has a greater impact on Job Sat (Job Satisfaction) than Role Con (Role Conflict) (as indicated by standardized parameter values of -0.603 and -0.237 respectively). In contrast, Job Sat (Job Satisfaction) and Mkt Ort (Market Orientation) have approximately equal influence on Cust Foc (Customer Focus); the relevant standardized parameter estimates come to 0.418 and 0.421 respectively.

With regards to the nonsignificant link, this relates to the path between Role Con (Role Conflict) and Cust Foc (Customer Focus); the relevant standardized estimate is very low and close to zero (-0.05). This raises questions about the inclusion of this link in the model, an issue we will revisit in Chapter 7 which deals with model modification.

Power assessment

An important, but often neglected issue in model evaluation is the **statistical power** associated with testing one's model. In this context, 'the power of the test is defined as the probability that an incorrect model will be rejected'.[52] When we test a model's fit by, say, the chi-square test, we emphasize the probability of making a **Type I error**, i.e. rejecting a correct model; this probability is captured by the **significance level**, α, which is usually set at 0.05. A significant chi-square result indicates that *if* the null hypothesis is true (i.e. the model is correct in the population), then the probability of incorrectly rejecting it is low (i.e. less than five times out of 100 if $\alpha = 0.05$). However, another error that can occur is *not* to reject an incorrect model. This type of error is known as **Type II error** and the probability associated with it is denoted as β. The probability of avoiding a Type II error is, therefore, $1 - \beta$ and it is this probability that indicates the power of our test; thus the power of the test tells us how likely it is that a false null hypothesis (i.e. incorrect model) will be rejected.

As the different kinds of error can be confusing, Table 7.3 summarizes the possible outcomes resulting from testing a model. Two of these outcomes are desirable, representing correct decisions on our part; however,

Table 7.3   Errors in model testing

		Situation in population	
		Model is correct	Model is incorrect
Decision made	Do Not Reject Model	Correct decision $(1-\alpha)$	Type II Error (β)
	Reject Model	Type I Error (α)	Correct decision $(1-\beta)$

two are undesirable as they represent different kinds of error. In applying the chi-square test only *one* of these errors (Type I error) is explicitly taken into account. To also account for Type II error, a power analysis must be undertaken.

Conducting a power analysis is important because of the role that sample size plays in model testing. Specifically, 'for large samples we face the question of whether a statistically significant chi-square estimate of overall fit means that serious specification errors are present or whether the test has excessively high power. Nonsignificant chi-squares can occur in the face of substantial specification errors in small samples where the power is more likely to be low.'[53] What this means is that 'when a model contains small specification errors, large sample sizes will magnify their effects, leading to the rejection of the null hypothesis. When a model contains large specification errors, small sample sizes will mask their effects leading to acceptance of the null hypothesis.'[54] Thus, in evaluating a model's fit, we may be faced with any one of four possibilities as illustrated in Table 7.4.

If the test statistic (e.g. value of the chi-square test) is significant and the power is low (case 1 in Table 7.4), the model can be safely rejected because small misspecifications would not be detected by the test; the fact that the latter is significant is indicative of substantial misspecifications (i.e. the model must be wrong). In contrast, if the test is significant but power is high (case 2), then we have a problem because we do not know whether the high value of the test statistic is due to gross misspecifications or the high sensitivity of the test to even trivial misspecification errors. We also have a problem if the test is *not* significant but power is low (case 3) because we do not know whether the low value of the test statistic reflects the 'correctness' of our model or the lack of sensitivity to specification errors. Finally, in the ideal scenario (case 4), the model could be accepted because the high power of the test implies that any serious specification errors would be detected.

From the above discussion it becomes evident that any model evaluation that ignores power considerations would be incomplete. For example, for our illustrative model, recall that the value of the test statistic was significant (see Table 7.1). Does this reflect a poor model that ought to be rejected (case 1 in Table 7.5) or could it be the case that our sample size is such that it makes the test too sensitive to even small specification errors (case 2 in Table 7.5)?

Table 7.4 Model testing situations

		Power of the test	
		Low	High
Outcome of test	Significant	Reject model (1)	? (2)
	Not significant	? (3)	Accept model (4)

To answer the above question, we must calculate the power of the test for our model. There are two types of power calculations we can undertake.[55] First, we can estimate the power associated with a **test of exact fit** (i.e. testing the null hypothesis that the model fits *perfectly* in the population). This is the null hypothesis tested by the conventional chi-square test and, as noted previously, such a test is very restrictive since models are only *approximations* of reality (i.e. they never fit exactly even in the population). Second, we can estimate the power associated with a **test of close fit**, whereby the null hypothesis is that the model has a close, albeit imperfect fit in the population. This null hypothesis takes the error due to approximation into account (see earlier discussion and Appendix 7A) and is, therefore, more realistic.

Both types of power calculation utilize the RMSEA statistic discussed in an earlier section of this chapter. Let ε denote the RMSEA value in the population. If the model fits perfectly in the population, then the error due to approximation will be zero and, therefore, $\varepsilon = 0$. Thus, a null hypothesis of exact fit can be represented as:

$$H_o: \varepsilon_o = 0$$

We must now state a *specific* value for the alternative hypothesis, H_a, since 'power depends on the specific value of a parameter under the alternative hypothesis'.[56] A reasonable value is $\varepsilon_a = 0.05$ (recall that RMSEA values of less than 0.05 are indicative of good fit). Thus, in this case, we would be investigating the power of the test of $H_o: \varepsilon_o = 0$ when the true fit of the model was close, i.e. $\varepsilon_a = 0.05$.

A similar line of thinking can be applied to the examination of power under the more realistic hypothesis of close (rather than exact) fit. Specifically, the null and alternative hypotheses can be stated as:

$$H_o: \varepsilon_o \leq 0.05$$
$$H_a: \varepsilon_a = 0.08$$

The choice of values for ε_o and ε_a reflect the recommendations in the literature regarding RMSEA thresholds for close and mediocre fit respectively. Here we are asking the question: if the true fit of the model was mediocre (i.e. if H_a is correct), what is the power of the test that $Ho: \varepsilon_o \leq 0.05$ (i.e. that fit is close)?

Armed with the information on ε_o and ε_a and given a significance level α (typically 0.05) and a sample size N, the power of the test becomes a function of the degrees of freedom (v) in the model; the latter reflects the model specification (i.e. the number of over-identifying restrictions (see Chapters 3 and 5)). All other things being equal, the higher the degrees of freedom, the greater the power of the test.

For our illustrative model, to assess the power associated with testing for exact fit, we would set $\varepsilon_o = 0$, $\varepsilon_a = 0.05$, $\alpha = 0.05$, $N = 306$ and $v = 57$; to investigate the power of close fit, we would set $\varepsilon_o = 0.05$ and $\varepsilon_a = 0.08$ while keeping α, N and v unchanged. We now have two options. We can either consult some very useful power tables compiled by MacCallum, Browne and Sugawara (1996) or we can use an SAS program routine developed by these authors for analyzing power.[57] Use of the tables is the easy option, as one can simply read off power estimates associated with different sample sizes and degrees of freedom; however, since not all possible combinations of N and v are listed in the tables, for many models and sample sizes only approximate power estimates can be obtained. On the other hand, use of the power program allows one not only to input any value of N and v but also to specify any value for α, ε_o and ε_a;[58] this provides great flexibility in power assessment. The downside is, of course, that one has to do some computing and also have access to the SAS package.

For our purposes, we will opt for the easy option and get power estimates for our model from Table 2 of MacCallum, Browne and Sugawara (1996). For a model with 60 degrees of freedom (ours has 57) and a sample size of 300 (ours is 306), the power estimate for the test of exact fit is 0.941 and that for the test of close fit is 0.960. Thus, both power estimates indicate that our analysis is sufficiently powerful (usually power levels of about 0.80 are considered sufficient for most practical purposes).

An interesting point that is revealed by the power figures above is that we have an extremely high chance of rejecting a *good* (if not perfect) model with our sample size. Specifically, the likelihood of rejecting the hypothesis of exact fit is more than 0.90 even though the true fit is close! Going back to Table 7.4, our model falls clearly under case 2 (upper right cell), i.e. there is a clear danger of rejecting a close-fitting model. This demonstrates quite unequivocally the problems associated with relying exclusively on a test of exact fit (such as that performed by the chi-square statistic) and establishes 'a clear basis for recommending against the use of the test of exact fit for evaluating covariance structure models . . . use of this test would routinely result in rejection of close-fitting models in studies with moderate to large sample sizes'.[59]

What about the power associated with testing the hypothesis of close fit for our model? Would we be able to detect major specification errors? The answer is yes; the likelihood of rejecting the hypothesis of close fit when the true fit is mediocre is again in excess of 0.90. Thus, we can rest assured that serious misspecifications would be detected.

Another way of looking at the issue of power is to ask: given a model with v degrees of freedom, what is the minimum necessary sample size to attain a certain level of power (e.g. 0.80)? This question can be posed in connection with a test of exact fit or a test of close fit and is particularly relevant at the design stage of a study (so that a sufficient but not excessive sample size is chosen *before* data is collected). Again, MacCallum, Browne and Sugawara (1996) provide tables with the values of N necessary to attain power levels of 0.80 and 0.50 for models with different degrees of freedom, v; they also provide an SAS program for directly calculating N. For our illustrative model, an approximation of the minimum N necessary to have a power of 0.80 when testing for *close* fit, can be obtained by looking at their Table 4 for v = 60; this indicates that $N = 200$, which is comfortably exceeded by our sample size (in other words, we would have had sufficient power to test our model even if our sample size was about a third smaller than its actual size). For a test of exact fit, $N = 218$.

Our discussion of power issues has so far focused on the determination of power for the model as a whole. However, one can also undertake power calculations for individual parameters. For example, recall from the previous section that the link between Role Con (Role Conflict) and Cust Foc (Customer Focus) turned out to be nonsignificant. Is this because the relevant link is zero in the population or is it that our sample size is too small to detect its existence? To answer this question, we must estimate the power associated with testing that $\gamma_{22} = 0$ against some alternative value (e.g. that $\gamma_{22} = 0.20$). There are several ways for doing this[60] and we will consider one of them in the context of model modification in Chapter 8.

Having evaluated the fit of our model from a variety of angles, we are now in a position to consider possible modifications to improve the model. As mentioned in Chapter 1, this is the stage in LISREL modeling most likely to be abused. Indeed, as Chapter 8 will demonstrate, model modification is fraught with danger and should be approached with great caution; otherwise, 'modifications may merely fit chance characteristics of the original sample, rather than represent aspects of the model that generalize to other samples and to the population'.[61]

Notes

1 Strictly speaking, 'the covariance structure hypothesis is that $\Sigma = \Sigma(\theta)$. The overall fit measures help to assess whether this is valid, and if not, they help to measure the departure of Σ from $\Sigma(\theta)$. Being population parameters, Σ and $\Sigma(\theta)$ are unavailable, so researchers examine their counterparts S and $\Sigma(\hat{\theta})$' (Bollen, 1989, p. 256). See also note 1 in Chapter 6.

2 Bollen (1989), p. 256.

3 Byrne (1998), p. 119, emphasis in the original.

4 Darden (1983), p. 28, emphasis in the original.

5 Byrne (1998), p. 103.

6 Bagozzi and Yi (1988), p. 90.

7 Bagozzi and Yi (1988), p. 92.

8   Sobel and Bohrnstedt (1985), p. 158.
9   For a review and discussion of different fit indices and their statistical properties, see
    Marsh, Balla and McDonald (1988), Mulaik et al. (1989), Tanaka (1993), Gerbing and
    Anderson (1993), Hu and Bentler (1995) and Marsh, Balla and Hau (1996).
10 Byrne (1998), p. 118.
11 Hayduk (1996), p. 201.
12 For example, Maruyama (1998) cites Mulaik et al. (1989) and does not recommend use of
    the adjusted goodness-of-fit index (AGFI), while Hayduk's (1996) recommendation is
    precisely the opposite!
13 Of course, if you do not wish to follow these recommendations 'on faith', you are more
    than welcome to make up your own mind by consulting the relevant literature (see note 9
    above); be warned, however, that this literature is not exactly bedtime reading!
14 Jaccard and Wan (1996), p. 18.
15 Note that the null hypothesis can also be specified as H_0: $\Sigma - \Sigma(\theta) = 0$ which is equivalent
    to testing that all residuals are zero. Again, in testing this hypothesis, we use S instead of
    Σ, and $\hat{\Sigma}$ instead of $\Sigma(\theta)$, since both Σ and $\Sigma(\theta)$ are unknown population covariance
    matrices (see also note 1 above).
16 See also Chapter 5 on model identification. Note in particular that the degrees of freedom
    calculated for the illustrative model equals the degrees of freedom in Table 7.1.
17 LISREL 8.20 can produce a total of four different chi-square statistics (denoted as C1,
    C2, C3 and C4) depending upon (a) the method of estimation, and (b) whether an
    asymptotic covariance matrix is provided or not; see the program's on-line Help file
    'Introduction to LISREL 8.20'.
18 With small samples, the distribution of the test statistic does not adequately approximate
    the χ^2-distribution. With large samples, on the other hand, 'almost any model with
    positive degrees of freedom is likely to be rejected as providing a statistically unacceptable
    fit' (Long, 1983b), p. 75; this is because the probability of detecting a false model
    increases with sample size even with a 'minimally false' model (i.e. when the differences
    between S and $\hat{\Sigma}$ are trivial (Bentler and Bonett, 1980)). Thus 'a poor fit based on a small
    sample size may result in a non-significant χ^2, whereas a good fit based on a large sample
    size may result in a statistically significant χ^2' (Marsh, Balla and McDonald, 1988, p. 392).
19 Jöreskog and Sörbom (1989), p. 43. A well-fitting model would ideally be indicated by a
    chi-square value that approximates the degrees of freedom; in practice, χ^2/df ratios of 5
    (Wheaton et al., 1977) or even 2 (Carmines and McIver, 1981) have been used as
    thresholds. However, for reasons explained by Wheaton (1987), the use of this 'normed'
    chi-square statistic is no longer recommended for assessing fit.
20 Browne and Cudeck (1993), p. 137.
21 The central χ^2-distribution is a special case of the non-central χ^2-distribution when $\lambda = 0$.
22 In calculating the NCP in LISREL 8.20, the Normal Theory Weighted Least
    Squares Chi-Square is used.
23 Confidence intervals are also normally provided for the RMSEA, F_0 and the ECVI.
    However, the calculation of such intervals is partly dependent upon the chi-square value;
    when the latter is too large, the confidence limits cannot be established (see warning note
    at bottom of Table 7.1).
24 If the model fits perfectly in the population, then $F_0 = 0$ and, therefore, RMSEA = 0.
25 Browne and Cudeck (1993), pp. 137–138.
26 These thresholds are based on the recommendations of Browne and Cudeck (1993) and
    MacCallum, Browne and Sugawara (1996).
27 Byrne (1998), p. 113. We will have more to say about cross-validation in general and the
    ECVI in particular in Chapter 9.
28 Jöreskog and Sörbom (1989), p. 32. Note, however, that because full-information
    estimation techniques (such as maximum likelihood) *simultaneously* fit all the parameters
    in all model equations, specification errors in one equation can affect the estimation of
    other correctly specified equations (see Chapter 6). Therefore, standardized residuals are
    not independent but correlated from cell to cell; moreover, they are calculated under

assumptions of multivariate normality and will be biased when this assumption is violated (Steenkamp and van Trijp, 1991).

29 Gerbing and Anderson (1993), p. 43.

30 Hu and Bentler (1995), p. 82.

31 Note that it is theoretically possible for the GFI and AGFI to take on negative values; however, this should not happen as it means that 'the model fits worse than no model at all' (Jöreskog and Sörbom, 1993, p. 123).

32 Mulaik et al. (1989), p. 439.

33 Jöreskog and Sörbom (1993), p. 125.

34 The NNFI is also sometimes referred to as the Tucker-Lewis index (TLI).

35 Hoelter (1983), p. 330.

36 For example, Hu and Bentler (1995, p. 93) argue that with samples of 250 plus, 'a cutoff value that is substantially greater than 200 would be required to evaluate appropriately the fit of the model'.

37 Schumacker and Lomax (1996), p. 135, emphasis in the original.

38 Bagozzi and Yi (1988), p. 80.

39 Jöreskog and Sörbom (1989), p. 45.

40 For general discussions of validity and reliability, see Heeler and Ray (1972), Carmines and Zeller (1979), Peter (1979, 1981), Zeller and Carmines (1980), Brinberg and McGrath (1982), Nunnally and Bernstein (1994) and Traub (1994). For discussions within a LISREL context, see Anderson and Gerbing (1982), Danes and Mann (1984), Darden, Carlson and Hampton (1984), Gerbing and Anderson (1988), Bollen (1989), Steenkamp and van Trijp (1991) and Homburg and Giering (1996).

41 Specifically, VAR(ε_5) = 0.048, t-value = 0.0653, not significant; see fourth equation in the SIMPLIS output (Table 6.2) and the THETA-EPS matrix in the LISREL output (Table 6.3).

42 Bagozzi and Yi (1988), p. 77. See also note 27 in Chapter 6.

43 Note also that since the loading of the reference variable is a *fixed* parameter, no standard errors or t-values are computed by the program (see Chapter 6, Tables 6.2 and 6.3).

44 Recall from Chapter 6 that it is only in the Completely Standardized Solution that *both* the latent *and* the manifest variables (i.e. indicators) are standardized; in the Standardized Solution only the latent variables are standardized. To obtain these solutions, it is necessary to specify the SS and/or SC keywords on the LISREL Output command line of the input file (see Table 6.1).

45 When indicators measure more than one latent variable (i.e. when the indicators are not unidimensional), there are additional measures of validity that can be computed from the program output; for a good discussion, see Bollen (1989).

46 Note that indicator reliabilities (as measured by the squared multiple correlations) are also sometimes referred to as 'convergent validities' (e.g. see Jöreskog and Sörbom, 1989); this can cause confusion, so beware!

47 See Bagozzi and Yi (1988).

48 Fornell and Larcker (1981), p. 45.

49 Again the Completely Standardized Solution should be used in applying the formula in equation (3).

50 Assuming, of course, that they are in the hypothesized direction (i.e. they have the 'correct' signs).

51 As the latent variables are standardized in both the Standardized Solution and the Completely Standardized Solution, the parameter estimates in the BETA, GAMMA and PSI matrices are identical across the two solutions (see Table 6.5).

52 Saris and Satorra (1993), p. 188.

53 Bollen (1989), p. 338.

54 Kaplan (1995), p. 101.

55 Strictly speaking, there are three types of power calculations relating to hypotheses of exact, close and not-close fit (see MacCallum, Browne and Sugawara, 1996); for our purposes, consideration of the first two types is sufficient.

56 Bollen (1989), p. 340.
57 This program is listed as an Appendix in MacCallum, Browne and Sugawara (1996); it can also be found in the following website: *http://quantrm2.psy.ohio-state.edu/maccallum/power.htm*
58 In the power tables of MacCallum, Browne and Sugawara (1996) the default settings are: $\alpha = 0.05$, $\varepsilon_o = 0$ and $\varepsilon_a = 0.05$ for exact fit and $\alpha = 0.05$, $\varepsilon_o = 0.05$ and $\varepsilon_a = 0.08$ for close fit (so if you want to, say, estimate the power when $\alpha = 0.01$, $\varepsilon_o = 0.07$ and $\varepsilon_a = 0.10$, you cannot rely on the tabled values but have to use the program instead).
59 MacCallum, Browne and Sugawara (1996), p. 145.
60 See, for example, Bollen (1989), Saris and Satorra (1993) and Kaplan (1995) and references given therein.
61 MacCallum, Roznowski and Necowitz (1992), p. 491.

APPENDIX 7A

Different types of discrepancy in evaluating a LISREL model

If one subscribes to the notion that models are only approximations to reality, then a hypothesized model cannot fit *perfectly* in the population. The lack of fit in the population is represented by the discrepancy between Σ (the population covariance matrix) and $\Sigma(\theta)$ (the model-based covariance matrix). This is the **discrepancy of approximation**; in practice, this discrepancy cannot be exactly determined, as neither Σ nor θ is known (see Appendix 1B in Chapter 1).

A second type of discrepancy is that between S (the sample covariance matrix) and $\hat{\Sigma}$ (where $\hat{\Sigma} = \Sigma(\hat{\theta})$, representing the lack of fit of the model in the sample. This is known as the **sample discrepancy** and can be exactly determined during the estimation process (see Chapter 6).

A third type of discrepancy is the one between $\Sigma(\theta)$ and $\hat{\Sigma}$ and reflects the lack of correspondence between the actual parameter values and the parameter estimates obtained from a given sample. This is known as the **discrepancy of estimation**.

Finally, the discrepancy of approximation and discrepancy of estimation combine to produce the **overall discrepancy**, representing the difference between the population covariance matrix, Σ, and the model implied covariance matrix, $\hat{\Sigma}$, based upon fitting the model to a sample.

A detailed discussion of the four types of discrepancy can be found in Cudeck and Henly (1991).

8 MODEL MODIFICATION

At first glance, the rationale behind model modification is both simple and intuitively appealing: having estimated a particular model and assessed its fit (following the procedures outlined in Chapters 6 and 7), are there any changes that can be made to improve the model? By 'changes' we mean here alterations to the model specification via the addition/deletion of certain parameters (see Chapter 4), while by 'improvement' we mean a better-fitting and/or more parsimonious model *which is substantively interpretable*. The last point is critical: model modifications, however tempting, should be firmly resisted, unless 'a clear and well-founded interpretation'[1] can be offered. The reason for this is that data-driven model modifications are particularly susceptible to **capitalization on chance** in that 'idiosyncratic characteristics of the sample may influence the particular modifications that are performed'.[2] As a result, the modified model, while demonstrating a good (or even excellent) fit in one particular sample, may fail miserably when applied to a different sample or the population. In short, 'it is of utmost importance that any modifications made to an original model must be substantively meaningful and justifiable'.[3]

Model modifications may be considered in two instances. First, one may seek to *further* improve an already well-fitting model. Although most researchers would not even consider this step under this scenario (they'd probably be out celebrating), there still may be opportunities for either improving fit or for simplifying the model (e.g. deletion of some parameters may result in a more parsimonious model that fits almost as well as the original version). Unfortunately, research has shown that modifications to a well-fitting model can be very unstable (i.e. they may not replicate in other samples). Therefore, it is recommended that 'when an initial model fits well, it is probably unwise to modify it to achieve even better fit because the modifications may simply be fitting small idiosyncratic characteristics of the sample'.[4]

The second and, by far, most common reason for contemplating model modifications, is that the fit of the original model is *not* good. There are several reasons for a model's poor fit, including violations of distributional assumptions, non-linearities, missing data and specification error.[5] It is the detection and correction of specification errors that model modification seeks to accomplish. As you may recall from Chapter 2, specification errors come in all sorts of shapes and forms (e.g. omissions of relevant exogenous variables from the model, omissions of important linkages among included variables, and inclusion of irrelevant linkages). Model modification procedures can only deal with **internal specification errors**, i.e. omission (inclusion) of important (irrelevant) parameters given the set of variables in the model; **external specification errors**, in the sense of omitted variables, cannot be addressed by the procedures discussed in this chapter.[6]

Specification searches

The process of identifying and correcting (internal) specification errors is known as **specification search**; during such a search 'the investigator alters the model specification, perhaps numerous times, in search of a parsimonious, substantively meaningful model that fits the data well . . . The ultimate objective of a specification search is to arrive at the model that correctly represents the network of relations among the MVs [manifest variables] and LVs [latent variables] in the population'.[7]

Several points become apparent from the above definition. First, and most important, 'the nature of the analysis is no longer *confirmatory* (i.e. testing a pre-determined system of hypotheses as reflected in the original model specification) but becomes *exploratory*'.[8] What this means is that any model finally arrived at via a specification search is only tentative and in need of independent verification (i.e. it must be tested and validated on a different sample). It is *not* acceptable to use the same data set for both model generation and model testing purposes; indeed, 'the entire logic of confirmatory analysis is undermined when the same data set is used both to develop a model and to evaluate its fit'.[9]

Second, in effect, a specification search leads to a *new* model which may or may not be similar to the one originally proposed (depending upon the number and nature of modifications undertaken). In any case, it cannot be taken for granted that the new model will be identified (see Chapter 5); consequently 'the user must prove identification for each model estimated in a specification search'.[10]

Third, there is a question of 'knowing when to stop' as modifying the model beyond a certain point may lead to an **overfitting model**. Such a model 'can result from the inclusion of additional parameters that: (a) are "fragile" in the sense of representing weak effects that are not likely replicable, (b) lead to a significant inflation of standard errors, and (c) influence primary parameters in the model, albeit their own substantive meaningfulness is somewhat equivocal'.[11] Indeed, taken to extremes, a specification search may well lead to a saturated model with zero degrees of freedom and, therefore, perfect fit![12] This model, however, is not disconfirmable because it is not possible for it to be inconsistent with observed data (it will *always* fit perfectly). In this context, 'if a model is not disconfirmable to any reasonable degree, then a finding of good fit is essentially useless and meaningless. Therefore, in the model modification process, researchers are very strongly encouraged to keep in mind the principle of disconfirmability and to construct models that are not highly parameterized'.[13]

Table 8.1   Possible modifications to a LISREL model

	Reduce constraints[a]	Increase constraints[b]
Measurement model	Free measurement parameters	Fix measurement parameters
Structural model	Free structural parameters	Fix structural parameters

[a] Reducing constraints typically involves freeing a parameter previously fixed to zero but may also involve the cancellation of an equality constraint.

[b] Increasing constraints typically involves setting parameters to zero but many also involve setting equality constraints (i.e. constraining the values of two parameters to be equal).

Bearing the above points in mind, what are possible modifications to a model resulting from a specification search? Recall from Chapter 4 that the formal specification of a LISREL model is reflected in the pattern of fixed and free parameters in eight parameter matrices (see Appendix 4D). Therefore, any change in this pattern (by freeing previously fixed parameters and/or fixing previously free parameters) will change the original model specification. Table 8.1 summarizes the range of possible modifications that can be made to a LISREL model.

Modifications to the measurement part of the model can be made by (a) changing the loadings (λ's) linking the indicators to the latent variables from fixed to free or vice versa (hence changing the pattern of LAMBDA-X and/or LAMBDA-Y matrices), and (b) allowing or constraining correlations among measurement errors (i.e. δ's and ε's) (thus changing the THETA-DELTA and/or THETA-EPSILON matrices). Modifications to the structural part of the model include (a) changing the path coefficients (γ's and β's) linking the exogenous and endogenous latent variables from fixed to free or vice versa (thus changing the pattern of the GAMMA and/or BETA matrices), (b) allowing or constraining correlations (ϕ's) among the exogenous latent variables (thus changing the PHI matrix), and (c) allowing or constraining correlations among disturbance terms (ζ's) (thus changing the PSI matrix). If all this sounds like Greek to you, it is probably a good idea to revisit Chapter 4 at this stage (and, in particular, Appendices 4D and 4E).

While there is a lot of choice when it comes to modifying one's model, some kinds of modifications are much harder to justify than others. For example, allowing measurement errors to correlate is nearly always viewed with suspicion because 'correlated measurement residuals imply that one or more omitted variables exist causing common variation in the measurements whose residuals covary. The omitted variables may be underlying theoretical variables, methods confounds, or other systematic contaminators. The problem is that it is not possible to ascertain what causes the covariation by simply allowing for correlated residuals'.[14]

It should also be appreciated that the broad type of modification made (i.e. increasing versus reducing constraints) has very different implications for the model's specification and fit. Increasing the number of constraints typically means that previously free parameters are now fixed to zero;

therefore, fewer parameters will be estimated and there will be a corresponding increase in the degrees of freedom. The value of the chi-square statistic will always increase if parameters are deleted but it is hoped that such an increase will be small so as to justify the more parsimonious model. In contrast, reducing the number of constraints by adding parameters (even irrelevant ones) will *always* result in a reduction of the chi-square statistic and a better fitting model (albeit at the expense of parsimony as reflected in the loss of degrees of freedom); indeed, 'the inclusion of an irrelevant parameter may not be of substantive interest and will result in a loss of a degree-of-freedom, but it will not harm, and most likely rather improve, the fit of the model'.[15] What this shows is that the effects of adding versus eliminating parameters are non-symmetrical and qualitatively different. Consequently, 'it is preferable to make modifications involving the addition of new parameters prior to deleting parameters. That is, it is recommended that modifications be made so as to improve the fit of the model prior to improving parsimony'.[16]

Finally, there is the issue of *where* and *how* to start a specification search; after all, 'an incredible number of major or minor alterations are possible, and the analyst needs some procedure to narrow the choices'.[17] Fortunately, the LISREL program output contains some helpful diagnostics that can guide a specification search (see next section). A specification search is also likely to be more productive if one is aware of some (often depressing!) findings from the literature; these are summarized in Table 8.2. Finally, one should always keep in mind that the 'potentially richest source of ideas for respecification is theoretical or substantive knowledge of the researcher'.[18]

Diagnostics for model modification

Focusing initially on modifications aiming to improve a model's fit, relevant diagnostic information can be obtained by examining the **residual statistics** and **modification indices** which form part of the program output. Table 8.3 shows this information for our illustrative model in SIMPLIS format (we will consider the output in LISREL format later in this section).

In terms of residual statistics, information is provided on both the fitted and the standardized residuals. Recall from Chapter 7, that the size of the former is dependent upon the unit of measurement of the observed variables, whereas standardized residuals do not display such a dependence (hence they are easier to interpret). Recall also that standardized residuals can be interpreted as standard normal deviates (i.e. z-scores) with absolute values greater than 2.58 being considered 'large'.[19] In addition to showing the lowest, highest and median ('middle') residual values (under Summary Statistics for Fitted Standardized Residuals), the SIMPLIS output also provides **stem-leaf residual plots**; the latter capture the

Table 8.2   Specification search guidelines

Research finding	Comments
• Specification searches very often do not lead to the 'correct' model (i.e. the model which best approximates the situation in the population)	• A specification search is no substitute for careful initial model conceptualization
• Type II error (i.e. failure to reject a misspecified model) is frequent in specification searches	• Ensure that sample size offers sufficient power for the model examined; do not interpret a nonsignificant chi-square test as a sign to stop the search (but also bear in mind the test's sensitivity to sample size)
• The greater the number of specification errors, the less successful the search	• Do your homework before specifying your initial model
• Search more likely to be successful if misspecification is limited to the structural part of the model only	• Pay as much attention to the specification of your measures as to the substantive relationships among the constructs in your model
• 'Unrestricted' (i.e. purely data-driven) searches are less successful than 'restricted' searches (i.e. those guided by theory)	• Do not use diagnostic information for model modification in a mechanistic fashion
• Assigning priority to the measurement model during a specification search does not help and may even prove counterproductive	• Look for the most important, substantially meaningful modification in your model, regardless of its location
• Specific modifications carried out during a specification search can be very unstable in small-to-moderately large samples; searches on samples of the same size may produce a quite different set of modifications. Search is almost certain to fail if $N \leq 100$	• Use as large a sample as possible (but beware of the dangers of 'excessive' power)
• Goodness-of-fit measures can be unstable for both original and modified model across repeated samples of the same size in small-to-moderately large samples	• If your sample is large enough, split it into two halves and undertake 'parallel' specification searches on each half
• Modified models do not cross-validate well, unless sample size is very large	• Undertake double cross-validation (see Chapter 9) following a parallel specification search

individual residual values. Specifically, the values to the left of the dashed line constitute the 'stem', whereas those to the left of the line constitute the 'leaf' and represent the second digit of the residual value. Thus, the number of leaves is equal to the number of elements in the residual covariance matrix ($\mathbf{S}-\hat{\mathbf{\Sigma}}$); in our example, this comes to 91.[20] Reading these plots is straightforward. For example, looking at the standardized residuals we can see that there are nine residuals with values greater than 4 (i.e. 4.1, 4.1, 4.2, 4.3, 4.3, 4.9, 6.7, 6.7, 6.7 (see last three rows of the second stem-and-leaf plot)); the last value reflects the largest standardized residual (6.74) but expressed to a single decimal point.

If a model fits well, the stem-leaf plots will be characterized by residuals which are clustered symmetrically around the zero point, with most residuals lying in the middle of the distribution and fewer in the tails. An excess of residuals on either tail suggests that covariances are systematically

Table 8.3   Residual analysis and modification indices: SIMPLIS output

```
!ILLUSTRATIVE MODEL OF JOB SATISFACTION AND CUSTOMER FOCUS

Summary Statistics for Fitted Residuals

Smallest Fitted Residual =   -0.067
  Median Fitted Residual =    0.029
 Largest Fitted Residual =    0.205

Stemleaf Plot

 - 0|7665
 - 0|433322111100000000000000000
   0|111122222222333333333444
   0|555555666666777777888899
   1|00011234
   1|58
   2|1

Summary Statistics for Standardized Residuals

Smallest Standardized Residual =   -2.746
  Median Standardized Residual =    1.120
 Largest Standardized Residual =    6.746

Stemleaf Plot

 - 2|76664
 - 1|93
 - 0|88776332100000000000000
   0|1122335667889
   1|11112223333566788999
   2|00134579
   3|01233335569
   4|112339
   5|
   6|777
Largest Negative Standardized Residuals
Residual for Ambig and Supervis     -2.746
Residual for Conflict and Supervis  -2.634
Largest Positive Standardized Residuals
Residual for      Sell and      Pay   3.191
Residual for      Sell and     Sell   6.746
Residual for     Solve and      Pay   4.051
Residual for     Solve and     Sell   6.746
Residual for     Clear and  Promote   3.145
Residual for     Ambig and     Work   3.005
Residual for     Ambig and    Clear   6.746
Residual for    Compat and      Pay   2.738
Residual for    Compat and    Solve   4.912
Residual for  Conflict and      Pay   3.482
Residual for  Conflict and    Solve   3.267
Residual for   Custort and     Work   3.497
Residual for   Custort and Supervis   3.340
Residual for   Custort and     Sell   4.075
Residual for   Custort and    Solve   3.297
Residual for   Comport and     Work   3.265
Residual for   Comport and Supervis   3.916
Residual for   Comport and      Pay   4.348
Residual for   Comport and  Promote   4.277
Residual for   Intcord and     Work   3.630
Residual for   Intcord and Supervis   4.209
Residual for   Intcord and  Promote   2.900
```

Table 8.3   (continued)

The Modification Indices Suggest to Add the			
Path to	from	Decrease in Chi-Square	New Estimate
Clear	Mkt Ort	8.0	0.27
Job Sat	Cust Foc	19.7	0.11
Job Sat	Mkt Ort	45.5	0.15

The Modification Indices Suggest to Add an Error Covariance			
Between	and	Decrease in Chi-Square	New Estimate
Solve	Pay	8.1	0.06
Ambig	Work	16.8	0.08
Ambig	Clear	45.5	0.83
Compat	Solve	9.3	0.08
Conflict	Compat	43.6	19.43
Comport	Pay	8.7	0.08
Comport	Promote	8.1	0.11

under- or overestimated by the model. Recall from Chapter 6 that a large positive residual indicates that the model underestimates the covariance between the manifest variables involved (underfitting); the model should, therefore, be modified through the *addition* of paths (i.e. through the freeing of parameters) in order to account better for the covariance between the two variables. In contrast, a large negative residual indicates that the model overestimates a given covariance (overfitting); consequently, the models should be modified through the *deletion* of paths (i.e. through the fixing of parameters) that are associated with the covariance concerned.

Inspection of the standardized stem-leaf plot for our illustrative model indicates a marked non-symmetrical distribution of residuals, with most of them having positive values (see Table 8.3). This suggests that our model underestimates the covariances among the observed variables. In fact, there are only two large negative residuals (i.e. greater than −2.58) as opposed to twenty-two large positive residuals (i.e. greater than 2.58). The *specific* residuals involved are identified in the next portion of the output under Largest Negative (Positive) Standardized Residuals.

Inspection of the variables associated with large standardized residuals can often reveal clear patterns to guide model modification. For example, in Table 8.3 nine of the largest positive standardized residuals involve indicators of Mkt Ort (Market Orientation) and Job Sat (Job Satisfaction); this suggests that the addition of a direct path from Mkt Ort to Job Sat should be considered. However, when there are a lot of observed variables and many large residuals, it can be quite difficult to draw a clear picture as to possible modifications. Under these circumstances, one has to rely more on the modification indices. A **modification index** shows the minimum decrease in the model's chi-squared value if a previously fixed parameter is set free and the model re-estimated;[21] thus, the largest modification index indicates which parameter should be set free to improve fit maximally. Statistically, a modification index can be interpreted by means of an χ^2-distribution with 1 degree of freedom; thus, modification indices larger than 3.84 are considered to be 'large' (since 3.84 is the critical value of the chi-square statistic, with 1 degree of freedom at the 5% significance level).

For our illustrative model, there are ten large modification indices, the largest being 45.5 (with two parameters having the same value) and the smallest 8.

Although an inspection of modification indices immediately reveals which paths, when added to the model, will have the most impact in terms of improving the model's fit, several words of caution are in order.

First, there is no guarantee that freeing the parameter with the largest modification index will make sense from a substantive point of view; for example, the sign of the freed parameter may be 'wrong' (i.e. opposite to what could be defended theoretically) or the path represented by the parameter may be conceptually suspect (e.g. a covariance between measurement errors). Therefore, 'one examines the modification indices and relaxes the parameter with the largest modification index *if this parameter can be interpreted substantively*. If it does not make sense to relax the parameter with the largest modification index, consider that with the second largest modification index and so on'.[22]

Secondly, although there may be several modification indices with high values, parameters should be relaxed *one at a time* because 'freeing one parameter may reduce or eliminate the improvement in fit possible by freeing a second parameter';[23] thus 'wholesale' relaxation of model constraints based on modification indices is not a good idea!

Thirdly, modification indices should be used in conjunction with the **expected parameter change** (EPC) values; the latter show the predicted changes (either positive or negative) for the fixed parameter concerned and are indicated under New Estimate in Table 8.3. For example, allowing the path between Mkt Ort (Market Orientation) and Job Sat (Job Satisfaction) to be freely estimated is expected to result in a parameter estimate of 0.27. Table 8.4 shows four possible scenarios based upon the size of the modification indices and associated expected parameter changes; each of these scenarios has different implication for model modification.

In scenario 1, a large modification index is associated with a large EPC; thus, provided it makes substantive sense, one would be inclined to free the parameter concerned because doing so will lead to a big change in the parameter value and a big drop in the chi-square statistic. In scenario 2, a large modification index is associated with a small EPC. Here, although the reduction in the test statistic would be large, the small change in the parameter suggests that the latter is probably trivial (i.e. the specification error resulting from fixing that parameter is very small); thus relaxing this parameter makes little sense. In scenario 3, a small modification index is accompanied by a large EPC. What to do in this case is not very clear since the large EPC may be due to either sampling variability or to insensitivity of the chi-square test to that parameter. In this context, it should be borne in mind that the 'test has unequal power for misspecifications of the same size in different places in the model';[24] therefore, modification indices are much more sensitive to specification errors in some fixed parameters than in others. Finally, in scenario 4, a small modification index is associated

Table 8.4   Modification indices and expected parameter change

		Expected parameter change	
		Large	Small
Modification	Large	Scenario 1	Scenario 2
index	Small	Scenario 3	Scenario 4

with a small EPC; obviously, in this case, freeing the parameter concerned would bring no benefit.

One problem with the expected parameter values in Table 8.3 is that they are unstandardized (and therefore, influenced by the units of measurement of the variables involved). Thus, if the observed variables are measured on widely different scales, it becomes difficult to determine what is a 'small' or a 'large' value. To overcome this, one may consult the **standardized expected parameter change** (SEPC) which makes it possible to compare values for all fixed parameters; the interpretation of the latter is identical to that of any standardized parameter estimate (see Chapter 6). Unfortunately, the standardized version of the EPC is not routinely provided as part of the SIMPLIS output. They are, however, obtainable if output is specified in LISREL format; the latter is shown in Table 8.5.[25]

The output in LISREL format includes *exactly* the same information on the fitted and standardized residuals (i.e. summary statistics and stem-leaf plots), so this part of the output has been deleted from Table 8.5. However, the LISREL output also provides an additional graphical display of residuals, namely a **normal probability (or Q-) plot**; the latter plots the standardized residuals (horizontal axis) against the quantiles of the normal distribution. The best possible fit would be indicated if all residuals were lying in a straight vertical line (i.e. parallel to the ordinate), whereas the worst possible fit would be indicated if all residuals were lying in a horizontal straight line (i.e. parallel to the abscissd). An acceptable fit is indicated when the residuals lie approximately along the diagonal, with steeper plots (i.e. greater than 45 degrees) representing the better fits. If the pattern of residuals is nonlinear, this is indicative of departures from normality, nonlinearity and/or specification errors in the model; specification errors are also indicated by the presence of outliers in the Q-plot.

For our illustrative model, the Q-plot of standardized residuals is both shallower than 45 degrees and decidedly nonlinear. This confirms the conclusions drawn from both the examination of model fit in Chapter 7 and the patterns revealed by the stem-leaf plot in Table 8.3; as presently specified, the model does not fit the empirical data adequately.

Regarding modification indices, whereas the SIMPLIS output only displays those parameters with 'large' indices, the LISREL output shows the modification indices (as well as the expected parameter changes both unstandardized and standardized) for *all* fixed parameters in the model.

Table 8.5   Residual analysis and modification indices: LISREL output

```
!ILLUSTRATIVE MODEL OF JOB SATISFACTION AND CUSTOMER FOCUS

        Standardized Residuals

            Work    Supervis      Pay    Promote      Sell     Solve
          --------  --------  --------  --------  --------  --------
    Work     - -
 Supervis  -1.857      - -
      Pay   2.494    -2.551      - -
  Promote   0.190     0.483     1.254      - -
     Sell   1.985     1.328     3.191     1.537     6.746
    Solve   2.428     0.810     4.051     1.156     6.746      - -
    Clear  -0.594    -0.162     0.887     3.145     1.921     1.679
    Ambig   3.005    -2.746     1.649     2.022     1.151     1.831
   Compat  -0.057    -2.559     2.738     0.344     0.051     4.912
 Conflict  -0.276    -2.634     3.482     0.614    -0.834     3.267
  Custort   3.497     3.340     1.886     1.277     4.075     3.297
  Comport   3.265     3.916     4.348     4.277     2.293     1.050
  Intcord   3.630     4.209     1.350     2.900     0.692     1.068

        Standardized Residuals

            Clear     Ambig    Compat  Conflict   Custort   Comport
          --------  --------  --------  --------  --------  --------
    Clear     - -
    Ambig   6.746      - -
   Compat  -0.712     1.164      - -
 Conflict  -1.270     0.753      - -       - -
  Custort   1.070     0.630    -0.311     0.212      - -
  Comport   1.637     0.136    -0.726    -0.808    -2.355      - -
  Intcord   2.114     1.780     1.891     1.120     0.261     1.845

        Standardized Residuals

           Intcord
          --------
  Intcord     - -

  Summary Statistics for Standardized Residuals

Smallest Standardized Residual =    -2.746
  Median Standardized Residual =     1.120
 Largest Standardized Residual =     6.746

Stemleaf Plot

 - 2|76664
 - 1|93
 - 0|887763321000000000000
   0|1122335667889
   1|111122233335667888999
   2|00134579
   3|01233335569
   4|112339
   5|
   6|777
Largest Negative Standardized Residuals
Residual for     Ambig and Supervis  -2.746
Residual for Conflict and Supervis  -2.634
Largest Positive Standardized Residuals
Residual for      Sell and      Pay   3.191
Residual for      Sell and     Sell   6.746
Residual for     Solve and      Pay   4.051
Residual for     Solve and     Sell   6.746
Residual for     Clear and  Promote   3.145
Residual for     Ambig and     Work   3.005
```

Table 8.5 (continued)

!ILLUSTRATIVE MODEL OF JOB SATISFACTION AND CUSTOMER FOCUS (continued)

```
Residual for    Ambig and    Clear   6.746
Residual for   Compat and      Pay   2.738
Residual for   Compat and    Solve   4.912
Residual for Conflict and      Pay   3.482
Residual for Conflict and    Solve   3.267
Residual for  Custort and     Work   3.497
Residual for  Custort and Supervis   3.340
Residual for  Custort and     Sell   4.075
Residual for  Custort and    Solve   3.297
Residual for  Comport and     Work   3.265
Residual for  Comport and Supervis   3.916
Residual for  Comport and      Pay   4.348
Residual for  Comport and  Promote   4.277
Residual for  Intcord and     Work   3.630
Residual for  Intcord and Supervis   4.209
Residual for  Intcord and  Promote   2.900
```

Qplot of Standardized Residuals

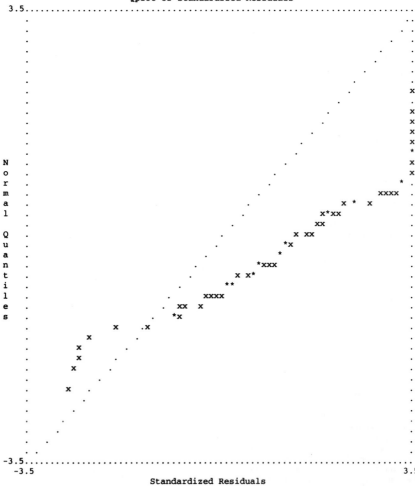

Standardized Residuals

Table 8.5 (continued)

!ILLUSTRATIVE MODEL OF JOB SATISFACTION AND CUSTOMER FOCUS (continued)

Modification Indices and Expected Change

     Modification Indices for LAMBDA-Y

	Job Sat	Cust Foc
Work	- -	1.662
Supervis	- -	0.037
Pay	- -	6.080
Promote	- -	0.483
Sell	0.197	- -
Solve	0.197	- -

     Expected Change for LAMBDA-Y

	Job Sat	Cust Foc
Work	- -	0.033
Supervis	- -	0.008
Pay	- -	0.111
Promote	- -	0.043
Sell	-0.286	- -
Solve	0.166	- -

     Standardized Expected Change for LAMBDA-Y

	Job Sat	Cust Foc
Work	- -	0.042
Supervis	- -	0.010
Pay	- -	0.140
Promote	- -	0.054
Sell	-0.068	- -
Solve	0.039	- -

     Completely Standardized Expected Change for LAMBDA-Y

	Job Sat	Cust Foc
Work	- -	0.105
Supervis	- -	0.016
Pay	- -	0.200
Promote	- -	0.056
Sell	-0.053	- -
Solve	0.042	- -

     Modification Indices for LAMBDA-X

	Role Amb	Role Con	Mkt Ort
Clear	- -	1.469	7.973
Ambig	- -	1.469	6.273
Compat	0.240	- -	0.819
Conflict	0.189	- -	0.157
Custort	0.320	0.228	- -
Comport	0.710	1.390	- -
Intcord	1.109	2.491	- -

Table 8.5 (continued)

!ILLUSTRATIVE MODEL OF JOB SATISFACTION AND CUSTOMER FOCUS (continued)

Expected Change for LAMBDA-X

	Role Amb	Role Con	Mkt Ort
Clear	- -	-0.067	0.266
Ambig	- -	0.111	0.388
Compat	0.099	- -	0.084
Conflict	-0.089	- -	0.038
Custort	-0.069	-0.024	- -
Comport	-0.096	-0.058	- -
Intcord	0.112	0.071	- -

Standardized Expected Change for LAMBDA-X

	Role Amb	Role Con	Mkt Ort
Clear	- -	-0.081	0.263
Ambig	- -	0.134	0.384
Compat	0.075	- -	0.083
Conflict	-0.067	- -	0.037
Custort	-0.052	-0.029	- -
Comport	-0.073	-0.071	- -
Intcord	0.085	0.086	- -

Completely Standardized Expected Change for LAMBDA-X

	Role Amb	Role Con	Mkt Ort
Clear	- -	-0.080	0.261
Ambig	- -	0.093	0.267
Compat	0.056	- -	0.063
Conflict	-0.047	- -	0.026
Custort	-0.045	-0.025	- -
Comport	-0.065	-0.064	- -
Intcord	0.081	0.083	- -

Modification Indices for BETA

	Job Sat	Cust Foc
Job Sat	- -	19.717
Cust Foc	- -	- -

Expected Change for BETA

	Job Sat	Cust Foc
Job Sat	- -	0.106
Cust Foc	- -	- -

Standardized Expected Change for BETA

	Job Sat	Cust Foc
Job Sat	- -	0.357
Cust Foc	- -	- -

Modification Indices for GAMMA

	Role Amb	Role Con	Mkt Ort
Job Sat	- -	- -	45.507
Cust Foc	0.663	- -	- -

Table 8.5 (continued)

!ILLUSTRATIVE MODEL OF JOB SATISFACTION AND CUSTOMER FOCUS (continued)

Expected Change for GAMMA

	Role Amb	Role Con	Mkt Ort
Job Sat	- -	- -	0.151
Cust Foc	0.140	- -	- -

Standardized Expected Change for GAMMA

	Role Amb	Role Con	Mkt Ort
Job Sat	- -	- -	0.630
Cust Foc	0.084	- -	- -

No Non-Zero Modification Indices for PHI

Modification Indices for PSI

	Job Sat	Cust Foc
Job Sat	- -	
Cust Foc	0.663	- -

Expected Change for PSI

	Job Sat	Cust Foc
Job Sat	- -	
Cust Foc	0.018	- -

Standardized Expected Change for PSI

	Job Sat	Cust Foc
Job Sat	- -	
Cust Foc	0.060	- -

Modification Indices for THETA-EPS

	Work	Supervis	Pay	Promote	Sell	Solve
Work	- -					
Supervis	3.447	- -				
Pay	6.219	6.506	- -			
Promote	0.036	0.233	1.573	- -		
Sell	1.021	1.274	0.040	0.000	- -	
Solve	2.244	0.032	8.068	0.032	- -	- -

Expected Change for THETA-EPS

	Work	Supervis	Pay	Promote	Sell	Solve
Work	- -					
Supervis	-0.020	- -				
Pay	0.031	-0.049	- -			
Promote	0.003	0.013	0.038	- -		
Sell	-0.014	-0.024	-0.005	0.000	- -	
Solve	0.018	-0.003	0.058	0.005	- -	- -

Table 8.5 (continued)

!ILLUSTRATIVE MODEL OF JOB SATISFACTION AND CUSTOMER FOCUS (continued)

Completely Standardized Expected Change for THETA-EPS

	Work	Supervis	Pay	Promote	Sell	Solve
Work	- -					
Supervis	-0.083	- -				
Pay	0.112	-0.115	- -			
Promote	0.009	0.022	0.056	- -		
Sell	-0.028	-0.030	-0.006	0.000	- -	
Solve	0.047	-0.005	0.089	0.006	- -	- -

Modification Indices for THETA-DELTA-EPS

	Work	Supervis	Pay	Promote	Sell	Solve
Clear	3.747	0.842	0.001	6.147	0.225	0.002
Ambig	16.829	4.525	1.575	0.669	0.315	1.187
Compat	0.108	0.208	0.172	0.011	3.213	9.283
Conflict	0.119	1.351	4.465	0.165	0.506	0.103
Custort	1.865	0.009	0.169	3.217	0.104	2.700
Comport	0.000	0.026	8.714	8.100	0.026	0.641
Intcord	2.937	4.729	1.436	3.094	1.961	0.294

Expected Change for THETA-DELTA-EPS

	Work	Supervis	Pay	Promote	Sell	Solve
Clear	-0.028	0.019	-0.001	0.086	0.014	0.001
Ambig	0.079	-0.060	0.042	0.038	-0.022	0.036
Compat	0.005	-0.011	0.011	-0.004	-0.062	0.084
Conflict	-0.006	-0.029	0.063	0.017	-0.026	0.010
Custort	0.020	-0.002	-0.010	-0.063	0.011	0.044
Comport	0.000	0.004	0.081	0.108	0.005	-0.023
Intcord	0.024	0.044	-0.029	0.059	-0.042	0.014

Completely Standardized Expected Change for THETA-DELTA-EPS

	Work	Supervis	Pay	Promote	Sell	Solve
Clear	-0.070	0.031	-0.001	0.089	0.011	0.001
Ambig	0.138	-0.069	0.042	0.027	-0.012	0.027
Compat	0.010	-0.013	0.012	-0.003	-0.037	0.068
Conflict	-0.010	-0.033	0.063	0.012	-0.014	0.007
Custort	0.043	-0.003	-0.013	-0.057	0.007	0.040
Comport	0.000	0.005	0.104	0.101	0.004	-0.022
Intcord	0.058	0.068	-0.040	0.059	-0.032	0.014

Modification Indices for THETA-DELTA

	Clear	Ambig	Compat	Conflict	Custort	Comport
Clear	- -					
Ambig	45.507	- -				
Compat	0.157	0.304	- -			
Conflict	0.518	0.427	43.610	- -		
Custort	0.143	0.029	0.621	0.595	- -	
Comport	2.355	0.117	0.016	0.043	5.544	- -
Intcord	0.566	1.065	2.035	0.030	0.068	3.403

Modification Indices for THETA-DELTA

	Intcord
Intcord	- -

Table 8.5 (continued)

!ILLUSTRATIVE MODEL OF JOB SATISFACTION AND CUSTOMER FOCUS (continued)

Expected Change for THETA-DELTA

	Clear	Ambig	Compat	Conflict	Custort	Comport
Clear	- -					
Ambig	0.827	- -				
Compat	0.014	0.026	- -			
Conflict	-0.027	0.033	19.431	- -		
Custort	-0.012	0.008	-0.028	0.030	- -	
Comport	0.053	0.016	0.005	-0.009	-0.123	- -
Intcord	0.023	0.042	0.047	-0.006	0.014	0.081

Expected Change for THETA-DELTA

	Intcord
Intcord	- -

Completely Standardized Expected Change for THETA-DELTA

	Clear	Ambig	Compat	Conflict	Custort	Comport
Clear	- -					
Ambig	0.570	- -				
Compat	0.010	0.014	- -			
Conflict	-0.019	0.016	10.195	- -		
Custort	-0.011	0.004	-0.018	0.018	- -	
Comport	0.047	0.010	0.003	-0.005	-0.095	- -
Intcord	0.022	0.028	0.034	-0.004	0.012	0.070

Completely Standardized Expected Change for THETA-DELTA

	Intcord
Intcord	- -

Maximum Modification Index is 45.51 for Element (2, 1) of THETA-DELTA

This information is presented in the same order as that for the parameter estimates, i.e. LAMBDA-*Y*, LAMBDA-*X*, BETA, GAMMA, PHI, PSI, THETA-EPSILON AND THETA-DELTA. The additional detail provided by the LISREL output is important, not least because it enables one to detect fixed parameters with small modification indices but large SEPC values (i.e. those falling under scenario 3 in Table 8.4); such parameters would not normally be detectable from the SIMPLIS output in Table 8.3. Having said that, in our illustrative model, there do not appear to be any parameters falling in this category; inspection of the SEPC results shows that large values are invariably associated with substantial modification indices.

We are now ready to take the plunge and undertake some modifications to our illustrative model; we do this by first considering modifications to improve its fit and follow this by considering possible changes for simplifying the model.

Modification of illustrative model: fit improvement

As previously noted, improvement in fit is attained through the addition (i.e. freeing) of model parameters. Inspection of the modification indices shows that two fixed parameters share the same value (45.507).[26] The first is the path between Mkt Ort (Market Orientation) and Job Sat (Job Satisfaction); as no link between these variables has been proposed at the conceptualization stage (see path diagrams in Figures 3.1 and 3.2), this path has implicitly been set to zero (i.e. $\gamma_{13} = 0$) when the model was formally specified (see Chapter 4). The EPC associated with this path comes to 0.151 and its standardized counterpart to 0.630 (see Table 8.5). The positive sign of the parameter makes conceptual sense, since it implies that the job satisfaction of salespeople is likely to be greater in companies which are more market-oriented.[27] The size of the parameter is also substantial; for example, the literature suggests 'choosing 0.1 as a reasonable value for a standardized parameter. An effect of 0.1 represents an effect of some importance which one does not want to overlook'.[28] Here the SEPC value comes to 0.630 which comfortably exceeds the suggested threshold. In short, allowing the path between Mkt Ort and Job Sat to be freely estimated would appear to be a viable option.

The second fixed parameter with a modification index of 45.507 is the covariance between the measurement errors of the indicators of Role Amb (Role Ambiguity), i.e. Ambig (Ambiguity) and Clear (Clarity). By default, measurement errors are assumed to be independent in a LISREL model (see discussion of parameter specifications in Chapter 4 and, in particular, assumption 5 in Table 4.1). As noted earlier (see section on Specification Searches), allowing measurement errors to covary is not easy to defend. In fact, the advice in the literature is that the introduction of correlated measurement errors should be avoided unless there are clear theoretical or methodological reasons for doing so; for example, 'a theoretical reason for correlated measurement residuals is that each measure was taken at a different point in time. A methodological reason for them is that all measurements share a common data collection bias . . . Correlated measurement residuals are fall-back options nearly always detracting from the theoretical elegance and empirical interpretability of the study'.[29] In our case, given that we are dealing with cross-sectional data and given that all measures were collected by the same method (a survey of salespeople), it becomes difficult to justify the incorporation of any correlated measurement errors. Moreover, inspection of the standardized expected parameter (i.e. the SEPC) estimate resulting from freeing the covariance between the measurement errors of Ambig and Clear indicates that an 'improper' solution would be obtained. Specifically a value of 10.195 is expected, which given that it represents a correlation between error terms, is clearly outside the admissible range for correlation coefficients (the latter always lie between −1 and +1). Thus, in addition to theoretical difficulties, there are clear statistical reasons arguing against freeing the error covariance concerned.

In the light of the above, we decided to free the path between Mkt Ort and Job Sat and re-estimate the model. To do this we modified the SIMPLIS input file (see Table 6.1) by amending the `'Job Sat'` equation under `Relationships` as follows:[30]

`'Job Sat' = 'Role Amb' 'Role Conf' 'Mkt Ort'`

Table 8.6 shows selected output (in SIMPLIS format) for the modified model; here, we limit ourselves to a presentation of the fit statistics and relevant diagnostic information for possible further modifications.

The first thing to note from Table 8.6 is that all measures of overall fit show a marked improvement over the corresponding values for the original model (see Table 7.1 in Chapter 7). For example, the RMSEA is now 0.06 (indicating 'fair fit'),[31] the standardized RMR is less than 0.05, while the NNFI and CFI are both greater than 0.95.

Secondly, while there has been a loss of one degree of freedom, this has been more than compensated by the (large) reduction in the value of the chi-square statistic. In fact we can formally evaluate the improvement in fit by performing what is known as a **chi-square difference test** (D^2). To do this, we simply take the difference in the chi-square values of the original and modified modules and evaluate the result as a chi-square with one degree of freedom (the latter reflecting the difference in the degrees of freedom between the two models). In our case

$$D^2 = 168.310 - 118.776 = 49.534$$

which is highly significant ($p < 0.001$). Note that the *actual* reduction in the chi-square statistic (49.534) is higher than the *expected* reduction as indicated by the modification index (45.507); this confirms the role of the modification index as representing 'the *minimum* decrease in the overall chi-square value that would be achieved if the corresponding parameter were freed'.[32] Note that all the caveats associated with applying the chi-square test for fit assessment purposes (see Chapter 7) also apply to D^2 tests.

Thirdly, inspection of the summary statistics for the residuals and the associated stem-leaf plots also shows a big improvement. There are now only seven large residuals (i.e. > |2.58|) as opposed to 24 in the original model (see Table 8.3). Also the stem-leaf plot of the standardized residuals is now much more symmetrical and concentrated around zero (the Q-plot of standardized residuals – not included in Table 8.6 – is also steeper and much more linear).

Fourthly, while there are still a few large modification indices, none of them are as large as the ones for the original model. Moreover, they all relate to paths reflecting covariances among measurement errors which, as noted previously, cannot be substantively justified in the present case. It is also interesting to note that whereas the modification indices of the original model suggested the addition of *three* paths (see Table 8.3), freeing a *single* path (i.e. the link between Mkt Ort and Job Sat) has eliminated the need for the other two. Similarly, whereas originally there were seven error

Table 8.6   Selected output for modified model (round 1)

```
!ILLUSTRATIVE MODEL OF JOB SATISFACTION AND CUSTOMER FOCUS

                    Goodness of Fit Statistics

                    Degrees of Freedom = 56
         Minimum Fit Function Chi-Square = 118.462 (P = 0.00000225)
 Normal Theory Weighted Least Squares Chi-Square = 118.776 (P = 0.00000206)
             Estimated Non-centrality Parameter (NCP) = 62.776

                 Minimum Fit Function Value = 0.388
            Population Discrepancy Function Value (F0) = 0.206
        Root Mean Square Error of Approximation (RMSEA) = 0.0606

              Expected Cross-Validation Index (ECVI) = 0.619
                    ECVI for saturated Model = 0.597
                  ECVI for Independence Model = 6.826

   Chi-Square for Independence Model with 78 Degrees of Freedom = 2056.035
                    Independence AIC = 2082.035
                        Model AIC = 188.776
                      Saturated AIC = 182.000
                    Independence CAIC = 2143.441
                      Model CAIC = 354.101
                     Saturated CAIC = 611.846

              Root Mean Square Residual (RMR) = 0.0405
                    Standardized RMR = 0.0410
                Goodness of Fit Index (GFI) = 0.943
            Adjusted Goodness of Fit Index (AGFI) = 0.908
            Parsimony Goodness of Fit Index (PGFI) = 0.581

                  Normed Fit Index (NFI) = 0.942
                Non-Normed Fit Index (NNFI) = 0.956
            Parsimony Normed Fit Index (PNFI) = 0.677
                Comparative Fit Index (CFI) = 0.968
                Incremental Fit Index (IFI) = 0.969
                  Relative Fit Index (RFI) = 0.920

                      Critical N (CN) = 216.021

CONFIDENCE LIMITS COULD NOT BE COMPUTED DUE TO TOO SMALL P-VALUE FOR CHI-SQUARE

!ILLUSTRATIVE MODEL OF JOB SATISFACTION AND CUSTOMER FOCUS

Summary Statistics for Fitted Residuals

Smallest Fitted Residual =   -0.080
  Median Fitted Residual =    0.000
 Largest Fitted Residual =    0.174

Stemleaf Plot

 - 0|887655
 - 0|443333333322221111111111100000000000000000000000000
   0|111111112222222333334444
   0|56667778
   1|13
   1|7

Summary Statistics for Standardized Residuals

Smallest Standardized Residual =   -3.383
  Median Standardized Residual =    0.000
 Largest Standardized Residual =    4.753
```

Table 8.6   (continued)

```
Stemleaf Plot

 - 3|4
 - 2|7642100
 - 1|964431
 - 0|999887754444332222210000000000000000000000
   0|11333556677888889
   1|012444678
   2|0012455
   3|122
   4|8
Largest Negative Standardized Residuals
Residual for      Ambig and Supervis   -3.383
Residual for     Compat and Supervis   -2.640
Residual for Conflict and Supervis   -2.730
Largest Positive Standardized Residuals
Residual for      Solve and      Pay    3.207
Residual for     Compat and    Solve    4.753
Residual for Conflict and      Pay    3.214
Residual for Conflict and    Solve    3.114

The Modification Indices Suggest to Add an Error Covariance
  Between     and    Decrease in Chi-Square    New Estimate
  Clear     Work              8.2                  -0.04
  Ambig     Work             13.9                   0.07
  Compat    Solve             8.8                   0.08

        The Problem used    29872 Bytes (= 0.0% of Available Workspace)

                    Time used:   2.08 Seconds
```

covariances with high modification indices, there are only three in the modified model.[33] This serves to highlight the importance of making only one modification at a time, since freeing a particular parameter may cure problems in a different part of the model.[34] In our example, no further relaxation of restrictions is warranted.

Finally, an inspection of the parameter estimates (not shown in Table 8.6), shows that the unstandardized estimate for the freed path between Mkt Ort and Job Sat (i.e. γ_{13}) comes to 0.141 with a standard error of 0.023; this estimate is highly significant (t-value = 6.237, $p < 0.01$) and close to the EPC estimate (0.15) earlier observed in Table 8.3. Similarly, the actual standardized estimate obtained (0.569) is close to the SEPC estimate (0.630) shown in Table 8.5. More importantly, the inclusion of γ_{13} has improved considerably the proportion of variance explained in the Job Sat variable; the latter's R^2 is now 0.692, as compared to 0.571 in the original model.[35]

The comparison of the modified and original models can also be used to highlight a more general situation often encountered in covariance structure analysis, namely that of **nested models**. A model, $M1$, is said to be nested within another model, $M2$, 'if $M1$ can be obtained from $M2$ by constraining one or more of the free parameters in $M2$ to be fixed or equal to other parameters. Thus, $M1$ can be thought of as a special case of $M2$.'[36] In our example, the *original* illustrative model is nested within the *modified* model, because the former can be obtained from the latter by constraining the path between Mkt Ort and Job Sat to zero (i.e. by setting $\gamma_{13} = 0$). Similarly, the independence (i.e. null model) mentioned in Chapter 7 is nested within the original illustrative model since it can be obtained by setting all parameters of the former to zero.[37] In contrast, both the original and modified models are themselves nested within the saturated model (also discussed in Chapter 7), as the latter includes *all possible links* among the observed and latent variables; clearly, by fixing appropriate parameters to zero one can arrive at the original and modified models used in our example.[38]

Nested models can be compared by means of chi-square difference (D^2) tests with degrees of freedom equal to the difference in the degrees of freedom between the two models. For example, if $M1$ is nested within $M2$ and $M2$ is nested within $M3$ we can set up the following model comparisons:

Comparison	D^2	Degrees of freedom
$M1 - M2$	$\chi_1^2 - \chi_2^2$	$v_1 - v_2$
$M2 - M3$	$\chi_2^2 - \chi_3^2$	$v_2 - v_3$
$M1 - M3$	$\chi_1^2 - \chi_3^2$	$v_1 - v_3$

In undertaking nested model comparisons 'a large change in χ^2 compared to the difference in degrees of freedom, indicates that the freed parameters constitute a real improvement. Alternatively, a change in χ^2 close to the difference in the number of degrees of freedom suggests that any improvement in fit is merely due to capitalization on chance and that restrictions therefore are supported'.[39]

Modification of illustrative model: model simplification

Having improved the original model's fit by introducing a substantively justified parameter, we now focus attention on 'trimming' our modified model, i.e. on eliminating possibly unnecessary parameters. Our prime concern therefore is with model parsimony rather than model fit (although if a more parsimonious model is only obtainable at the expense of a major sacrifice in terms of fit, we may have to think again!).

Insights into which parameters to eliminate (i.e. fix to zero) can be gained by looking at nonsignificant t-values. As noted in Chapters 6 and 7, nonsignificant t-values imply that the parameter estimates concerned do not 'deviate significantly from zero. This would mean that the hypothesis that they are zero cannot be rejected. In such cases one might as well fix these parameter values at zero'.[40] Having said that, two issues must still be considered. First, as was the case with adding parameters to the model, deletion of parameters must be based primarily on theoretical rather than statistical considerations; after all 'there are generally some parameters that are definitely required on the basis of past research'.[41] Second, a parameter may turn out to be insignificant because of insufficient power; in this case, 'if the substantive theory suggests that a particular parameter should be included in the model, it is probably better to retain it even though it is not significant, because the sample size may be too small to detect its real significance'.[42]

In our modified illustrative model, there are only two parameters with nonsignificant *t*-values. These are the same parameters identified as nonsignificant when we estimated the original model (see Chapter 7) and include the measurement error for Sell (Selling Behavior) and the coefficient of the path from Role Con (Role Conflict) to Cust Foc (Customer Focus).[43] Regarding the former, as mentioned in Chapter 7, a nonsignificant error term suggests that the indicator concerned is free from measurement error; as this is highly unlikely in most real-life measurement situations,[44] fixing the error term to zero represents a rather implausible assumption that cannot be defended substantively. We thus chose to retain the error term concerned and attribute its lack of significance to a sampling idiosyncrasy.

With regards to the path between Role Con and Cust Foc (i.e. γ_{22}), the nonsignificant coefficient seems to suggest that the former variable does not have a *direct* effect on the latter and that its influence is mediated through the Job Sat (Job Satisfaction) variable (in other words, Role Con influences Cust Foc only indirectly).[45] Let us for the moment assume that this is a theoretically defensible position and decide to eliminate the parameter concerned (i.e. set $\gamma_{22} = 0$). To do this we amend the SIMPLIS input file by changing the 'Cust Foc' equation under Relationships as follows:[46]

'Cust Foc' = 'Mkt Ort' 'Job Sat'

Table 8.7 shows selected output (in SIMPLIS format) for the illustrative model following the second modification introduced.

Comparing Table 8.7 with Table 8.6 indicates very little difference in fit. The fit statistics are practically identical and the same applies to the pattern of residuals and modification indices. A comparison of the two models by means of the D^2 test also produced a nonsignificant result ($D^2 = 1.466$, $\nu = 1$, $p > 0.10$) indicating that only a minimal reduction in fit has resulted from fixing the parameter concerned to zero. Finally, the R^2 for Cust Foc has now increased (it now comes to 0.620 as compared to 0.602) although the relevant structural equation includes fewer predictors.[47] In short, a more parsimonious model has been obtained with minimal loss in fit. Having said that, it seems prudent, at this stage, to revisit our decision to eliminate the path between Role Con and Cust Foc by undertaking a power analysis.

Unlike in Chapter 7 where our assessment of statistical power focused on the entire model, here our concern is with the power associated with a *specific* model restriction. The question we ask here is whether 'for a given fixed parameter, the test is powerful enough to reject the null hypothesis, given that it is false'.[48] To answer this question we must make use of the non-central χ^2-distribution with one degree of freedom and non-centrality

Table 8.7   Selected output for modified model (round 2)

!ILLUSTRATIVE MODEL OF JOB SATISFACTION AND CUSTOMER FOCUS

Goodness of Fit Statistics

Degrees of Freedom = 57
Minimum Fit Function Chi-Square = 119.721 (P = 0.00000236)
Normal Theory Weighted Least Squares Chi-Square = 120.242 (P = 0.00000204)
Estimated Non-centrality Parameter (NCP) = 63.242

Minimum Fit Function Value = 0.393
Population Discrepancy Function Value (F0) = 0.207
Root Mean Square Error of Approximation (RMSEA) = 0.0603

Expected Cross-Validation Index (ECVI) = 0.617
ECVI for saturated Model = 0.597
ECVI for Independence Model = 6.826

Chi-Square for Independence Model with 78 Degrees of Freedom = 2056.035
Independence AIC = 2082.035
Model AIC = 188.242
Saturated AIC = 182.000
Independence CAIC = 2143.441
Model CAIC = 348.844
Saturated CAIC = 611.846

Root Mean Square Residual (RMR) = 0.0400
Standardized RMR = 0.0402
Goodness of Fit Index (GFI) = 0.943
Adjusted Goodness of Fit Index (AGFI) = 0.909
Parsimony Goodness of Fit Index (PGFI) = 0.591

Normed Fit Index (NFI) = 0.942
Non-Normed Fit Index (NNFI) = 0.957
Parsimony Normed Fit Index (PNFI) = 0.688
Comparative Fit Index (CFI) = 0.968
Incremental Fit Index (IFI) = 0.969
Relative Fit Index (RFI) = 0.920

Critical N (CN) = 216.867

CONFIDENCE LIMITS COULD NOT BE COMPUTED DUE TO TOO SMALL P-VALUE FOR CHI-SQUARE

Summary Statistics for Fitted Residuals

Smallest Fitted Residual = -0.083
  Median Fitted Residual = 0.000
 Largest Fitted Residual = 0.152

Stemleaf Plot

 - 8|3
 - 6|935
 - 4|72971
 - 2|7109987776000
 - 0|98631199865510000000000000000000
   0|125578811224577
   2|123550237
   4|0045867
   6|3825
   8|4
  10|79
  12|
  14|2

Table 8.7   (continued)

```
Summary Statistics for Standardized Residuals

Smallest Standardized Residual =   -3.250
  Median Standardized Residual =    0.000
 Largest Standardized Residual =    3.426

Stemleaf Plot

 - 3|3
 - 2|442111
 - 1|887664332
 - 0|9987777666654333221000000000000000000000
   0|223345667778888999
   1|0014445889
   2|0112567
   3|034
Largest Negative Standardized Residuals
Residual for     Ambig and Supervis  -3.250
Largest Positive Standardized Residuals
Residual for     Solve and     Pay    2.964
Residual for    Compat and     Pay    2.679
Residual for    Compat and    Solve   3.426
Residual for Conflict and      Pay    3.345

The Modification Indices Suggest to Add an Error Covariance
  Between     and    Decrease in Chi-Square    New Estimate
 Clear     Work              8.2                  -0.04
 Ambig     Work             13.7                   0.07
 Compat    Solve             8.9                   0.08

          The Problem used    29272 Bytes (= 0.0% of Available Workspace)

                     Time used:    0.88 Seconds
```

parameter, λ; this is the distribution of the test statistic when the null hypothesis (here that $\gamma_{22} = 0$) is false.[49] There are various ways of determining the value of λ,[50] but the easiest is to use the modification index (MI) as it has been found that 'the MI could be used to approximate the non-centrality parameter for each restriction in the model . . . Because there is an MI associated with each fixed parameter, a unit degree-of-freedom assessment of power can be obtained for each univariate restriction in the model'.[51]

For our modified model in its final form, the value of the modification index for the (now fixed to zero) path between Role Con and Cust Foc is 1.102 (we obtained this by requesting the output in LISREL format so as to obtain the modification indices for all fixed parameters). This is our estimate for λ. We now refer to Saris and Stronkhorst (1984) who provide tables of the non-central χ^2-distribution for different degrees of freedom (v), and values of λ (assuming $\alpha = 0.05$). With $\lambda = 1.10$ and $v = 1$ we find that the power of the test is 0.18 which is very low (it means that an incorrect null hypothesis that $\gamma_{22} = 0$ will only be rejected very infrequently). This clearly raises questions as to the sensitivity of the test statistic to misspecification in this parameter. Thus, while we took the decision to modify our model by excluding the path between Role Con and Cust Foc, we should keep in mind that power is low for this particular parameter.[52]

Table 8.8   Comparison of original and final models

	ECVI	AIC	CAIC
Independence model	6.826	2082.035	2143.441
Original model	0.775	236.310	396.912
Final model	0.617	188.242	348.844
Saturated model	0.597	182.000	611.846

As a final point, it is worth comparing our initial model formulation with our latest modified version. Both models have 57 degrees of freedom, yet the modified one has a much better fit than the original model (compare the fit statistics in Table 8.7 with those in Table 7.1). Note that the two models are *not* nested; one cannot arrive at one model by placing restrictions on the other[53] (however, as we have seen, both are nested within the first modified model (i.e. the one in Table 8.6)). If we wanted to formally compare the original and our 'final' models' we could not do so by means of D^2 tests; we could, however, use other criteria such as the ECVI, AIC and CAIC statistics which are appropriate for non-nested model comparisons. Table 8.8 shows such a comparison and includes the null and saturated models as benchmarks. It can be seen that the 'final' model outperforms the original across all criteria. Another type of comparison that we could undertake is to examine the degree to which each model is stable across different samples; this raises the issue of model cross-validation which is the topic of the next chapter.

Notes

1   MacCallum, Roznowski and Necowitz (1992), p. 492.
2   MacCallum (1995), p. 33. Note, however, that 'even when substantive justifications for model modification are offered, one may be concerned as to the rigor and validity of those justifications . . . If a model modification is highly interpretable, then why was it not represented in the original model' (MacCallum, Roznowski and Necowitz, 1992, pp. 491–492). On this issue, see Bollen (1989) and Steiger (1990).
3   MacCallum, Roznowski and Necowitz (1992), p. 491.
4   MacCallum, Roznowski and Necowitz (1992), p. 501.
5   Discussions of possible causes of poor fit can be found in Bentler and Chou (1987) and Kaplan (1990); the impact of specification error on model estimation, testing, and improvement is discussed by Kaplan (1988, 1989).
6   Hence the importance of ensuring that no omission of key variables has taken place at the model conceptualization stage (see Figures 2.1 and 2.2 in Chapter 2).
7   MacCallum (1986), pp. 107–108.
8   Diamantopoulos (1994), p. 123, emphasis in the original.
9   Breckler (1990), p. 268. Similarly, Biddle and Marlin (1987), p. 15 state that 'ex-post-facto mucking around with the data can generate insights; it certainly does not "confirm" a causal model that was stated in advance of data analysis'.
10   Long (1983a), p. 69.
11   Byrne (1998), p. 125.

12   Recall from Chapter 7 that a saturated model has $k(k+1)/2$ parameters and is just-identified (where k is the number of observed variables).

13   MacCallum (1995), p. 30.

14   Bagozzi (1983), p. 450. See also Gerbing and Anderson (1984) and references given therein.

15   Kaplan (1990), pp. 148–149.

16   MacCallum (1986), p. 109.

17   Bollen (1989), p. 296.

18   Bollen (1989), p. 297.

19   More formally, a standardized residual indicates the number of standard deviations that observed residuals depart from zero residuals; the latter would exist if the model fit was perfect.

20   Given that the residual matrix $(S-\hat{\Sigma})$ has exactly the same number of elements as the sample matrix, S, and given that the size of the latter is a function of the number of observed variables, the total number of elements in the residual matrix is equal to $k(k+1)/2$, where k = number of observed variables. In our illustrative model, $k = 13$ and, therefore, the number of elements is $(13 \cdot 14)/2 = 91$ (see also Chapter 5 on the calculation of degrees of freedom for our model).

21   Obviously, freely estimated parameters have modification indices equal to zero.

22   Jöreskog (1993), p. 312.

23   Long (1983a), p. 69.

24   Saris, Satorra and Sörbom (1987), p. 112.

25   This part of the output is produced as a result of including the keywords RS (residual analysis), MI (modification indices), SS (standardized solution) and SC (completely standardized solution) in the LISREL Output command line. See the discussion on the specification of the SIMPLIS input file in Chapter 4 and the interpretation of the output file in LISREL format in Chapter 6.

26   The equality of modification indices raises the issue of **equivalent models**; this issue will be discussed in detail in Chapter 9.

27   For a theoretical discussion in support of this link, see Siguaw, Brown and Widing (1994).

28   Saris and Stronkhorst (1984), p. 205.

29   Bagozzi (1983), p. 450.

30   In terms of the formal specification of our model in LISREL notation (see Chapter 4), we have in effect amended the first equation in the structural part of the model to read as follows:

$$\eta_1 = \gamma_{11}\xi_1 + \gamma_{12}\xi_2 + \gamma_{13}\xi_3 + \zeta_1$$

31   See thresholds proposed by MacCallum, Browne and Sugawara (1996).

32   MacCallum (1986), p. 109, emphasis added.

33   Note in particular that the high modification index for the error covariance between Ambig and Clear noted earlier has now disappeared.

34   An important reason for this has to do with the estimation technique used. With full-information techniques (such as maximum likelihood), specification errors in one model equation can affect the estimation of other correctly specified equations; consequently, when a misspecification is corrected, the effects can be 'felt' throughout the model (see also Chapter 6).

35   See discussion of structural model evaluation in Chapter 7 and also Tables 6.2 and 6.3 in Chapter 6.

36   Long (1983a), p. 65.

37   The only parameters estimated in this model are the variances of the observed variables; as the latter are assumed independent, the covariance matrix is diagonal. The independence model has k parameters, where k is the number of observed variables. See also Chapter 7.

38   The maximum possible number of parameters are estimated in this model, namely

$k(k+1)/2$, where k = number of observed variables. As a result the saturated model has zero degrees of freedom and, therefore, *always* fits the data perfectly. See also Chapter 7.

39   Bagozzi and Yi (1988), p. 78. Note that there are additional types of comparisons that can be undertaken between nested models; however, these involve quite advanced knowledge of covariance structure modeling and are therefore, not considered here (see, for example, Raykov and Penev, 1998).

40   Saris and Stronkhorst (1984), p. 247.

41   Long (1983b), p. 77.

42   Jöreskog and Sörbom (1989), p. 225.

43   In the path model in Figure 3.3 of Chapter 3, the parameters concerned are VAR(ε_5) and γ_{22}.

44   On this issue, see the assessment of the measurement part of the model in Chapter 7 and comments made therein.

45   See the discussion of direct, indirect and total effects in Chapter 6.

46   Note that we are further amending the already modified input file (i.e. which now also includes a link between Mkt Ort and Job Sat). In terms of the formal specification of the model using LISREL notation (see Chapter 4), the second structural equation would now read:

$$\eta_2 = \beta_{21}\eta_1 + \gamma_{23}\xi_3 + \zeta_2$$

47   Again, the reason for this is that since a full-information estimation technique is used, elimination of parameters influences other parameters which may be better estimated as a result (see also note 34 above).

48   Kaplan (1995), p. 103.

49   See also Chapter 7 for a discussion of the non-central χ^2-distribution.

50   See Saris and Stronkhorst (1984), Satorra and Saris (1985), Matsuelda and Bielby (1986), Satorra, Saris and de Pipjer (1985), Saris and Satorra (1987, 1993) and Saris, Satorra and Sörbom (1987).

51   Kaplan (1995), p. 103.

52   An alternative way to compute the power of the test is to use the squared t-value (i.e. t^2) as an approximation of the non-centrality parameter λ. Clearly we would do this *before* fixing a parameter and the question we would be asking would be: did the test not reject the null hypothesis because of a small estimated value or because the sample size was small? In our case, the t-statistic with γ_{22} prior to freeing it came to -1.233; therefore $t^2 \approx \lambda = 1.640$. Inspection of Saris and Stronkhorst's (1984) power tables when $\lambda = 1.60$ and $v = 1$ gives a power estimate of 0.244. Again, this is quite low.

53   The fact that they both have the same degrees of freedom precludes nesting; see definition of nested models earlier in this chapter. Also note that 'models based on different sets of variables cannot be nested' (Hayduk, 1987, p. 164).

9 MODEL CROSS-VALIDATION

In the previous three chapters we estimated our illustrative model, evaluated its fit and undertook some modifications to arrive at a 'better' model; the latter was shown to have better fit than our original model and was also considered to make substantive sense. The question that now arises is: how confident can we be in our final model? If the final version of our model is likely to be of any use, 'the model should work not only for the given sample but also for other samples'.[1] In this context, 'the possibility exists that the accepted model only fits the set of data for which the model has been developed. One ought to be aware of this possibility, especially if the model has been improved using the same data set again and again'.[2]

To examine the extent to which a model replicates in samples other than the one on which it was derived, one has to undertake a **cross-validation analysis**. Such an analysis is also necessary if one wants to select the 'best' model among a set of alternative models, since 'the model that fits best in a given sample is not necessarily the model with the best cross-validity, especially when sample size is not large'.[3] For example, going back to Chapter 8, it was concluded that the final modified model (following the addition of one parameter and the deletion of another)[4] had a better fit than the original illustrative model. However, this conclusion was reached on the basis of a *single* sample and there is no guarantee that the modified model's performance with a different sample will be any better (it could, in fact, be worse) than that of the original model. The same rationale applies if there are several *a-priori* specified models (i.e. 'alternative' or 'competing' models perhaps representing different theories) and one wants to select the one 'that will have the greatest predictive validity in future samples rather than a model that best reproduces structures of one specific sample that may be inappropriate to future observations from the same population'.[5]

As discussions of cross-validation in the literature approach the topic from different angles (and can, thus, be confusing to the novice), Table 9.1 classifies the main forms of cross-validation in covariance structure modeling.

Under **model stability**, the objective is to assess whether a single model is likely to be fit well when estimated on a different sample from the *same* general population. This is the most basic form of cross-validation analysis and could involve either the collection of data from an independent sample or the **split-sample approach** whereby the total sample is randomly split (usually 50:50) to a **calibration sample** and a **validation sample**. The former is then used to develop the model (and undertake any modifications deemed necessary), while the latter is used to test the derived model;

Table 9.1   Forms of model cross-validation

		Validation sample	
		Same population	Different population
Number of models	Single model	Model stability	Validity extension
	Model comparison	Model selection	Validity generalization

therefore, 'in this sense, cross-validation simulates prediction of an independent sample'.[6] Needless to say, that one needs to have a large enough sample to implement a split-sample approach; a suggested lower threshold is 300 cases but the complexity of the model (in terms of number of parameters to be estimated) ought to be taken into account as well.[7]

Validity extension, as a form of model cross-validation,[8] is procedurally very similar to stability assessment, the only difference being that the validation sample is drawn from a *different* population (e.g. a different industry or a different country). Obviously, here a split-sample approach cannot be used since the very aim of the analysis is to determine whether the validity of the model will extend to a different population. Note also that validity extension makes more sense *after* model stability has been established; talking about extending the model's validity to a second population implicitly assumes that the model already replicates in samples of a particular population.

Under **model selection**, the objective is to choose one model from several competing or alternative models based upon the model's stability when replicated on different samples drawn from the *same* population. The underlying rationale here is that 'comparing a set of competing models will give better insights into the relative explanatory power of a proposed model than will give a consideration of only the proposed model'.[9] In this form of cross-validation a split-sample approach is feasible as long as the sample is large enough (see above) and 'since competing models are evaluated on the same sample, conclusions about the relative adequacy of models are not affected by sample size'.[10]

Finally, under **validity generalization** the objective is to identify the model from a set of competing alternatives that replicates best across *different* populations. Say, for example, that you have three competing models A, B and C and through the application of model selection procedures you found that, in population #1, the relative ordering of the models (from best to worse) is B, A, C. Cross-validating the models in population #2, however, produces the order C, A, B. Thus, although model A is not the optimal model for either population #1 or population #2, it nevertheless does better than model B or model C if *both* populations are considered simultaneously.[11] Validity generalization, therefore, involves the application of model selection procedures on different populations, followed by a comparison of the results.

Another way of looking at cross-validation is in terms of the **cross-validation strategy** employed. Let us assume that we have estimated a model on a calibration sample and want to cross-validate it on a validation sample. One way of doing this is to use the same model specification as that in the calibration sample (i.e. the same pattern of measurement and structural paths) but allow all parameters to be freely estimated on the validation sample. Under this **loose replication strategy**, the values of all parameters are allowed to differ between the calibration and validation samples. Alternatively, we may decide to not only use the same model specification but also to fix all parameters at the values estimated from the calibration sample before fitting the model to the validation sample. Here, we would be following a **tight replication strategy** whereby identical parameter estimates would be assumed between the calibration and the validation sample. Finally, under a **moderate replication strategy**, some critical parameters reflecting measurement and/or structural paths are fixed to values estimated from the calibration sample, while other parameters (e.g. error variances) are set free and subsequently estimated on the validation sample.[12]

In the next two sections, we illustrate the key principles of cross-validation and demonstrate different ways in which the LISREL program can be used for this purpose. We first focus on cross-validating our illustrative model (as modified in Chapter 8) on a different sample and then show how cross-validation procedures can be employed to compare alternative models.

Cross-validating the illustrative model (final version)

To cross-validate the final version of our illustrative model, we collected data from another sample of 160 salespeople and computed the covariance matrix among the observed variables; the latter looks very much like the one in Appendix 4A in Chapter 4, the only difference being that the numerical entries are, of course, different (which is not surprising given that this covariance matrix is based on a completely different sample). Table 9.2 shows the goodness-of-fit measures resulting from fitting our model to this new sample; the relevant SIMPLIS input file is shown in Appendix 9A.

On the whole, the goodness-of-fit measures paint a positive picture as all the key fit criteria take values consistent with recommended thresholds (see Chapter 7); for example, the chi-square statistic is nonsignificant, the RMSEA is low, and the NNFI and CFI are greater than 0.95 (inspection of residuals – not shown in Table 9.2 – also confirms a good fit). An important point to note from the information in Table 9.2 is the 90% confidence intervals for the NCP, F_0, RMSEA and ECVI (as well as the test of close fit for the RMSEA); as you may recall from Chapter 7, such intervals could not be computed for the original version of the model due

Table 9.2   Overall fit measures for validation sample

!ILLUSTRATIVE MODEL OF JOB SATISFACTION AND CUSTOMER FOCUS

Goodness of Fit Statistics

Degrees of Freedom = 57
Minimum Fit Function Chi-Square = 62.288 (P = 0.294)
Normal Theory Weighted Least Squares Chi-Square = 62.408 (P = 0.290)
Estimated Non-centrality Parameter (NCP) = 5.408
90 Percent Confidence Interval for NCP = (0.0 ; 28.809)

Minimum Fit Function Value = 0.392
Population Discrepancy Function Value (F0) = 0.0340
90 Percent Confidence Interval for F0 = (0.0 ; 0.181)
Root Mean Square Error of Approximation (RMSEA) = 0.0244
90 Percent Confidence Interval for RMSEA = (0.0 ; 0.0564)
P-Value for Test of Close Fit (RMSEA < 0.05) = 0.893

Expected Cross-Validation Index (ECVI) = 0.820
90 Percent Confidence Interval for ECVI = (0.786 ; 0.967)
ECVI for saturated Model = 1.145
ECVI for Independence Model = 6.882

Chi-Square for Independence Model with 78 Degrees of Freedom = 1068.277
Independence AIC = 1094.277
Model AIC = 130.408
Saturated AIC = 182.000
Independence CAIC = 1147.255
Model CAIC = 268.964
Saturated CAIC = 552.841

Root Mean Square Residual (RMR) = 0.0403
Standardized RMR = 0.0407
Goodness of Fit Index (GFI) = 0.943
Adjusted Goodness of Fit Index (AGFI) = 0.909
Parsimony Goodness of Fit Index (PGFI) = 0.591

Normed Fit Index (NFI) = 0.942
Non-Normed Fit Index (NNFI) = 0.993
Parsimony Normed Fit Index (PNFI) = 0.688
Comparative Fit Index (CFI) = 0.995
Incremental Fit Index (IFI) = 0.995
Relative Fit Index (RFI) = 0.920

Critical N (CN) = 217.295

---

to its very poor overall fit. Here, however, the error due to approximation (see Chapter 7 and, in particular, Appendix 7A) is not very high and, therefore, appropriate confidence limits can be determined.

Although the results from fitting our final model to the validation sample are very encouraging, two issues must be raised. The first is that there has been a loss in statistical power as a result of the much smaller size of the validation sample ($N = 160$) compared to the calibration sample ($N = 306$). Whereby previously power was in excess of 0.90, it is now below 0.70;[13] thus the danger of making a Type II error (i.e. not rejecting an incorrect model) is now higher.[14] Secondly, the fact that we allowed all parameters to be freely estimated on the validation sample implies that we have been following a loose replication strategy. However, strictly speaking, 'this strategy is not truly cross-validation since the analysis of the validation sample in no way depends on results from analysis of the calibration sample'.[15] Thus a more rigorous cross-validation test of the model would be obtained if a tight, or, at least, moderate replication strategy was employed.

Tight and moderate replication strategies can be easily implemented by using LISREL's **multi-sample analysis** facility. The latter allows models to be fitted to several samples simultaneously and enables the specification of **invariance constraints** (i.e. setting all or a subset of parameters to be equal across groups).[16] A particularly nice feature of the program is that, in multi-sample analyses, all parameters are, by default, assumed to be equal across groups, unless one tells the program otherwise. This means that only those parameters on which groups are allowed to differ need to be specified. In other words, LISREL assumes that a tight replication strategy is to be followed by default;[17] the latter, however, can be transformed to a moderate replication strategy by selectively removing invariance constraints (i.e. by allowing certain parameters to be freely estimated in each group). *Which* invariance constraints to remove, of course, is a decision that has to be taken by the analyst in the light of the particular model at hand.[18]

Table 9.3 shows the SIMPLIS input file for a two-sample LISREL analysis under a tight replication strategy. The program knows that more than one sample is to be analyzed as a result of the insertion of the Group 1 and Group 2 command lines and the fact that two covariance matrices and sample sizes are provided as input; here ex1.cov is the covariance matrix for the original (i.e. calibration) sample and crossmod.cov is the corresponding covariance matrix for the validation sample.[19] Note that the model is only specified once (under Group 1); the model specification reflects the final illustrative model and is identical to the one in Appendix 9A. The fact that no Relationships command line appears under Group 2 implies that *all* model parameters are supposed to be equal across groups (we will see how to relax such constraints shortly).

The full output resulting from running the input file in Table 9.3 begins with a listing of the covariance matrix of each sample and follows this with a listing of the parameter estimates for Group 1. Subsequently, residual statistics, stem-leaf plots and modification indices for Group 1 are shown but not fit statistics. The latter are displayed after the parameter estimates for Group 2 have been listed (which, in this case, are identical to those in Group 1 given that all parameters are assumed to be equal); finally, residual statistics, stem-leaf plots and modification indices for Group 2 are provided.

As the full output contains a lot of redundant information for our purposes, we focus here on the overall fit of the model to the two samples as indicated by the chi-square test (Table 9.4). Note that the latter is an aggregate measure 'of the fit of all LISREL models in all groups, including all constraints, to the data from all groups'.[20] The degrees of freedom for this analysis are calculated as:

Table 9.3   SIMPLIS input file for two-sample analysis

```
!ILLUSTRATIVE MODEL OF JOB SATISFACTION AND CUSTOMER FOCUS
Group 1: Tight Replication of Final Model
Observed Variables: Work Supervise Pay Promote Sell Solve Clear Ambig
Compat Conflict Custort Comport Intcord
Covariance Matrix from File ex1.cov
Sample Size: 306
Latent Variables: 'Job Sat' 'Cust Foc' 'Role Amb' 'Role Conf' 'Mkt Ort'
Relationships:
'Job Sat' = 'Role Amb' 'Role Conf' 'Mkt Ort'
'Cust Foc' = 'Mkt Ort' 'Job Sat'
Clear = 1*'Role Amb'
Ambig = 'Role Amb'
Compat = 1*'Role Conf'
Conflict = 'Role Conf'
Custort = 1*'Mkt Ort'
Comport Intcord = 'Mkt Ort'
Work = 1*'Job Sat'
Supervise - Promote = 'Job Sat'
Sell = 1*'Cust Foc'
Solve = 'Cust Foc'

Group 2: Tight Replication of Final Model
Covariance Matrix from File crossmod.cov
Sample Size: 160
Options: ND=3
End of Problem
```

Table 9.4   Final model fit: tight replication strategy

$$
\begin{array}{c}
\text{Goodness of Fit Statistics} \\
\text{Degrees of Freedom = 148} \\
\text{Minimum Fit Function Chi-Square = 182.159 (P = 0.0295)} \\
\text{Normal Theory Weighted Least Squares Chi-Square = 182.773 (P = 0.0275)} \\
\text{Contribution to Chi-Square = 62.384} \\
\text{Percentage Contribution to Chi-Square = 34.132}
\end{array}
$$

$$(G \cdot s/2) - t$$

where G = the number of groups
   t = the number of parameters to be estimated
   s = the number of variances and covariances among the manifest variables, calculated as $(p + q)(p + q + 1)$
   p = the number of y-variables
   q = the number of x-variables

Here $G = 2$, $t = 34$, $p = 6$ and $q = 7$. Thus $s/2 = [(6 + 7) \times (6 + 7 + 1)]/2 = 91$ and the degrees of freedom are $2 \times 91 - 34 = 148$.

The only unfamiliar pieces of information in Table 9.4 are the Contribution to Chi-Square and the Percentage Contribution to Chi-Square. These show the contribution of Group 2 to the overall chi-square statistic and thus reflect the relative influence of this group on the fit of the model; in this case, it appears that Group 1 (the calibration sample) is more influential than Group 2 (the validation sample) since it accounts for two-thirds of the overall model chi-square.[21]

Table 9.5   Final model fit: moderate replication strategy

Goodness of Fit Statistics
Degrees of Freedom = 144
Minimum Fit Function Chi-Square = 182.133 (P = 0.0173)
Normal Theory Weighted Least Squares Chi-Square = 182.755 (P = 0.0160)
Contribution to Chi-Square = 62.368
Percentage Contribution to Chi-Square = 34.127

For interpretation purposes, it is instructive to compare the cross-validation results in Table 9.4 with those that would result had a moderate replication strategy been adopted (i.e. certain parameters had been allowed to vary across the calibration and validation samples). Table 9.5 shows the results obtained from implementing such a strategy. In this case we have allowed the covariances of the exogenous latent variables and the error variances of the endogenous latent variables to be estimated freely across groups; all other parameters (e.g. measurement and structural paths) have been constrained to be equal. To relax the above-mentioned constraints, we have modified the latter part of the input file in Table 9.3 to read as follows:

```
Group 2: Moderate Replication of Final Model
Covariance Matrix from File crossmod.cov
Sample Size: 160
Relationships:
Set covariances of 'Role Amb' 'Role Conf' 'Mkt Ort' free
Set the error variance of 'Job Sat' free
Options: ND = 3
End of Problem
```

We can now formally compare the results of the tight and moderate replication strategies by means of a chi-square difference (D^2) test. We can do this because we have a nested comparison situation since the tight replication strategy can be derived from the moderate replication strategy by introducing additional equality constraints. Specifically, $D^2 = 182.773 - 182.755 = 0.018$, while the degrees of freedom are $v = 148 - 144 = 4$. A chi-square value of 0.018 with four degrees of freedom is *not* significant which implies that a tight replication of the model works just as well as a more moderate replication.[22] This is, of course, a positive sign as it shows that our final model replicates well even under strict conditions.

Cross-validation and model comparison

So far we have looked at cross-validation from the perspective of seeing how our final illustrative model performs when fitted to a different sample. In this section, we demonstrate how cross-validation procedures can be used to *compare* different models. We do this by using the **cross-validation index** (CVI) which, is, again, easily obtainable from the LISREL program.

To understand how the CVI works, assume that we have a sample of size N which we split into two sub-samples of equal size, say, A and B. Let us denote the covariance matrices for these samples S_A and S_B. Initially, we employ sample A as the calibration sample and sample B as the validation sample. Specifically, we fit the model on sample A and obtain the fitted covariance matrix (see Chapter 6), which we denote as $\hat{\Sigma}_A$. We then form the fitting function F (S_B, $\hat{\Sigma}_A$) which provides 'a measure of the discrepancy between the validation-sample covariance matrix . . . and the calibration-sample reproduced covariance matrix'.[23] This is the cross-validation index. Note that no estimation as such takes place at the validation stage, i.e. the model is not really 'fitted' to the validation data; instead, the calibration sample 'imposes' the model structure on the covariance matrix of the validation sample. This procedure is repeated for each model of interest; subsequently 'the choice of the model with the greatest estimated "predictive validity" is made by selecting the model which yields the smallest cross-validation index'.[24]

A **double cross-validation** can also be implemented by reversing the role of the first and second sub-samples. In other words, sample B now acts as the calibration sample, while sample A becomes the validation sample; the resulting CVI is then F (S_A, $\hat{\Sigma}_B$). Under double cross-validation, each model of interest has two CVIs and the 'model(s) that achieves the smallest cross-validation index in each of the two rounds of cross-validation may be regarded as the one(s) with the greatest predictive validity'.[25]

To illustrate the use of the CVI we pooled our initial sample ($N = 306$) together with the second sample ($N = 160$) used in the previous section. Subsequently, we randomly split the resulting total sample into two halves of 233 cases each and used them to perform a double cross-validation of (a) the original version of our model (as originally specified in Chapter 4), and (b) the final version of our model (as finally modified in Chapter 8). To generate the CVIs for each of the models in each of the two cross-validation rounds, we used the cross-validation feature of the LISREL program. Table 9.6 shows the input for one of the cross-validation rounds for the original model; note that *four* such input files had to be constructed (two models times two cross-validation rounds).

Three points should be noticed from Table 9.6. First, the file `split2.cov` contains the covariance matrix of the validation sample. Secondly, the sample size stated is half the total sample size (see above). Thirdly, the key command of interest is in the line `Crossvalidate File Sigma1.cov`. This command refers the program to the fitted covariance matrix derived from the calibration sample; in our case this has been saved in a file entitled `Sigma1.cov`. To save the latter we only had to include the keyword `SI = Sigma1.cov` in the `Options` command line of the SIMPLIS input file in Table 6.1 (see also the discussion of the SIMPLIS command structure in Chapter 4). The output from running the input file in Table 9.6 is very basic: it first lists the elements of the covariance matrix of the validation sample (here `split2.cov`), then the elements of the

Table 9.6   Input file for cross-validation index (CVI) calculation

```
!CROSS-VALIDATING ILLUSTRATIVE MODEL
Observed Variables: Work Supervise Pay Promote Sell Solve Clear Ambig
Compat Conflict Custort Comport Intcord
Covariance Matrix from File split2.cov
Sample Size: 233
Crossvalidate File Sigma1.cov
End of problem
```

Table 9.7   Double cross-validation results

		Original model	Final model
Sample combinations	$S_B, \hat{\Sigma}_A$	CVI = 4.58	CVI = 4.39
	$S_A, \hat{\Sigma}_B$	CVI = 4.37	CVI = 4.35

S = Covariance matrix of validation sample.
$\hat{\Sigma}$ = Implied covariance matrix of calibration sample.

fitted covariance matrix based on the calibration sample (here Sigma1.cov) and, finally, it prints the value of the CVI (as well as a 90% confidence interval for the latter).

Table 9.7 summarizes the results of the double cross-validation procedure described above; each CVI value was obtained by a separate LISREL run using an input file similar to the one in Table 9.6.

It can be seen that the CVI values of the final model are lower than those of the original model (for both cross-validation rounds). This suggests that the former ought to be selected as it has the greatest predictive validity. Note, however, that double-cross validation does not always work as smoothly as in our example. It is entirely possible that the two cross-validation rounds may favor a *different* model. Should this happen, then considerations such as model interpretability and parsimony should be given greater weight; after all, 'the need for judgment on the part of an experimenter cannot be avoided'.[26]

An obvious drawback of cross-validation is that one must have a large enough sample size to enable it to be split into calibration and validation subsamples.[27] If sample size is a problem then, instead of the CVI, one may rely on the expected cross-validation index (ECVI) which was introduced in Chapter 7. The latter is a single sample approximation of the CVI, whereby 'the cross-validation coefficient is replaced by a calibration sample statistic with approximately the same expected value'.[28] A drawback of the ECVI is that it is more sensitive to distributional assumptions than the CVI; moreover, there is some evidence to suggest that the ECVI 'is probably not appropriate for evaluating sequences of models produced by specification searches'[29] (hence it is more suitable for comparisons of a-priori models).

A second drawback of cross-validation is that it may produce unstable results, particularly in smaller samples; in other words, depending upon *how* the sample happens to be split into calibration and validation subsamples, different models may be associated with the lowest CVI value. One solution to this problem is to employ some sort of sample-splitting algorithm to ensure 'that neither the calibration sample nor the validation sample alone contains a subset of observations that could bias the cross-validation'.[30] In addition, instead of using one-half of the sample to develop and modify a model and the other half to validate it, one may try a **parallel specification search** procedure (see Table 8.2 in Chapter 8). The latter involves 'conducting the specification search process on independent samples and obtaining goodness-of-fit measures for each model in each sample. One would also obtain two sets of two-sample cross-validation measures by carrying out a double cross-validation analysis, exchanging the designation of calibration and cross-validation samples'.[31]

Equivalent models

Imagine that you developed and estimated a model, evaluated its fit and found it to be acceptable and also established that the model cross-validates well. You may thus feel (and quite understandably so) that your model is in fact the 'best' model for explaining the relationships among the constraints of interest. Well, not *quite*.

A problem with modeling in general and covariance structure modeling in particular is that 'for any given model, there will generally be alternative models, represented by different patterns of relations among the variables, that are *indistinguishable* from the original model in terms of goodness-of-fit to sample data'.[32] These alternative models are known as **equivalent models** and 'will always yield exactly the same fit to any sample data . . . such models can be distinguished only in terms of other criteria such as interpretability of parameter estimates and meaningfulness of the model'.[33]

To illustrate the principle of equivalent models, consider the situation where one has two variables X and Y. Figure 9.1 shows three substantively different models, all of which, however, will produce an identical fit to data. This will be the case, irrespective of the particular data set or sample size involved because 'model equivalence is a property of models independently of the data being analyzed'.[34] In terms of Figure 9.1, given that the observed data only include the variances of X and Y and the covariance between them, it is not possible to determine whether X causes Y (case A), or Y causes X (case B); all we can do is say whether or not X and Y are correlated (case C). Thus, if our substantive model of interest is that X causes Y (case A), then we would have to defend our model on a basis *other* than goodness of fit.[35] For example, it could be the case that X was experimentally manipulated to produce effects on Y (thus logically excluding cases B and C), or that data collection was undertaken in a longitudinal fashion with measurement of X preceding that of Y (thus excluding case B).[36]

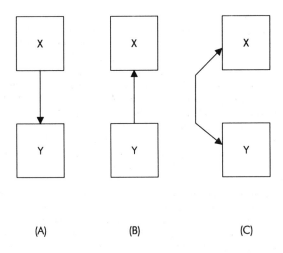

(A)   (B)   (C)

Figure 9.1   Equivalent models

Although, as Figure 9.1 indicates, equivalent models can arise even with two variables, as the number of variables increases, the number of equivalent models increases at a much faster rate.[37] In fact, there is substantial evidence in the literature that 'the problem is a severe one in practice, with equivalent models occurring routinely and often in very large numbers'.[38] Much more worrying is the fact that 'in the majority of instances, plausible and theoretically compelling alternative models could be easily formulated'.[39]

From the above, it becomes clear that, no matter what its fit, one should not regard one's model as *the* model for explaining the linkages among the variables involved. Indeed, an effort should be made to construct alternative equivalent models and thus explicitly confront alternative theoretical interpretations. There are several rules for identifying equivalent models[40] and a specialized computer package (namely TETRAD II)[41] can also be used for this purpose. Although the mechanics of generating equivalent models clearly fall outside the scope of the present text, we do encourage the reader to consult these sources and bring his/her awareness of equivalent models into the model conceptualization process (see Chapter 2); after all 'if one finds that it is possible to generate a substantial number of such models, and if many of those models seem to be substantively plausible, then there is relatively little point in conducting a study of one's original model and arguing for its validity'.[42]

Notes

1   Yi and Nassen (1992), p. 409.
2   Saris and Stronkhorst (1984), p. 28.

3   MacCallum et al. (1994), p. 28.

4   Namely, the addition of a path from Mkt Ort (Market Orientation) to Job Sat (Job Satisfaction) and the deletion of the path from Role Con (Role Conflict) to Cust Foc (Customer Focus); in LISREL notation, γ_{13} was set free while γ_{22} was fixed to zero.

5   Homburg (1991), p. 138. According to Bagozzi and Yi (1988, p. 85), 'cross-validation is relevant under at least four conditions: a) when one needs to establish validity by separating estimation from evaluation of a model in order to ascertain that the fit is not the result of idiosyncratic sample characteristics, b) when specification searches or model explorations are done by modification of a hypothesized model in the light of fit to data, c) when one best fitting model has been chosen out of several models on the current data and there is a need to check whether capitalization on chance has occurred . . ., and d) when the objective of a study is to identify models that can predict future data well'.

6   Yi and Nassen (1992), p. 409.

7   Based on simulation study, Homburg (1991) found that cross-validation performed best with sample sizes in the 300 to 500 range. In contrast, MacCallum, Roznowski and Necowitz (1992) reported that cross-validation results can be unstable unless sample size exceeds 800. Homburg (1991) also found that cross-validation results are much more consistent if a formal sample-splitting algorithm (namely Snee's (1977) DUPLEX algorithm) is used rather than a random split; however, one should be warned that such algorithms 'tend to be very intensive in terms of computer time' (Diamantopoulos, 1994, p. 129). As far as the impact of model complexity is concerned, Bentler (1995, p. 6) states that 'the ratio of sample size to the number of free parameters to be estimated may be able to go as low as 5:1 under normal and elliptical theory . . . a ratio of at least 10:1 may be more appropriate for arbitrary distributions. These ratios used to be larger to obtain trustworthy z-tests on the significance of parameters, and still larger to yield correct model evaluation chi-square probabilities'. So, now you know!

8   In the literature, often no distinction is made between validity extension and validity generalization and both forms of cross-validation are subsumed under the latter term. However, we feel that such a distinction is important because a model can replicate well in a different population but another model may replicate even better; in this case, the latter model would be considered superior than the first in terms of validity generalization potential.

9   Yi and Nassen (1992), p. 408.

10 Yi and Nassen (1992), p. 408.

11 Of course, one may decide that no one model is appropriate for both populations and settle for different models in each (i.e. model B in population #1 and model C in population #2). This will depend on several factors, including the interpretability and parsimony of the three models and the substantive difference in performance between model A and the other two models (i.e. by how much is A outperformed by B and C in populations #1 and #2 respectively).

12 There can, of course, be different variations of the moderate replication strategy, depending upon the *specific* combination of parameters that are set equal or allowed to vary between the calibration and validation samples. Such variations are discussed in detail by MacCallum et al. (1994).

13 For power calculation procedures, see Chapter 7 and references given therein.

14 In terms of the four model-testing scenarios in Table 7.4, the model now falls in cell 3.

15 MacCallum et al. (1994), p. 13.

16 Invariance constraints are also known as 'equality constraints' or 'group restrictions'.

17 Note that the tight replication strategy implemented under LISREL's multi-sample facility differs somewhat from the tight replication strategy earlier described in which the parameter values of the validation sample are *fixed* to those of the calibration sample. Instead, LISREL first computes initial estimates by IV and TSLS (see Chapter 6) and then replaces parameters specified to be equal across groups by their mean value.

18 Relaxing *all* invariance constraints, however, makes little sense in multi-group analysis

since doing so implies that all model parameters will be independently estimated in each group (i.e. one would be reverting to a loose replication strategy).

19   Note that multi-sample analysis in LISREL is not limited to two groups; any number of groups can be simultaneously analyzed. See Jöreskog and Sörbom (1989, 1993, 1996a).

20   Jöreskog and Sörbom (1989), p. 228.

21   The influence of Group 1 is readily computed by subtracting the contribution of Group 2 from the overall chi-square value; this comes to 182.159 – 62.384 = 119.775 or about 66% of the overall chi-square. Note that the Minimum Fit Function Chi-Square is used in these calculations.

22   Of course, this conclusion applies in connection with the *specific* moderate replication strategy adopted. Had additional equality constraints (e.g. measurement paths) been removed, it is possible that a significant improvement over a tight replication could have been obtained.

23   Cudeck and Browne (1983), p. 152.

24   Cudeck and Browne (1983), p. 152.

25   Bagozzi and Yi (1988), p. 84.

26   Cudeck and Browne (1983), p. 153.

27   Or, alternatively, that one has the time, access and resources to collect data from an independent sample.

28   Browne and Cudeck (1989), p. 446.

29   MacCallum, Roznowski and Necowitz (1992), p. 500.

30   Homburg (1991), p. 138. See also note 7 above.

31   MacCallum, Roznowski and Necowitz (1992), p. 502.

32   MacCallum et al. (1993), p. 185, emphasis added.

33   MacCallum et al. (1993), p. 185.

34   Jöreskog and Sörbom (1989).

35   In Figure 9.1, all three models will produce perfect fit because they are saturated (i.e. they have different degrees of freedom). However, model equivalence is just as much of an issue if non-saturated (i.e. overidentified) models are involved; for relevant examples, see Breckler (1990), MacCallum et al. (1993) and Williams, Bozdogan and Aiman-Smith (1996).

36   The nature of the specific variables involved will also influence the plausibility of alternative equivalent models; for example if X = age and Y = incidence of illness, then it is clear that model B (and probably model C) can be safely excluded. For a comprehensive discussion on the factors that influence the plausibility and meaningfulness of alternative equivalent models, see MacCallum et al. (1993).

37   For example, considering only recursive models (i.e. allowing no reciprocal paths) with three variables, ten possible models can be generated, whereas with four variables, no fewer than 24 models can be obtained (these examples assume that each variable is in some way connected to all the rest, i.e. a saturated model is involved).

38   MacCallum (1995), p. 31.

39   Breckler (1990), p. 266.

40   See Stelzl (1986), Lee and Hershberger (1990), Hershberger (1994), Hayduk (1996) and Williams, Bozdogan and Aiman-Smith (1996). Note that equal modification indices suggest the existence of equivalent models; see Jöreskog and Sörbom (1989).

41   See Scheines et al. (1994).

42   MacCallum (1995), p. 31.

APPENDIX 9A

SIMPLIS input file for validation sample

```
!ILLUSTRATIVE MODEL OF JOB SATISFACTION AND CUSTOMER FOCUS
 Observed Variables: Work Supervise Pay Promote Sell Solve Clear Ambig
 Compat Conflict Custort Comport Intcord
 Covariance Matrix from File crossmod.cov
 Sample Size: 160
 Latent Variables: 'Job Sat' 'Cust Foc' 'Role Amb' 'Role Conf' 'Mkt Ort'
 Relationships:
 'Job Sat' = 'Role Amb' 'Role Conf' 'Mkt Ort'
 'Cust Foc' ='Mkt Ort' 'Job Sat'
 Clear = 1*'Role Amb'
 Ambig = 'Role Amb'
 Compat = 1*'Role Conf'
 Conflict = 'Role Conf'
 Custort = 1*'Mkt Ort'
 Comport Intcord = 'Mkt Ort'
 Work = 1*'Job Sat'
 Supervise - Promote = 'Job Sat'
 Sell = 1*'Cust Foc'
 Solve = 'Cust Foc'
 Options: ND=3
 End of Problem
```

Note that the above input file is very similar to the SIMPLIS input file in Table 6.1 of Chapter 6. The only differences are that (a) a different covariance matrix is being used (i.e. that of the validation sample), (b) the sample size is 160 instead of 306 (reflecting the differences in size between the calibration and validation samples), and (c) the equations for Job Sat (Job Satisfaction) and Cust Foc (Customer Focus) now reflect the modifications made to the model in Chapter 8 (also we have not bothered asking for a path diagram).

10 AN INTRODUCTION TO PRELIS 2

PRELIS 2 (hereafter referred to as PRELIS) is a program used for the purpose of preprocessing raw data and computing the appropriate matrix for input into the LISREL program.[1] However, it can also function as a stand-alone program to provide an initial descriptive overview of the raw data, manipulate data files, etc. Access to PRELIS is obtained automatically when one starts the interactive versions of LISREL 8 (i.e. versions 8.20 and 8.30); in earlier versions of the program, PRELIS was accessed as a separate program.

The rationale underlying the development of PRELIS was based on the fact that users of LISREL 'are not always sufficiently familiar with characteristics and problems of their raw data when they set out to estimate and test a LISREL model'.[2] Indeed, in previous chapters, we only made passing reference to some of the key assumptions underlying a LISREL model. Thus, in Chapter 2 we assumed that all our manifest variables were metric (i.e. continuous), while in Chapter 6 we assumed that departures from multivariate normality were not too severe (otherwise our use of maximum likelihood (ML) estimation would be questionable); the multivariate normality assumption was also implicit in our interpretation of standard errors and chi-square statistics (see Chapter 7). However, violations in the above assumptions as well as problems relating to missing data[3] 'can often account for peculiarities that occur when estimating and testing LISREL models'.[4] By using PRELIS one can pinpoint any particular characteristics with the raw data that may account for idiosyncrasies in the LISREL output.[5]

Although PRELIS has a wide range of uses,[6] we will limit ourselves to those most likely to be useful to non-experts, i.e. data screening, testing assumptions, incorporation of non-metric variables, and generation of an asymptotic covariance matrix; the latter is needed whenever one chooses to use generally weighted least squares (WLS) as the estimation technique (see Chapter 6).[7]

For illustration purposes, we will use our original sample of 306 salespeople (see Chapter 2) and run PRELIS on the raw data relating to seven variables defined as follows (of course, any number of variables could have been used):

RANK = respondents' organizational position (coded 1 to 6, with higher numbers indicating more senior positions).

SEX = respondents' gender (coded 1 = male, 2 = female).

SCALE1 to SCALE5 = five composite variables capturing different aspects of salesforce behavior; each composite is computed as the average of several scale items.

Note that RANK and SEX are **categorical variables** and will be treated as ordinal in the analysis. On the other hand, SCALE1 to SCALE5 are assumed to be interval-scaled and will, thus, be declared as **continuous variables**. Note also that, although PRELIS has the facility for creating new variables, we have opted to create our composite variables (SCALE1 to SCALE5) using the SPSS program and then inputting the resulting raw data file into PRELIS. In our experience, this is much less problematic than trying to create combinations of items *within* PRELIS (particularly when a lot of items are involved) as the program has a tendency to become unstable. Be careful, however, when using the SPSS program to create the raw data file since missing data values are left as blank spaces by default. PRELIS, however, does not interpret blanks as missing values and, instead, looks for the next actual number. Thus, in our example, 'system-missing' values represented by blanks in SPSS were replaced by a specific missing value code (i.e. '99') and declared as such in the PRELIS input file (see below).

Table 10.1 shows the PRELIS input file for our example and highlights the different command syntax compared to the SIMPLIS language. There are only three required command lines in the input file namely DA (data specifications), RA (raw data) and OU (output); everything else is optional.

The first line of the input file is an optional title line. Any combination of words can be used as long as the first two characters are not DA (whether in upper or lower case or any combination thereof). To be on the safe side, start your title line with an exclamation mark (!) and then you can use whatever words you fancy wherever you fancy them. In fact, you can insert comments throughout the input file as long as you start the relevant lines with an exclamation mark.

The second line, DA (data specifications), specifies the characteristics of the raw data by using the keywords NI (number of input variables), NO (number of observations), TR (treatment of missing values) and MI (global missing value code for all variables). In our example NI=7, NO=306, TR=LI (listwise deletion; the other option is PA for pairwise deletion)[8] and MI=99. Note that if the missing value codes are not the same for *all* variables in the data file, one should use a separate MI command (*after* the LA line – see below) to specify the missing value codes for each variable concerned (in which case, no MI keyword is needed on the DA line).

The third line, LA (variable labels), is optional and assigns names to the variables in the raw data file. If this line is not included, default labels (namely VAR1, VAR2, VAR3, etc.) are assigned by the program.

Table 10.1   PRELIS input file

```
!ILLUSTRATIVE USE OF PRELIS
 DA NI=7 NO=306 TR=LI MI=99
 LA RANK SEX SCALE1 SCALE2 SCALE3 SCALE4 SCALE5
 RA FI=prel.dat
 OR RANK SEX
 CO SCALE1 SCALE2 SCALE3 SCALE4 SCALE5
 OU MA=PM SM=new.cor AC=asymptot.cov PK ND=3
```

However, it is advisable to use some easily remembered labels as one might have a problem recalling what, say, VAR239 represents! Variable labels cannot be longer than eight characters and the guidelines given in Chapter 4 (regarding the assignment of value labels in the SIMPLIS input file) apply here too.

The fourth line, RA, tells the PRELIS program the location of the raw data as indicated by the FI (file) keyword. In our example, these are located in a file called prel.dat. Note that the specified file must *only* contain raw data and no variable names or other information. If NO has not been specified in the DA command line (or if DA=0 has been entered), the program will automatically determine the sample size. If the NO included in the DA command is larger than the number of cases included in the raw data file, the program will use the latter as the sample size. Finally, if the NO is smaller than the actual number of cases in the raw data file, the program will stop after reading the last case specified in the NO keyword; any additional cases will be ignored.

The fifth and sixth lines designate the scale type of each variable in the raw data file. The OR command indicates that RANK and SEX are designated as ordinal variables, whereas the CO command shows that SCALE1 to SCALE5 have been declared as continuous variables (see earlier discussion). By default, PRELIS assumes that variables with less than 16 distinct values are ordinal, whereas those with 16 or more values are continuous. However, one can override the former specification for variables with less than 16 values via the CO command. On the other hand, variables with 16 or more distinct values are *always* treated as continuous, irrespective of whether they are declared ordinal by means of the OR command or not.[9]

The final line, OU (output), identifies the type of output you wish to obtain. The MA (matrix) keyword specifies the kind of matrix that you want LISREL to construct from the raw data. Here, we have requested a correlation matrix by setting MA=PM; this matrix contains product moment, polyserial and/or polychoric correlations, depending upon the combination of continuous and ordinal variables involved (we will revisit this matrix when we discuss the PRELIS output file). Other options include AM (augmented moment matrix), CM (covariance matrix), KM (product moment correlation matrix), MM (moment matrix), OM (optimal correlations), RM (Spearman rank correlations) and TM (Kendall correlations).[10] The matrix requested can also be saved in an external (i.e. separate) file by using the

SM (save matrix) keyword. In our example, we have requested that the PM matrix is saved in a file called new.cor. In addition, we have asked the program to compute an asymptotic covariance matrix (AC) and save it in a file titled asymptot.cov. Lastly, we have asked for a test of multivariate kurtosis with the PK keyword (in order to check the extent to which our data depart from multivariate normality) and specified three decimal places (ND=3) for printed output.

Table 10.2 shows the output resulting from running the PRELIS input file in Table 10.1; a discussion of the various parts of the output follows.

Following a reproduction of the input file (not shown in Table 10.2), the program provides an analysis of missing values both per variable and overall. For example, the variable with the most missing cases is SCALE4 and that with the fewest is SCALE5. Similarly, across cases, out of a total of 306 respondents, 271 provided responses to all seven variables, 24 did not respond to one of the seven variables, eight respondents did not respond to two variables and another three respondents to three variables. Thus, the Total Effective Sample Size (i.e. number of cases with responses on *all* variables) is 271 and, given that listwise deletion was specified in the PRELIS input file (see Table 10.1), a total of 271 cases are used in all other computations. Note that the number under Total Sample Size should be identical with that specified by the NO keyword on the DA command line of the input file; if not, then you have a problem with your raw data file and you should check it carefully before proceeding any further.

The next part of the output provides descriptive information for those variables that have been declared as ordinal in the input file. The Thresholds for Ordinal Variables indicate the cut-off points in the underlying continuous variables which define the categories of the observed ordinal variables (see Appendix 10A for a discussion of threshold values). These are followed by a listing of absolute and relative frequencies of each ordinal variable (under Univariate Distributions for Ordinal Variables) and a cross-tabulation of absolute and relative frequency counts (under Bivariate Distributions for Ordinal Variables); graphical displays in the form of bar charts are also provided. This information is useful as it gives a 'feel' for the data at hand; for example, it can be seen by looking at the SEX variable that most respondents (over 80%) are male with only a few being female. Consequently, it could be argued that the salesforce behaviors captured by the SCALE1 to SCALE7 composite variables (see below) are more representative of male rather than female salespeople.

The type of information presented for variables that have been denoted as continuous is much more extensive than that for ordinal variables. Thus, in addition to absolute and relative frequency displays and associated histograms (under Histograms for Continuous Variables), several descriptive statistics are also provided. Therefore, under Univariate Summary Statistics for Continuous Variables, the means,

Table 10.2   PRELIS output file

```
Number of Missing Values per Variable

    RANK      SEX    SCALE1    SCALE2    SCALE3    SCALE4    SCALE5
 --------  --------  --------  --------  --------  --------  --------
       3         7         3         3         5        26         2

Distribution of Missing Values

Total Sample Size =     306

Number of Missing Values      0    1    2    3
          Number of Cases   271   24    8    3

Listwise Deletion

Total Effective Sample Size =      271

Thresholds for Ordinal Variables

    RANK   -1.113   -0.153    0.334    1.047    1.888
    SEX     0.898

Univariate Distributions for Ordinal Variables

  RANK Frequency Percentage Bar Chart
    1       36       13.3    [IIIIIIIIIIIIIIIIIIII]
    2       83       30.6    [IIIIIIIIIIIIIIIIIIIIIIIIIIIIIIIIIIIIIIIIIIIIIIIIIIII]
    3       52       19.2    [IIIIIIIIIIIIIIIIIIIIIIIIIIIIIIIII]
    4       60       22.1    [IIIIIIIIIIIIIIIIIIIIIIIIIIIIIIIIIIIIIII]
    5       32       11.8    [IIIIIIIIIIIIIIIIIIIII]
    6        8        3.0    [IIIII]

  SEX Frequency Percentage Bar Chart
    1      221       81.5    [IIIIIIIIIIIIIIIIIIIIIIIIIIIIIIIIIIIIIIIIIIIIIIIIIIIIIIIIIII]
    2       50       18.5    [IIIIIIIIIIIII]

Bivariate Distributions for Ordinal Variables (Frequencies)

            SEX
          --------
  RANK     1    2
          --------
    1      23   13
    2      67   16
    3      47    5
    4      55    5
    5      22   10
    6       7    1


Bivariate Distributions for Ordinal Variables (Percentages)

            SEX
          --------
  RANK     1    2
          --------
    1     8.5  4.8
    2    24.7  5.9
    3    17.3  1.8
    4    20.3  1.8
    5     8.1  3.7
    6     2.6  0.4
```

Table 10.2   (continued)

Univariate Summary Statistics for Continuous Variables

Variable	Mean	St. Dev.	T-Value	Skewness	Kurtosis	Minimum	Freq.	Maximum	Freq.
SCALE1	3.654	0.475	126.518	0.228	-0.138	2.330	2	5.000	1
SCALE2	3.666	1.308	46.135	0.047	-0.716	1.000	2	7.000	1
SCALE3	4.774	0.956	82.191	-0.697	0.302	1.670	1	6.870	1
SCALE4	2.200	0.408	88.722	-0.598	-0.124	0.930	1	2.960	1
SCALE5	5.208	1.178	72.766	-0.815	-0.077	2.130	2	7.000	3

Test of Univariate Normality for Continuous Variables

	Skewness		Kurtosis		Skewness and Kurtosis	
Variable	Z-Score	P-Value	Z-Score	P-Value	Chi-Square	P-Value
SCALE1	1.707	0.088	-0.301	0.763	3.003	0.223
SCALE2	0.497	0.620	-3.599	0.000	13.202	0.001
SCALE3	-2.869	0.004	1.127	0.260	9.504	0.009
SCALE4	-2.706	0.007	-0.245	0.807	7.382	0.025
SCALE5	-3.036	0.002	-0.065	0.948	9.224	0.010

Test of Multivariate Normality for Continuous Variables

Skewness		Kurtosis		Skewness and Kurtosis	
Z-Score	P-Value	Z-Score	P-Value	Chi-Square	P-Value
6.376	0.000	2.302	0.021	45.946	0.000

Histograms for Continuous Variables

SCALE1

Frequency	Percentage	Lower Class Limit	
2	0.7	2.330	⊔
10	3.7	2.597	⊔⊔⊔⊔⊔
15	5.5	2.864	⊔⊔⊔⊔⊔⊔⊔⊔
64	23.6	3.131	⊔⊔⊔⊔⊔⊔⊔⊔⊔⊔⊔⊔⊔⊔⊔⊔⊔⊔⊔⊔⊔⊔⊔⊔⊔⊔⊔⊔⊔⊔⊔⊔⊔⊔
36	13.3	3.398	⊔⊔⊔⊔⊔⊔⊔⊔⊔⊔⊔⊔⊔⊔⊔⊔⊔⊔⊔
67	24.7	3.665	⊔⊔⊔⊔⊔⊔⊔⊔⊔⊔⊔⊔⊔⊔⊔⊔⊔⊔⊔⊔⊔⊔⊔⊔⊔⊔⊔⊔⊔⊔⊔⊔⊔⊔⊔⊔
42	15.5	3.932	⊔⊔⊔⊔⊔⊔⊔⊔⊔⊔⊔⊔⊔⊔⊔⊔⊔⊔⊔⊔⊔⊔⊔
15	5.5	4.199	⊔⊔⊔⊔⊔⊔⊔⊔
17	6.3	4.466	⊔⊔⊔⊔⊔⊔⊔⊔⊔
3	1.1	4.733	⊔

SCALE2

Frequency	Percentage	Lower Class Limit	
13	4.8	1.000	⊔⊔⊔⊔⊔⊔⊔
27	10.0	1.600	⊔⊔⊔⊔⊔⊔⊔⊔⊔⊔⊔⊔⊔⊔
43	15.9	2.200	⊔⊔⊔⊔⊔⊔⊔⊔⊔⊔⊔⊔⊔⊔⊔⊔⊔⊔⊔⊔⊔⊔
33	12.2	2.800	⊔⊔⊔⊔⊔⊔⊔⊔⊔⊔⊔⊔⊔⊔⊔⊔⊔
48	17.7	3.400	⊔⊔⊔⊔⊔⊔⊔⊔⊔⊔⊔⊔⊔⊔⊔⊔⊔⊔⊔⊔⊔⊔⊔⊔⊔
36	13.3	4.000	⊔⊔⊔⊔⊔⊔⊔⊔⊔⊔⊔⊔⊔⊔⊔⊔⊔⊔
37	13.7	4.600	⊔⊔⊔⊔⊔⊔⊔⊔⊔⊔⊔⊔⊔⊔⊔⊔⊔⊔⊔
20	7.4	5.200	⊔⊔⊔⊔⊔⊔⊔⊔⊔⊔
12	4.4	5.800	⊔⊔⊔⊔⊔⊔
2	0.7	6.400	⊔

Table 10.2   (continued)

```
SCALE3
Frequency Percentage Lower Class Limit
    1        0.4        1.670
   10        3.7        2.190      |IIIII|
    9        3.3        2.710      |IIIII|
   18        6.6        3.230      |IIIIIIIIII|
   31       11.4        3.750      |IIIIIIIIIIIIIIIIII|
   52       19.2        4.270      |IIIIIIIIIIIIIIIIIIIIIIIIIIIIIII|
   64       23.6        4.790      |IIIIIIIIIIIIIIIIIIIIIIIIIIIIIII|IIIIIIIIII|
   52       19.2        5.310      |IIIIIIIIIIIIIIIIIIIIIIIIIIIIIIII|
   29       10.7        5.830      |IIIIIIIIIIIIIIIII|
    5        1.8        6.350      |I|


SCALE4
Frequency Percentage Lower Class Limit
    2        0.7        0.930      |I|
    9        3.3        1.133      |IIIIII|
    9        3.3        1.336      |IIIIII|
   19        7.0        1.539      |IIIIIIIIIIIII|
   29       10.7        1.742      |IIIIIIIIIIIIIIIIIIII|
   39       14.4        1.945      |IIIIIIIIIIIIIIIIIIIIIIIIII|
   56       20.7        2.148      |IIIIIIIIIIIIIIIIIIIIIIIIIIIIIIIIIIIIIIII|
   49       18.1        2.351      |IIIIIIIIIIIIIIIIIIIIIIIIIIIIIIIIIII|
   43       15.9        2.554      |IIIIIIIIIIIIIIIIIIIIIIIIIIIIIIII|
   16        5.9        2.757      |IIIIIIIIIII|


SCALE5
Frequency Percentage Lower Class Limit
   12        4.4        2.130      |IIIIIIII|
    8        3.0        2.617      |IIIII|
   12        4.4        3.104      |IIIIIIII|
   19        7.0        3.591      |IIIIIIIIIIIII|
   16        5.9        4.078      |IIIIIIIIIIII|
   32       11.8        4.565      |IIIIIIIIIIIIIIIIIIIIII|
   48       17.7        5.052      |IIIIIIIIIIIIIIIIIIIIIIIIIIIIIIIIII|
   45       16.6        5.539      |IIIIIIIIIIIIIIIIIIIIIIIIIIIIIIII|
   52       19.2        6.026      |IIIIIIIIIIIIIIIIIIIIIIIIIIIIIIIIIIIIII|
   27       10.0        6.513      |IIIIIIIIIIIIIIIIIII|
```

Bivariate Summary Statistics for Pairs of Variables
(The First Variable is Ordinal and the Second is Continuous)

RANK vs.   SCALE1

Category	Number of Observations	Mean	Standard Deviation
1	36	3.607	0.432
2	83	3.672	0.465
3	52	3.654	0.526
4	60	3.669	0.464
5	32	3.693	0.508
6	8	3.416	0.437

SEX vs.   SCALE1

Category	Number of Observations	Mean	Standard Deviation
1	221	3.645	0.470
2	50	3.693	0.504

Table 10.2 (continued)

RANK vs.   SCALE2

Category	Number of Observations	Mean	Standard Deviation
1	36	3.995	1.170
2	83	3.856	1.333
3	52	3.459	1.416
4	60	3.563	1.277
5	32	3.471	1.200
6	8	3.111	1.303

SEX vs.   SCALE2

Category	Number of Observations	Mean	Standard Deviation
1	221	3.679	1.319
2	50	3.610	1.269

RANK vs.   SCALE3

Category	Number of Observations	Mean	Standard Deviation
1	36	4.721	1.035
2	83	4.877	0.902
3	52	4.717	1.032
4	60	4.745	0.941
5	32	4.702	0.961
6	8	4.808	0.925

SEX vs.   SCALE3

Category	Number of Observations	Mean	Standard Deviation
1	221	4.774	0.997
2	50	4.773	0.759

RANK vs.   SCALE4

Category	Number of Observations	Mean	Standard Deviation
1	36	2.226	0.369
2	83	2.131	0.396
3	52	2.242	0.444
4	60	2.222	0.420
5	32	2.261	0.372
6	8	2.128	0.526

SEX vs.   SCALE4

Category	Number of Observations	Mean	Standard Deviation
1	221	2.200	0.415
2	50	2.201	0.381

RANK vs.   SCALE5

Category	Number of Observations	Mean	Standard Deviation
1	36	5.059	1.229
2	83	5.207	1.076
3	52	5.328	1.287
4	60	5.212	1.150
5	32	5.187	1.256
6	8	5.157	1.408

Table 10.2 (continued)

SEX vs.	SCALE5		

Category	Number of Observations	Mean	Standard Deviation
1	221	5.275	1.136
2	50	4.910	1.322

Correlations and Test Statistics

(PE=Pearson Product Moment, PC=Polychoric, PS=Polyserial)

Variable vs. Variable	Correlation		Test of Model			Test of Close Fit	
			Chi-Squ.	D.F.	P-Value	RMSEA	P-Value
SEX vs.	RANK	-0.149 (PC)	14.782	4	0.005	0.100	0.054
RANK vs.	SCALE1	-0.001 (PS)	5.250	9	0.812	0.000	0.970
SEX vs.	SCALE1	0.056 (PS)	0.337	1	0.561	0.000	0.676
RANK vs.	SCALE2	-0.158 (PS)	3.890	9	0.918	0.000	0.990
SEX vs.	SCALE2	-0.030 (PS)	0.175	1	0.675	0.000	0.764
SCALE2 vs.	SCALE1	0.207 (PE)					
RANK vs.	SCALE3	-0.025 (PS)	3.039	9	0.963	0.000	0.996
SEX vs.	SCALE3	0.000 (PS)	5.685	1	0.017	0.131	0.060
SCALE3 vs.	SCALE1	-0.235 (PE)					
SCALE3 vs.	SCALE2	-0.393 (PE)					
RANK vs.	SCALE4	0.042 (PS)	6.918	9	0.646	0.000	0.922
SEX vs.	SCALE4	0.002 (PS)	0.681	1	0.409	0.000	0.549
SCALE4 vs.	SCALE1	-0.223 (PE)					
SCALE4 vs.	SCALE2	-0.464 (PE)					
SCALE4 vs.	SCALE3	0.632 (PE)					
RANK vs.	SCALE5	0.026 (PS)	3.667	9	0.932	0.000	0.992
SEX vs.	SCALE5	-0.168 (PS)	1.944	1	0.163	0.059	0.297
SCALE5 vs.	SCALE1	-0.244 (PE)					
SCALE5 vs.	SCALE2	-0.448 (PE)					
SCALE5 vs.	SCALE3	0.637 (PE)					
SCALE5 vs.	SCALE4	0.599 (PE)					

Percentage of Tests Exceeding 0.5% Significance Level : 0.0%

Percentage of Tests Exceeding 1.0% Significance Level : 0.0%

Percentage of Tests Exceeding 5.0% Significance Level : 0.0%

Correlation Matrix

	RANK	SEX	SCALE1	SCALE2	SCALE3	SCALE4
RANK	1.000					
SEX	-0.149	1.000				
SCALE1	-0.001	0.056	1.000			
SCALE2	-0.158	-0.030	0.207	1.000		
SCALE3	-0.025	0.000	-0.235	-0.393	1.000	
SCALE4	0.042	0.002	-0.223	-0.464	0.632	1.000
SCALE5	0.026	-0.168	-0.244	-0.448	0.637	0.599

Correlation Matrix

	SCALE5
SCALE5	1.000

Means

	RANK	SEX	SCALE1	SCALE2	SCALE3	SCALE4
	0.000	0.000	3.654	3.666	4.774	2.200

Table 10.2   (continued)

```
        Means
            SCALE5
            --------
             5.208

        Standard Deviations

                RANK        SEX      SCALE1     SCALE2     SCALE3     SCALE4
            --------   --------   --------   --------   --------   --------
               1.000      1.000      0.475      1.308      0.956      0.408

        Standard Deviations

            SCALE5
            --------
             1.178

The Problem used 12000 Bytes (= 0.0% of available workspace)
```

standard deviations, minimum and maximum values (and associated frequencies) as well as measures of skewness and kurtosis are provided. The *t*-values associated with the means test the hypothesis that the latter take zero values in the population; this hypothesis is clearly rejected for all variables in our example. The more important information for diagnostic purposes is shown under the Tests of Univariate (Multivariate) Normality for Continuous Variables. The univariate tests examine each variable individually for departures from normality. This is done by calculating standardized (as indicated in *z*-scores) coefficients of skewness and kurtosis and examining whether they are significantly different from zero. Thus, departures from normality are indicated by significant skewness and/or kurtosis *p*-values (the former indicating that the distribution is non-symmetrical (i.e. it is skewed) and the latter that it is more or less 'peaked' than the normal distribution). In our example, it can be seen that, with the exception of SCALE1, all other variables depart from normality either due to skewness or kurtosis; the worst 'offender' is SCALE2 which is characterized by excessive negative kurtosis (i.e. it is very 'platykurtic'). The multivariate tests corroborate the univariate findings and show that the assumption of multivariate normality is not warranted for the variables at hand. In this context, you should note that 'if any of the observed variables deviate substantially from univariate normality, then the multivariate distribution cannot be multinormal. However, the converse is not true: theoretically, all of the univariate distributions may be normal, yet the joint distribution may be substantially multivariately non-normal. Consequently, it is also important to examine multivariate measures of skewness and kurtosis'.[11]

Following the histograms of the continuous variables, there is a list of Bivariate Summary Statistics for Pairs of Variables which cross-tabulate each ordinal variable against each continuous variable. More specifically, for each value (i.e. category) of each ordinal variable, the corresponding mean and standard deviation of the continuous variable under consideration is given. For example, we can see that women have higher scores than men on SCALE1 and lower on SCALE5; whether these (or any other) differences are significant, however, is not obvious as no significance tests accompany this information.

The part of the output titled `Correlations and Test Statistics` shows the different types of correlations computed by PRELIS following the specification `MA=PM` in the input file (see Table 10.1). When both variables are ordinal, **polychoric correlations** (PC) are computed; this is an estimated correlation between the underlying continuous variables that are assumed to be coarsely categorized (resulting in the observed ordinal variables). When both variables are continuous, normal **Pearson product moment correlations** (PE) are generated. Finally, when one variable is ordinal and the other continuous, **polyserial correlations** (PS) are computed; this is, again, an estimated correlation between the continuous variable and the latent continuous variable assumed to underlie the ordinal variable involved. For each pair of variables for which a polychoric correlation has been estimated, a goodness-of-fit test is performed of the model of an underlying bivariate normal distribution. A nonsignificant chi-square value indicates that the assumption of a bivariate normal distribution is warranted. In addition to the test of exact fit offered by the chi-square test, a test of close fit is provided by the RMSEA statistic (see Chapter 7). This tests whether the assumption of a bivariate normal distribution is a reasonable approximation (i.e. whether any departure from it is rather mild). This is indeed the case for all relevant pairs of variables in Table 10.2, as no significant RMSEA values (at $p < 0.05$ or better) were obtained.

The correlations computed above are also reproduced in matrix form in the `Correlation Matrix`; it is important to remember that this correlation matrix contains correlations of *different* types and is not, therefore, directly comparable to a correlation matrix obtained from a set of interval-scaled, continuous variables.

Finally, the `Means` and `Standard Deviations` of all variables are given. For the continuous variables, this largely involves a repetition of the same information as under `Univariate Summary Statistics for Continuous Variables`. For ordinal variables, means and standard deviations are computed by reference to their assumed underlying continuous variables and take the form of standard scores (hence they have a mean of zero and a standard deviation of 1).[12]

Just in case you were wondering, we *do* know that it is difficult to conceive of appropriate underlying continuous variables for the specific ordinal variables (RANK and SEX) in our example. The main reason we asked for polychoric and polyserial correlations via the PM keyword was to demonstrate the different types of correlation coefficients that are obtainable with the PRELIS program. In a substantive application, we would probably have requested a straightforward rank order correlation such as

Spearman's rho (keyword MA=RM) or Kendall's tau-*c* (MA=TM). Having said that, with the latter options, it is not possible to generate and save the asymptotic covariance matrix (see AC=asymptot.cov keywords in the input file).[13] However, as already mentioned, the latter is required if WLS estimation is contemplated.

So, having screened our data and obtained a detailed descriptive picture of them, what are the implications of the results in Table 10.2 for any LISREL model that we may wish to run with the variables concerned?

The key implication is that we need to think carefully about the choice of estimation method to use. The fact that we have both ordinal variables and continuous variables that are non-normal puts into question the use of ML estimation because 'if the observed variables are ordinal-scaled and/or extremely skewed or peaked (and thus non-normally distributed), then the ML estimates, standard errors, and chi-square test may not be appropriate'.[14] We now have three choices.[15] The first is to try some transformations on the continuous variables in order to improve their distributions. The second is to rely on the 'robustness' of the ML estimator (see Chapter 6) and still use it despite having non-normal data; this is clearly a judgment call and depends on how mild or severe we consider the normality departures to be. The final option is to opt for WLS estimation and use the asymptotic covariance matrix calculated by PRELIS for this purpose. One problem here is the question of sample size. The minimum sample size necessary to estimate an asymptotic covariance matrix (given that a PM correlation matrix has been specified) is $k(k - 1)/2$, where k = number of variables. However, 'there is no guarantee that sample sizes as low as these will give good estimates of the asymptotic covariance matrix. Rather, these values are to be regarded as absolute minimum values'.[16] In our example, $k(k - 1)/2 = (7 \cdot 6)/2 = 21$, which is comfortably exceeded by our total effective sample size of 271. Nevertheless, research has shown that WLS estimation can be problematic (particularly in terms of its chi-square test statistic) even with much larger samples; for example, 'sample sizes of 1000 appear to be necessary with relatively simple models under typical conditions of non-normality . . . Perhaps 5000 cases are necessary for more complex models, less favorable non-normal conditions, or both'.[17] You can never win, can you?

Our discussion of PRELIS concludes this basic introduction to LISREL modeling. By now you should have a sound grasp of the key decisions involved at each stage of the modeling process from model conceptualization to model cross-validation. More importantly, you should have developed a critical awareness of the assumptions and limitations associated with the use of LISREL and the importance of theory when specifying, testing and modifying LISREL models. Finally, we hope that you have acquired a taste for LISREL and that you will find the technique useful in your substantive area of interest. And remember: next time you try to fit a LISREL model and things don't work out, you can always blame us! Have fun.

Notes

1　In general, a covariance matrix is computed if all observed variables are continuous; however, one can also obtain several other types of matrices depending upon the types of variables involved.

2　Jöreskog and Sörbom (1996b), p. i.

3　See, for example, the potential estimation problems arising from pairwise deletion of missing data discussed in Appendix 6A of Chapter 6.

4　Jöreskog and Sörbom (1996b), p. i.

5　Recall from Chapter 8 that there are several reasons for poor fit other than specification error; most of these relate to violations of one assumption or another.

6　Uses of PRELIS include the creation and merging of data files; definition of new variables; transformation, weighting, recoding and deletion of existing variables; specification of continuous, ordinal and censored variables; selection of cases; alternative missing value treatments, including imputation; threshold specification for ordinal variables; computation of seven different moment matrices (including covariance and correlation matrix of observed variables); estimation of asymptotic covariance matrix; tests for univariate and multivariate normality; descriptive statistics; bivariate analysis; regression analysis; and facilities for undertaking bootstrapping and Monte Carlo simulations. Full details of the program's capabilities are given in Jöreskog and Sörbom (1996b).

7　The asymptotic (large sample) covariance matrix captures the *estimated* sample variances and covariances under arbitrary (i.e. non-normal) distributions. It is used to compute another matrix (known as a **weight matrix**) for use in WLS estimation). For more details, see Browne (1984) but be warned: the maths are not easy!

8　With pairwise deletion (PA), no multivariate statistics are included in the PRELIS output; also computation of the asymptotic covariance matrix is not possible.

9　PRELIS also offers the option to specify variables as CA (censored above), CB (censored below), CE (censored above and below) and FI (fixed); these options, however, are unlikely to be needed in most applications. For further details, see Jöreskog and Sörbom (1996b).

10　The different types of matrices obtainable under PRELIS are discussed in detail in Jöreskog and Sörbom (1989, 1996b) and references given therein.

11　West, Finch and Curran (1995), pp. 60–61. Note that it is excessive kurtosis (rather than skewness) that can be particularly problematic in LISREL modeling if ML or GLS estimation is used; for details, see Bollen (1989) and West, Finch and Curran (1995) and references given therein.

12　See also Appendix 10A.

13　Note that there *is* a way of estimating the asymptotic covariance matrix for RM and TM matrices. However, this involves the use of bootstrapping procedures and thus is not really an option for newcomers to LISREL.

14　Schumacker and Lomax (1996), p. 104.

15　For a discussion of each of these in detail, see Bollen (1989) and West, Finch and Curran (1995) and references given therein.

16　Jöreskog and Sörbom (1996b), p. 173.

17　West, Finch and Curran (1995), p. 68.

APPENDIX 10A

Thresholds for ordinal variables

With an ordinal response variable, X, different response categories are observed depending on the position of a respondent on an underlying continuous variable, X^*, relative to a set of cut-off points or *thresholds*. If X has c categories, there are c-1 thresholds. Say, for example, that X takes on the values of 1, 2, 3; the corresponding thresholds are illustrated below.

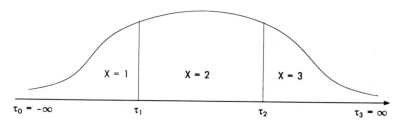

Thus, when $\quad -\infty < X^* \le \tau_1, \quad X = 1$

when $\quad \tau_1 \quad < X^* \le \tau_2, \quad X = 2$

and when $\quad \tau_2 \quad < X^* \le \infty, \quad X = 3$

where τ_1 and τ_2 are the threshold values (τ_0 and τ_c are always equal to $-\infty$ and $+\infty$ respectively, where c = number of categories). Note, that in PRELIS, it is assumed that the continuous underlying variable, X^*, is assumed to be normally distributed with mean zero and unit variance.

REFERENCES

Aaker, D.A. and Bagozzi, R.P. (1979) Unobservable variables in structural equation models with an application in industrial selling. *Journal of Marketing Research*, 16: 147–158.

Achen, C.H. (1992) *Interpreting and using regression*. Beverly Hills, CA: Sage.

Anderson, J.C. and Gerbing, D.W. (1982) Some methods for respecifying measurement models to obtain unidimensional construct measurement. *Journal of Marketing Research*, 19: 453–460.

Arbuckle, J.L. (1995) *AMOS user's guide*. Chicago: Smallwaters.

Asher, H.B. (1985) *Causal modeling* (2nd edn). Newbury Park, CA: Sage.

Austin, J.T. and Caldéron, R.F. (1996) Theoretical and technical contributions to structural equation modeling: An updated annotated bibliography. *Structural Equation Modeling*, 3 (2): 105–175.

Austin, J.T. and Wolfle, L.M. (1991) Annotated bibliography of structural equation modelling: Technical work. *British Journal of Mathematical and Statistical Psychology*, 44: 93–152.

Bagozzi, R.P. (1977) Structural equation models in experimental research. *Journal of Marketing Research*, 14: 209–226.

Bagozzi, R.P. (1980) *Causal models in marketing*. New York: Wiley.

Bagozzi, R.P. (1983) Issues in the application of covariance structure analysis: A further comment. *Journal of Consumer Research*, 9: 449–450.

Bagozzi, R.P. (1994) Structural equation models in marketing research: basic principles. In R. Bagozzi (ed.) *Principles of marketing research*. Oxford: Blackwell (pp. 317–385).

Bagozzi, R.P. and Yi, Y. (1988) On the evaluation of structural equation models. *Journal of the Academy of Marketing Science*, 16: 74–94.

Bagozzi, R.P. and Yi, Y. (1989) On the use of structural equation models in experimental designs. *Journal of Marketing Research*, 26: 271–284.

Bagozzi, R.P., Yi, Y. and Singh, S. (1991) On the use of structural equation models in experimental designs: Two extensions. *International Journal of Research in Marketing*, 8: 125–140.

Baumgartner, H. and Homburg, C. (1996) Applications of structural equation modeling in marketing and consumer research: A review. *International Journal of Research in Marketing*, 13: 139–161.

Bentler, P.M. (1995) *EQS: Structural equations program manual*. Encino, CA: Multivariate Software Inc.

Bentler, P.M. and Bonett, D.G. (1980) Significance tests and goodness of fit in the analysis of covariance structures. *Psychological Bulletin*, 88: 588–606.

Bentler, P.M. and Chou, C.P. (1987) Practical issues in structural modeling. *Sociological Methods and Research*, 16: 78–117.

Berry, W.D. (1984) *Nonrecursive causal models*. Beverly Hills, CA: Sage.

Biddle, B.J. and Marlin, M.M. (1987) Causality, confirmation, credulity and structural equation modeling. *Child Development*, 58: 4–17.

Blalock, H.M., Jr. (1964) *Causal inferences in non-experimental research*. Chapel Hill: University of North Carolina Press.

Blalock, H.M., Jr. (1967) Path coefficients versus regression coefficients. *American Journal of Sociology*, 72: 675–676.

Blalock, H.M., Jr. (1968) The measurement problem. In H.M. Blalock, Jr. and A. Blalock (eds) *Methodology in social research*. New York: McGraw-Hill (pp. 5–27).

Blalock, H.M., Jr. (ed.) (1971) *Causal models in the social sciences*. Chicago: Aldine.

Bollen, K.A. (1984) Multiple indicators: Internal consistency of no necessary relationship? *Quality and Quantity*, 18: 377–385.

Bollen, K.A. (1989) *Structural equations with latent variables*. New York: Wiley.

Bollen, K.A. and Lennox, R. (1991) Conventional wisdom on measurement: A structural equation perspective. *Psychological Bulletin*, 110 (2): 305–314.

Bollen, K.A. and Paxton, P. (1998) Interactions of latent variables in structural equation models. *Structural Equation Modeling*, 5: 267–293.

Boomsma, A. (1987) The robustness of maximum likelihood estimation in structural equation models. In P. Cuttance and R. Ecob (eds) *Structural modeling by example* (pp. 160–188). New York: Cambridge University Press.

Breckler, S.J. (1990) Applications of covariance structure modeling in psychology: Cause for concern? *Psychological Bulletin*, 107: 260–271.

Brinberg, D. and McGrath, J.E. (1982) A network of validity concepts within the research process. In D. Brinberg and L.H. Kidder (eds) *Forms of validity in research* (pp. 5–21). San Francisco: Jossey Bass.

Browne, M.W. (1984) The decomposition of multitrait-multimethod matrices. *British Journal of Mathematical and Statistical Psychology*, 37: 1–21.

Browne, M.W. and Cudeck, R. (1989) Single sample cross-validation indices for covariance structures. *Multivariate Behavioral Research*, 24: 445–455.

Browne, M.W. and Cudeck, R. (1993) Alternative ways of assessing model fit. In K.A. Bollen and J.S. Long (eds) *Testing structural equation models* (pp. 445–455). Newbury Park, CA: Sage.

Busemeyer, J.R. and Jones, L.E. (1983) Analysis of multiplicative combination rules when the causal variables are measured with error. *Psychological Bulletin*, 93: 549–562.

Byrne, B.M. (1995) One application of structural equation modeling from two perspectives: Exploring the EQS and LISREL strategies. In R.H. Hoyle (ed.) *Structural equation modeling: Concepts, issues and applications* (pp. 138–157). Thousand Oaks, CA: Sage.

Byrne, B.M. (1998) *Structural equation modeling with LISREL, PRELIS and SIMPLIS: Basic Concepts, Applications and Programming*. Mahwah, NJ: Lawrence Erlbaum Associates.

Carmines, E.G. and McIver, J.P. (1981) Analysing models with unobservable variables. In G.W. Bohrnstedt and E.F. Borgatta (eds) *Social Measurement: Current Issues* (pp. 65–115). Beverly Hills, CA: Sage.

Carmines, E.G. and Zeller, R.A. (1979) *Reliability and validity assessment*. Newbury Park, CA: Sage.

Cliff, N. (1983) Some cautions concerning the application of causal modeling methods. *Multivariate Behavioral Research*, 18: 115–126.

Cudeck, R. (1989) Analysis of correlation matrices using covariance structure models. *Psychological Bulletin*, 105: 317–327.

Cudeck, R. and Browne, M.W. (1983) Cross-validation of covariance structures. *Multivariate Behavioral Research*, 18: 147–167.

Cudeck, R. and Henly, S.J. (1991) Model selection in covariance structures analysis and the 'problem' of sample size: A clarification. *Psychological Bulletin*, 109: 512–519.

Danes, J.E. and Mann, K.O. (1984) Unidimensional measurement and structural equation models with latent variables. *Journal of Business Research*, 12: 337–352.

Darden, W.R. (1983) Review of behavioral modeling in marketing. In W.R. Darden, K.B.Monroe and W.R. Dillon (eds) *Research methods and causal modeling in marketing*. Chicago: American Marketing Association.

Darden, W.R., Carlson, S.M. and Hampton, R.D. (1984) Issues in fitting theoretical and measurement models in marketing. *Journal of Business Research*, 12: 273–296.

Davis, J.A. (1985) *The logic of causal order*. Newbury Park, CA: Sage.

Diamantopoulos, A. (1994) Modelling with LISREL: A guide for the uninitiated. *Journal of Marketing Management* (Special Issue on Quantitative Techniques in Marketing), 10: 105–136.

Diamantopoulos, A. and Winklhofer, H. (1999) Index construction with formative indicators: An application to scale development. In A. Menon and E. Sharma (eds) *Marketing theory and applications*, Vol. 10, February, p. 136. Proceedings Winter Educators' Conference of the American Marketing Association, St Petersburg, USA.

Dillon, W.R., Kumar, A. and Mulani, N. (1987) Offending estimates in covariance structure analysis: Comments on the causes of and solutions to Heywood cases. *Psychological Bulletin*, 101 (1): 126–135.

Ding, L., Velicer, W.F. and Harlow, L.L. (1995) Effects of estimation methods, number of indicators per factor, and improper solutions on structural equation modeling fit indices. *Structural Equation Modeling*, 2: 119–143.

Duncan, O.D. (1975) *Introduction to structural equation models*. New York: Academic Press.

Fornell, C. and Larcker, D.F. (1981) Structural equation models with unobservable variables and measurement error. *Journal of Marketing Research*, 18: 39–50.

Fornell, C., Rhee, B.-D., and Yi, Y. (1991) Direct regression, reverse regression, and covariance structure analysis. *Marketing Letters*, 2 (3): 309–320.

Fraser, C. (1988) *COSAN user's guide*. Centre for Behavioural Studies in Education, University of New England, Armidale, Australia.

Freedman, D.A. (1987) As others see us: A case study in path analysis. *Journal of Educational Statistics*, 12: 101–128, with a rejoinder after comments pp. 206–223.

Gerbing, D.W. and Anderson, J.C. (1984) On the meaning of within-factor correlated measurement errors. *Journal of Consumer Research*, 11: 572–580.

Gerbing, D.W. and Anderson, J.C. (1987) Improper solutions in the analysis of covariance structures: Their interpretability and a comparison of alternate respecifications. *Psychometrika*, 52: 99–111.

Gerbing, D.W. and Anderson, J.C. (1988) An updated paradigm for scale development incorporating unidimensionality and its assessment. *Journal of Marketing Research*, 25: 186–192.

Gerbing, D.W. and Anderson, J.C. (1993) Monte Carlo evaluations of goodness-of-fit indices for structural equation models. In K. Bollen and J.S. Long (eds) *Testing structural equation models* (pp. 40–65). Newbury Park, CA: Sage.

Goldberger, A.S. and Duncan, O.D. (eds) (1973) *Structural equation models in the social sciences*. New York: Seminar Press.

Hair, J.F., Anderson, R.E., Tatham, R.L. and Black, W.C. (1998) *Multivariate data analysis* (5th edn). Prentice Hall International: UK.

Harman, H.H. (1976) *Modern factor analysis*. Chicago: University of Chicago Press.

Hartmann, W.M. (1992) *The CALIS procedure: Extended user's guide*. Cary, NC: SAS Institute.

Hayduk, L.A. (1987) *Structural equation modeling with LISREL: Essentials and advances*. Baltimore, MD: Johns Hopkins University Press.

Hayduk, L.A. (1996) *LISREL issues, debates and strategies*. Baltimore, MD: Johns Hopkins University Press.

Heeler, R.M. and Ray, M.L. (1972) Measure validation in marketing. *Journal of Marketing Research*, 9: 361–370.

Heise, D.R. (1986) Estimating nonlinear models: Correcting for measurement error. *Sociological Methods and Research*, 14: 447–472.

Hershberger, S.L. (1994) The specification of equivalent models before the collection of data. In A. von Eye and C.C. Cogg (eds) *Latent variables analysis: Applications for developmental research* (pp. 69–105). Thousand Oaks, CA: Sage.

Hildebrandt, L. (1984) Kausalanalytische Validierung in der Marketing Forschung. *Marketing ZFP*, 6 (1): 41–51.

Hoelter, J.W. (1983) The analysis of covariance structures: Goodness-of-fit indices. *Sociological Methods and Research*, 11: 325–344.

Homburg, C. (1991) Cross-validation and information criteria in causal modeling. *Journal of Marketing Research*, 28: 137–144.

Homburg, C. and Giering, A. (1996) Konzeptualizierung und Operationalisierung komplexer Konstruckte – Ein Leitfaden für die Marketing Forschung. *Marketing ZFP*, 18 (1): 5–24.

Howell, R.D. (1987) Covariance structural modeling and measurement issues: A note on 'intercorrelations among a channel entity's power sources.' *Journal of Marketing Research*, 24: 119–126.

Hox, J.J. (1995) AMOS, EQS, and LISREL for Windows: A comparative review. *Structural Equation Modeling*, 2: 79–91.

Hoyle, R.H. (1995) The structural equation modeling approach: Basic concepts and fundamental issues. In R.H. Hoyle (ed) *Structural equation modeling: Concepts, issues and applications* (pp. 1–15). Thousand Oaks, CA: Sage.

Hoyle, R.H. and Panter, A.T. (1995) Writing about structural equation models. In R.H. Hoyle (ed.) *Structural equation modeling: Concepts, issues and applications* (pp. 158–176). Thousand Oaks, CA: Sage.

Hoyle, R.H. and Smith, G.T. (1994) Formulating clinical research hypotheses as structural equation models: A conceptual overview. *Journal of Consulting and Clinical Psychology*, 62: 429–440.

Hu, L.T. and Bentler, P.M. (1995) Evaluating model fit. In R.H. Hoyle (ed.) *Structural equation modeling: Concepts, issues and applications* (pp. 76–99). Thousand Oaks, CA: Sage.

Jaccard, J. and Wan, C.K. (1996) *LISREL approaches to interaction effects in multiple regression*. Thousand Oaks, CA: Sage.

James, L.R., Mulaik, S.A. and Brett, J.M. (1982) *Causal analysis: Assumptions, models and data*. Beverly Hills, CA: Sage.

Jöreskog, K.G. (1993) Testing structural equation models. In K.A. Bollen and J.S. Long (eds) *Testing structural equation models* (pp. 294–316). Newbury Park, CA: Sage.

Jöreskog, K.G. and Sörbom, D. (1989) *LISREL 7: A guide to the program and applications*. Chicago: SPSS Inc.

Jöreskog, K.G. and Sörbom, D. (1993) *LISREL 8: Structural equation modeling with the SIMPLIS command language*. Chicago: Scientific Software International.

Jöreskog, K.G. and Sörbom, D. (1996a) *LISREL 8: User's reference guide*. Chicago: Scientific Software International.

Jöreskog, K.G. and Sörbom, D. (1996b) *PRELIS 2: User's reference guide*. Chicago: Scientific Software International.

Jöreskog, K.G. and Yang, F. (1996) Nonlinear structural equation models: The Kenny-Judd model with interaction effects. In G.A. Marcoulides and R.E. Schumacker (eds) *Advanced structural equation modeling: Issues and techniques* (pp. 57–88). Mahwah, NJ: Lawrence Erlbaum Associates.

Kaplan, D. (1988) The impact of specification error on the estimation, testing and improvement of structural equation models. *Multivariate Behavioral Research*, 23: 69–86.

Kaplan, D. (1989) Model modifications in covariance structure analysis: Application of the expected parameter change statistic. *Multivariate Behavioral Research*, 24: 285–305.

Kaplan, D. (1990) Evaluating and modifying covariance structure models: A review and recommendation. *Multivariate Behavioral Research*, 25: 137–155.

Kaplan, D. (1995) Statistical power in structural equation modeling. In R.H. Hoyle (ed.) *Structural equation modeling: Concepts, issues and applications* (pp. 100–117). Thousand Oaks, CA: Sage.

Kenny, D.A. (1979) *Correlation and causality*. New York: Wiley.

Kenny, D.A. and Judd, C.M. (1984) Estimating the nonlinear and interactive effects of latent variables. *Psychological Bulletin*, 96: 201–210.

Kim, J.O. and Mueller, C.W. (1976) Standardized and unstandardized coefficients in causal analysis. *Sociological Methods and Research*, 4: 423–438.

Kim, J.O. and Mueller, C.W. (1978a) *Introduction to factor analysis: What it is and how to do it*. Beverly Hills, CA: Sage.

Kim, J.O. and Mueller, C.W. (1978b) *Factor analysis: Statistical methods and practical issues*. Beverly Hills, CA: Sage.

Lee, S. and Hershberger, S. (1990) A simple rule for generating equivalent models in structural equation modeling. *Multivariate Behavioral Research*, 25: 313–334.

Long, J.S. (1983a) *Confirmatory factor analysis*. Beverly Hills, CA: Sage.

Long, J.S. (1983b) *Covariance structure models: An introduction to LISREL*. Beverly Hills, CA: Sage.

MacCallum, R.C. (1986) Specification searches in covariance structure modelling. *Psychological Bulletin*, 100: 107–120.

MacCallum, R.C. (1995) Model specification: Procedures, strategies, and related issues. In R.H. Hoyle (ed.) *Structural equation modeling: Concepts, issues and applications* (pp. 16–36). Thousand Oaks, CA: Sage.

MacCallum, R.C. and Browne, M.W. (1993) The use of causal indicators in covariance structure models: Some practical issues. *Psychological Bulletin*, 114 (3): 533–541.

MacCallum, R.C., Browne, M.W. and Sugawara, H.M. (1996) Power analysis and determination of sample size for covariance structure modeling. *Psychological Methods*, 1 (2): 130–149.

MacCallum, R.C., Roznowski, M., Mar, C.M. and Reith, J.V. (1994) Alternative strategies for cross-validation of covariance structure models. *Multivariate Behavioral Research*, 29: 1–32.

MacCallum, R.C., Roznowski, M. and Necowitz, L.B. (1992) Model modifications in covariance structure analysis: The problem of capitalization on chance. *Psychological Bulletin*, 111: 490–504.

MacCallum, R.C., Wegener, D.T., Uchino, B.N. and Fabrigar, L.R. (1993) The problem of equivalent models in applications of covariance structure analysis. *Psychological Bulletin*, 114: 185–199.

Marsh, H.W., Balla, J.R. and Grayson, D. (1998) Is more ever too much?: The number of indicators per factor in confirmatory factor analysis. *Multivariate Behavioral Research*, 33 (2): 181–220.

Marsh, H.W., Balla, J.R. and Hau, K.-T. (1996) An evaluation of incremental fit indices: A clarification of mathematical and empirical properties. In G.A. Marcoulides and R.E. Schumacker (eds) *Advanced structural equation modeling: Issues and techniques* (pp. 315–353). Mahwah, NJ: Lawrence Erlbaum Associates.

Marsh, H.W., Balla, J.R. and McDonald, R.P. (1988) Goodness-of-fit indexes in confirmatory factor analysis: The effect of sample size. *Psychological Bulletin*, 103: 391–410.

Martin, J.A. (1987) Structural equation modeling: A guide for the perplexed. *Child Development*, 58: 33–37.

Maruyama, G.M. (1998) *Basics of structural equation modeling*. Thousand Oaks, CA: Sage.

Matsuelda, R.L. and Bielby, W.T. (1986) Statistical power in covariance structure models. In N.B. Tuma (ed.) *Sociological methodology 1986* (pp. 120–158). San Francisco: Jossey-Bass.

Miles, J. (1998) Multiple software review: Drawing path diagrams. *Structural Equation Modeling*, 5 (1).

Mulaik, S.A. (1986) Toward a synthesis of deterministic and probabilistic formulations of causal relations by the functional relation concept. *Philosophy of Science*, 52: 410–430.

Mulaik, S.A. (1987) Toward a conception of causality applicable to experimentation and causal modeling. *Child Development*, 58: 18–32.

Mulaik, S.A. (1993) Objectivity and multivariate statistics. *Multivariate Behavioral Research*, 28: 171–203.

Mulaik, S.A. and James, L.R. (1995) Objectivity and reasoning in science and structural equation modeling. In R.H. Hoyle (ed.) *Structural equation modeling: Concepts, issues and applications* (pp. 118–137). Thousand Oaks, CA: Sage.

Mulaik, S.A., James, L.R., Van Alstine, J. Bennett, N., Lind, S., and Stilwell, C.D. (1989) Evaluation of goodness-of-fit indices for structural equation models. *Psychological Bulletin*, 105: 430–445.

Muthén, B.O. (1988) *LISCOMP: Analysis of linear structural equations with a comprehensive measurement model*. Chicago: Scientific Software Inc.

Narver, J.C. and Slater, S.F. (1990) The effect of a market orientation on business profitability. *Journal of Marketing*, 54: 20–35.

Neale, M.C. (1993) *Mx structural equation modeling*. Richmond, VA: Medical College of Virginia.

Nunnally, J.C. and Bernstein, I.H. (1994) *Psychometric theory* (3rd edn). New York: McGraw-Hill.

Peter, J.P. (1979) Reliability: A review of psychometric basics and recent marketing practices. *Journal of Marketing Research*, 16: 6–17.

Peter, J.P. (1981) Construct validity: A review of basic issues and marketing practices. *Journal of Marketing Research*, 18: 133–145.

Ping, R.A. (1995) A parsimonious estimating technique for interaction and quadratic latent variables. *Journal of Marketing Research*, 32: 336–347.

Ping, R.A. (1996) Latent variable interaction and quadratic effect estimation: A two-step technique using structural equation analysis. *Psychological Bulletin*, 19: 166–175.

Raykov, T. and Penev, S. (1998) Nested structural equation models: Noncentrality and power of restriction test. *Structural Equation Modeling*, 5 (3): 229–246.

Rigdon, E. (1995) A necessary and sufficient identification rule for structural equation models estimated in practice. *Multivariate Behavioral Research*, 30: 359–383.

Rindskopf, D.M. (1984) Structural equation models: Empirical identification, Heywood cases and related problems. *Sociological Methods and Research*, 13: 109–119.

Rizzo, J.R., House, R.J. and Lirtzman, S.J. (1970) Role conflict and ambiguity in complex organizations. *Administrative Science Quarterly*, 15, 150–163.

Rust, R. and Schmittlein, D. (1985) A Bayesian cross-validated likelihood method for comparing alternative specifications of quantitative models. *Marketing Science*, 4: 20–40.

Saris, W.E. and Satorra, A. (1987) Characteristics of structural equation models which affect the power of the likelihood ratio test. In W.E. Saris and I.N. Gallhofer (eds) *Sociometric Research* (Vol. 2). London: Macmillan.

Saris, W.E. and Satorra, A. (1993) Power evaluations in structural equation models. In K. Bollen and J.S. Long (eds) *Testing structural equation models* (pp. 181–204). Newbury Park, CA: Sage.

Saris, W.E., Satorra, A. and Sörbom, D. (1987) The detection and correction of specification errors in structural equation models. In C.C. Clogg (ed.) *Sociological methodology 1987* (pp. 105–129). Washington: American Sociological Association.

Saris, W.E. and Stronkhorst, H. (1984) *Causal modeling in non experimental research: An introduction to the LISREL approach.* Amsterdam: Sociometric Research Foundation.

Satorra, A. and Saris, W.E. (1985) Power of the likelihood ratio test in covariance structure analysis. *Psychometrika*, 50: 83–90.

Satorra, A., Saris, W.E. and de Pipjer, W.M. (1985) *Several approximations to the power function for the likelihood ratio test in covariance structure analysis.* Amsterdam: Sociometric Research Foundation.

Saxe, R. and Weitz, B.A. (1982) The SOCO scale: A measure of the customer orientation of salespeople. *Journal of Marketing Research*, 19: 343–351.

Scheines, R., Sprites, P., Glymour, P. and Meek, C. (1994) *Tetrad II: Tools for causal modeling: User's manual.* Mahwah, NJ: Lawrence Erlbaum Associates.

Schoenberg, R. (1982) *MILS: A computer program to estimate the parameter of multiple indicator linear structural models.* Bethesda, MD: National Institute of Health.

Schoenberg, R. and Arminger, G. (1988) LINCS: Linear covariance structure analysis. *Multivariate Behavioral Research*, 23: 271–273.

Schumacker, R.E. and Lomax, R.G. (1996) *A beginner's guide to structural equation modeling.* Mahwah, NJ: Lawrence Erlbaum Associates.

Siguaw, J.A., Brown, G. and Widing, II, R.E. (1994) The influence of the market orientation of the firm on sales force behavior and attitudes. *Journal of Marketing Research*, 31: 106–116.

Smith, P., Kendall, L. and Hulin, C. (1969) *The measurement of satisfaction in work and retirement: a strategy for the study of attitudes*. Chicago, IL: Rand McNally.

Snee, R.D. (1977) Validation of regression models: Methods and examples. *Technometrics*, 19: 415–428.

Sobel, M.F. and Bohrnstedt, G.W. (1985) Use of null models in evaluating the fit of covariance structure models. In N.B. Tuma (ed.) *Sociological methodology 1985* (pp. 152–178). San Francisco: Jossey-Bass.

Sörbom, D. (1974) A general method for studying differences in factor means and factor structures between groups. *British Journal of Mathematical and Statistical Psychology*, 27: 229–239.

Sörbom, D. (1976) A statistical model for the measurement of change in true scores. In D.N.M. de Gruijter and J.L.Th. van der Kamp (eds) *Advances in psychological and educational measurement* (pp. 159–169). New York: Wiley.

Sörbom, D. (1982) Structural equation models with structured means. In K.G. Jöreskog and H. Wolds (eds) *Systems under direct observation* (pp. 183–195). Amsterdam: North Holland.

Steenkamp, J.-B.E.M. and van Trijp, H.C.M. (1991) The use of LISREL in validating marketing constructs. *International Journal of Research in Marketing*, 8 (4): 283–299.

Steiger, J.H. (1989) *EZPATH: A supplementary module for SYSTAT and SYSGRAPH*. Evanston, IL: SYSTAT.

Steiger, J.H. (1990) Structural model evaluation and modification: An interval estimation approach. *Multivariate Behavioral Research*, 25: 173–180.

Stelzl, I. (1986) Changing causal hypothesis without changing the fit: Some rules for generating equivalent path models. *Multivariate Behavioral Research*, 21: 309–331.

Sullivan, J.L. and Feldman, S. (1979) *Multiple indicators: An introduction*. Beverly Hills, CA: Sage.

Tanaka, J.S. (1993) Multifaceted conceptions of fit in structural equation models. In K.A. Bollen and J.S. Long (eds) *Testing structural equation models* (pp. 10–39). Newbury Park, CA: Sage.

Traub, R.E. (1994) *Reliability for the social sciences: Theory and applications*. Thousand Oaks, CA: Sage.

Waller, N.G. (1993) Seven confirmatory factor analysis programs: EQS, EZPATH, LINCS, LISCOMP, LISREL 7, SIMPLIS and CALIS. *Applied Psychological Measurement*, 17: 73–100.

Werts, C.E., Linn, R.L. and Jöreskog, K.G. (1974) Quantifying unmeasured variables. In H.M. Blalock (ed.) *Measurement in the social sciences: Theories and strategies*. Chicago: Aldine-Atherton.

West, S.G., Finch, J.F. and Curran, P.J. (1995) Structural equation models with non-normal variables: Problems and remedies. In R.H. Hoyle (ed.) *Structural equation modeling: Concepts, issues and applications* (pp. 56–75). Thousand Oaks, CA: Sage.

Wheaton, B. (1987) Assessment of fit in overidentified models with latent variables. *Sociological Methods and Research*, 16: 118–154.

Wheaton, B., Muthén, B., Alwin, D.F. and Summers, G.F. (1977) Assessing reliability and stability in panel models. In D.R. Heise (ed.) *Sociological methodology 1977* (pp. 84–136). San Francisco: Jossey-Bass.

Williams, L.J., Bozdogan, H. and Aiman-Smith, L. (1996) Inference problems with equivalent models. In G.A. Marcoulides and R.E. Schumacker (eds) *Advanced structural equation modeling: Issues and techniques* (pp. 279–314). Mahwah, NJ: Lawrence Erlbaum Associates.

Wold, H. (1982) Soft modeling: The basic design and some extensions. In K.G. Jöreskog and H. Wold (eds) *Systems under indirect observation: Causality, structure, prediction, Part II*. Amsterdam, North Holland Publishing.

Wold, H. (1985) Partial least squares. In *Encyclopaedia of Statistical Sciences* (Vol. 6, pp. 581–591). New York: Wiley.

Wothke, W. (1993) Nonpositive definite matrices in structural modeling. In K.A. Bollen and J.S. Long (eds) *Testing structural equation models* (pp. 256–293). Newbury Park, CA: Sage.

Wright, S. (1960) Path coefficients and path regressions: Alternative or complementary concepts? *Biometrics*, 16: 189–202.

Yadav, M.S. (1992) The effect of rescaling on the measurement and fit statistics of causal models: An exploratory study. In R.P. Leone and V. Kumar (eds) *Enhancing knowledge development in marketing*. Chicago: American Marketing Association.

Yi, Y. and Nassen, K. (1992) Multiple comparison and cross-validation in evaluating structural equation models. In V.L. Crittenden (ed.) *Developments in marketing science XV* (pp. 407–411). Miami, FL: Academy of Marketing Science.

Zeller, R.A. and Carmines, E.G. (1980) *Measurement in the social sciences: The link between theory and data*. New York: Cambridge University Press.

INDEX

absolute fit indices, 87
adjusted goodness-of-fit index (AGFI),
    87–88, 99n
admissibility test, 77
admissible solution, 56
Akaikes information criterion (AIC),
    86, 126
assessment of model fit (*see also* model
    fit), 7, 82–101
asymptotic covariance matrix, 98n
asymptotic covariance matrix (AC),
    146, 154, 155n,
asymptotic distribution-free (ADF),
    estimators 57, 74n
auxiliary theory, 19n
average variance extracted, 91

Beta, 24, 28, 38, 45, 62, 70, 92, 99n, 104,
    177

calibration sample, 129, 132, 133–138,
    140n, 142
capitalization on chance, 102, 140n
categorical variables, 144
causal indicators. See formative
    indicators
causal relationship, 26n, 28
censored variables, 155n
    censored above (CA), 155n
    censored below (CB), 155n
    censored above and below (CE), 155n
Chi-square statistic, 83–88, 93–96, 98n,
    105–106, 108–109, 119, 122–123,
    125, 128n, 131, 133–135, 140n,
    141n, 153–154
    chi-square difference test, 119, 135
    minimum fit function chi-square, 83,
        141n
    non-centrality chi-square 84–85,
        123–125, 128n, 135
    normal theory weighted least squares
        chi-square, 83

comparative fit index (CFI), 88, 119,
    131
competing models, 129, 130
completely standardized solution, 127n
composite reliability, 90–92
constrained parameters, 40n, 54n, 55
construct reliability. See composite
    reliability and reliability
constructs (*see also* latent variables), 1,
    50
continuous variables, 143, 145–146,
    152–154, 155n, 156
convergence, 56, 78, 83
consistent version of AIC (CAIC), 86,
    126
correlation coefficient, 11
covariance, 10, 40n, 42, 48–49, 51,
    53–55, 61–62, 65, 69, 73n, 74n, 78,
    85–87, 106, 108–109, 118, 119, 121
covariance matrix, 10, 18–19, 20n,
    33–34, 36, 39n, 42, 48, 50–51,
    55–56, 61–62, 73n, 74n, 76–77, 82,
    84–85, 87, 98, 101, 127n, 131, 133,
    136–137, 142, 155n
covariance structure analysis, 4, 8n
covariance structure hypothesis, 83, 97n
critical N (CN), 88
cross-validation analysis (*see also* model
    cross-validation), 129, 136–138,
    140n
cross-validation index (CVI) (*see also*
    expected cross-validation index),
    135–138
cross-validation strategy, 131
    loose replication 131, 132, 140n
    moderate replication 131, 133, 135,
        140n, 141n
    tight replication 131, 133–135, 140n,
        141n

data specifications (DA), 144–146
delta, 25, 28

dependent variables, 1,18
diagonally weighted least squares (DWLS), 55–57, 74n
direct effect, 69–70, 73, 128n
directional relationships, 24, 26n, 28
discrepancy of approximation, 101
discrepancy of estimation, 101
double cross-validation (*see also* cross-validation), 136–138

effect decomposition, 69
empirical underidentification (*see also* model identification), 53
endogenous variable, 2, 13–17, 22, 24–25, 28, 30, 33, 38–39, 46–47, 59, 61–62, 69–70, 72, 74n, 92–93, 104, 135
epsilon, 25, 28
equality constraints (*see also* invariance constraints), 51, 140n, 141n
equivalent models, 127n, 138, 139, l4ln
error, 2,24, 30–31, 34, 39n, 85, 89, 93, 95
error due to approximation, 85, 95, 132
error term, 13–14, 22, 24, 28, 31, 33, 123
error variance, 39n, 40n, 50–51, 60, 62, 75n, 89–90, 92, 135
estimation problems, 76–78
eta, 24, 28, 70, 72
exogenous variable, 2, 13–17, 22, 24–25, 28, 30, 33, 35, 38–39, 46–47, 61–62, 70, 72, 92, 102, 104, 135
expected cross-validation index (ECVI), 85–88, 98n, 126, 131, 136–137
expected parameter change (EPC), 109–110, 118, 121
external specification error, 103

fatal error, 77
file (FI), 144
fit, 52, 62, 65, 73n, 75n, 82–101–105, 109–110, 117–119, 122–123, 126n, 127n, 129, 131, 132, 133, 138, 140n, 155n
fit indices, fit criteria. See goodness-of fit indices
fitted residual, 87, 105, 110
fitting function, 55, 73n, 74n, 136

fixed parameter, 38, 47, 59, 73n, 99n, 104, 108–110, 117–118, 122–123, 125, 128n, 131
formative indicators, 14, 16, 21
free parameter, 38–39, 40n, 47, 49, 51, 53, 55–56, 59–60, 73n, 78, 104, 108, 109, 110, 118, 121, 122, 128n, 131–133, 140n
full-information techniques, 55

gamma, 24, 28, 39, 45, 70, 92, 99n, 104, 117
generalized least squares (GLS), 55–57, 74n, 155n
goodness-of-fit index (GEI), 87–88, 99n
goodness-of-fit indices, goodness-of-fit measures, 82–101, 106, 119, 123, 126, 131, 138, 153

Heywood case, 74n

identification (*see also* model identification), 30, 48–49, 51, 53, 103
implied covariance matrix, 11, 12
independence model (*see also* null model), 86, 88, 122, 127n
independent variables, 1, 18
indicator (*see also* reflective indicator or formative indicator), 9n, 16, 20n, 23, 25–26, 28, 34, 38, 40n, 49–52, 55, 59, 70, 72, 89–92
indirect effect, 69–70, 72–73, 80–81, 128n
information criteria, 86
information matrix, 54n
instrumental variables (IV), 55–57, 74n
internal specification error, 102
invariance constraint, 133, 140n
iterative procedures, 56

just-identified model, 49, 51–52, 127n

ksi, 24, 28, 70, 72

label line (LA), 144
lambda, 25, 28
lambda-X, 38, 45, 62, 65, 77, 89, 104, 117

lambda-Y, 38, 45, 62, 65, 77, 89, 104, 177

latent variables, 1–4, 8, 9n, 13–18, 20n, 21–22, 24–26, 27n, 28, 31, 34–35, 38, 39n, 40n, 46–47, 49–51, 54, 59, 61–62, 65, 69–70, 72, 74n, 76, 89–93, 99n, 103, 104, 122, 135, 153

limited-information techniques, 55

LISREL output, 36, 62, 65, 73, 83, 99n, 117

listwise deletion (LI), 144, 146

loadings, 34

local minimum, 74n

loose replication strategy, 131, 132, 140n

manifest variable, 1, 3–4, 14, 16–81, 22, 26n, 28, 31–32, 34–35, 39n, 48–49, 59, 61–62, 65, 89, 99n, 103, 108, 134, 143

mathematical specification, 26

matrix keyword (MA), 145, 155n
    augmented moment matrix (AM), 145
    correlation matrix (PM), 145, 153
    covariance matrix (CM), 145
    Kendall's Tau correlation matrix (TM), 145, 154, 155n
    moment matrix (MM), 145
    optimal correlation matrix (OM), 145
    product moment correlation matrix (KM), 145
    Spearman rank correlation matrix (RM), 145, 154, 155n

maximum likelihood (ML), 55–57, 74n, 143, 154, 155n

measurement error, 3,24, 26n, 61, 89, 91, 104, 118, 119, 123

measurement model, 4, 82, 88–89, 92, 104, 106, 128n

missing value code (MI), 145

model assumptions, 24

model-based covariance matrix, 12

model conceptualization, 6, 13–21, 106, 118, 126n, 139

model cross-validation (see also cross-validation), 8, 129–142

model estimation, 61, 73n, 126n, 138

model fit, 65, 75n, 82–101, 110, 122, 127n, 134

model identification (see also identification), 7, 39, 48–54, 98n

model modification, 7, 19, 62, 75n, 93, 97, 102–128, 129

model parsimony, 86

model selection, 130

model specification, 6, 30–47, 50–51, 55, 76, 78, 96, 102–104, 106, 131, 133

model stability, 129

moderate replication strategy 131, 133, 135, 140n, 141n

modification index, 105, 107–111, 117–119, 121, 123–125, 127n, 133, 141n

multi-sample analysis, 133

multivariate kurtosis, test of(PK), 146, 152

multivariate normality, test of, 152

nested models, 121, 122, 128n, 135

non-admissible (or improper) solution, 74n

non-centrality parameter (NCP) 84–85, 98n, 123, 125, 128n, 131

non-directional relationships, 24, 28

non-normed fit index (NNFI), 88, 99n, 119, 131

non-recursive model, 18, 20n, 78,

normal probability plot (see Q-plot)

null model (see also independence model), 86–87, 122, 126

number of decimal places (ND) 146

number of input variables (NI), 144

number of observations (NO), 144–145

options, 78, 136

ordinal variables (OR), 145–146, 152–154, 155n, 156

output (OU), 144–145

overall discrepancy, 101

overall error, 85

overfitting, 65, 103

overidentified model, 49, 52, 54, 96, 141n

pairwise deletion (PA), 144, 155n

parallel specification search, 138

parameter estimation,
7,50–51,55–81,93, 99n, 101, 109, 121
  DWLS, 55–57, 74n
  GLS, 55–57, 74n, 155n
  IV, 55–57, 74n
  ML, 55–57, 74n, 143, 154, 155n
  TSLS, 55–57, 74n
  ULS, 55–57, 74n
  WLS, 55–57, 74n, 143, 155n
parameter specification, 36–39, 62, 118
parsimony goodness-of-fit index (PGFI) 87–88
path diagram construction, 6, 22–29
path diagrams, 18, 22–23, 26, 27n, 28–29, 31–32, 47, 62, 70, 73, 74n, 76
Pearson product moment correlations (PE), 153
phi, 24, 28, 39, 45, 62, 77, 104, 117
polychoric correlations (PC), 153
polyserial correlations (PS), 153
positive definite, 76–77
power analysis, 94–97, 100n, 106, 123, 125, 128n, 132, 140n
PRELIS, 18, 143–156
psi, 28, 39, 45, 62, 77, 92, 99n, 104, 117

Q-plot, 110, 119

raw data (RA), 144–145
recursive model, 18, 141n
reference variable, 34–35, 39n, 50, 53, 54n, 59, 90
reflective indicators, 1, 14, 18, 21, 26n, 28
relative fit indices, 87
reliability, 3, 89–92, 99n, 123
residual (*see also* error term), 3, 13, 28. 34, 60, 65, 75n, 98, 106, 108, 110, 118–119, 123, 127n
residual analysis, 62, 65, 107, 111, 127n
residual matrix, 12, 56, 65, 87, 106, 127n
residual statistics, 105, 133
ridge option, 77
root mean square error of approximation (RMSEA) 85, 88, 95, 98n, 119, 131, 153

root mean square residual (RMR), 87, 119

sample discrepancy, 101
saturated model, 86, 122, 126, 127n, 128n, 141n
save matrix (SM), 146
scale-dependent methods, 57
scale-free methods, 57
significance level, 93
smoothing procedure, 77–78
specification error, 13–14, 55, 75n, 89, 94, 98n, 102, 109, 110, 127n, 155n
specification search, 103, 105–106, 118, 140n
split-sample approach, 129–130, 140n
squared multiple correlation, 60, 92–93, 99n
standard error, 59–62, 70, 74n, 87, 89, 99n, 103, 121, 154
standardized expected parameter change (SEPC), 110, 117–118, 121
standardized residual, 87, 98n, 105–106, 108, 110, 119, 127n
standardized root mean square residual, 87
standardized solution, 65, 73, 90, 99n, 127n
starting value, 55–56
statistical power (*see also* power analysis), 93
stem-leaf residual plot, 105–108, 110, 119, 133
structural error (*see also* error term), 3
structural model, 4, 13, 82, 88–89, 92, 104, 106, 127n
system of linear equations, 30, 48

test of close fit, 95
test of exact fit, 95
theta-delta, 39, 45, 62, 77, 104, 117
theta-epsilon, 39, 45, 62, 77, 99n, 104, 117
tight replication strategy, 131, 133–135, 140n, 141n
total effects, 70, 72–73, 80–81, 128n
treatment of missing values, 144
Tucker-Lewis Index (TLI). See NNFI

t-values, 73, 74n, 89, 99n, 122, 123, 128n, 152
Two-stages least squares (TSLS), 55–57, 74n
Type I error, 93
Type II error, 93, 132

underidentified (unidentified) model (*see also* empirical underidentification), 48–49, 52, 53–54, 54n
underfitting, 65, 108
unexplained variation, 3
univariate normality, test of, 152
unstandardized parameter estimate, 59–60, 70, 89
unweighted least squares (ULS), 55–57, 74n

validation sample, 129, 130–137, 140n, 142
validity, 3, 89, 92, 99n, 130, 136–137, 140n
validity extension, 130, 140n
validity generalization, 130, 140n
variance, 10, 50–51, 53–54, 54n, 55, 60–62, 73n, 74n, 78, 86–87, 90–92, 127n, 134
variance-covariance matrix (*see also* covariance matrix), 10

weight matrix, 155n
weighted least squares (WLS), 55–57, 74n, 143, 155n

zeta, 25, 28